# Cambridge

*Leo Jones*

Published by the Press Syndicate of the University of Cambridge
The Pitt Building, Trumpington Street, Cambridge CB2 1RP
40 West 20th Street, New York, NY 10011–4211, USA
10 Stamford Road, Oakleigh, Victoria 3166, Australia

© Cambridge University Press 1991

First published 1991
Third printing 1992

Printed in Great Britain at the
University Press, Cambridge

ISBN 0 521 33698 8    Teacher's Book
ISBN 0 521 33697 X    Student's Book
ISBN 0 521 33517 5    Set of 3 cassettes

VN

# Contents

Thanks   iv

Introduction   1

1   Desert islands   19

2   Around the world   31

3   That's show business!   45

4   Food and drink   57

5   Crossing the Channel   68

6   Buildings and homes   76

7   Put it in writing   85

8   Those were the days!   96

9   The third age   111

10   It takes all sorts . . .   118

11   Fame and fortune   126

12   Rich and poor   133

13   Communication   143

14   The English-speaking world   151

15   How strange!   160

16   Travellers   165

17   Love stories   172

18   Body and mind   181

19   On business   190

20   The natural world   201

21   Here is the news   213

22   Education   221

23   Science and technology   232

24   Utopia   242

Acknowledgements   250

# Thanks

First of all, I'd like to say how grateful I am to:

Jeanne McCarten for her inexhaustible patience, support and
   encouragement throughout my work on this book,
Alison Silver and Lindsay White for their editorial expertise,
Peter Ducker for the design of the book, and
Peter Taylor and Studio AVP for producing the recordings.

Thanks very much also to the following teachers who used the pilot
edition with their classes and contributed detailed comments on it
and who evaluated and reported on subsequent revised units.
Without their help, this book could not have been written:

Pat Biagi, Christ Church College ELTU, Canterbury
Jenny Bradshaw, Christ Church College, Department of Language
   Studies, Canterbury
Sylvie Dawid and Beverly Langsch and Monty Sufrin in Berne
George Drivas, Moraitis School, Athens
Tim Eyres, Godmer House, Oxford
David Gray
Amanda Hammersley, British School of Monza
Chris Higgins and staff, Teach In Language and Training
   Workshop, Rome
Tom Hinton
Roger Hunt, International House, Madrid
Ruth Jimack
Christine Margittai
Laura Matthews, Newnham Language Centre, Cambridge
Joy Morris and staff, British Institute, Barcelona
Jill Mountain and staff, British Institute, Rome
Julia Napier
Patricia Pringle, Université II, Lyons
Lesley Porte and Diann Gruber, ESIEE, Paris
Rachelle Porteous, London School of English
Tom Sagar and colleagues, Collège Rousseau, Geneva
Katy Shaw and colleagues, Eurocentre, Lee Green
Elizabeth Sim and staff, Eurocentre, Cambridge
Lynda Taylor
Kit Woods

Finally, thanks to Sue, Zoë and Thomas for everything.

# Introduction

## Who is this book for?

*Cambridge Advanced English* is for students who have completed an upper-intermediate course and have passed the Cambridge First Certificate in English examination (FCE) or reached an equivalent level.

Students using this course may be attending classes once or twice a week at a language institute, they may be doing a language course at a university, or they may be attending an intensive EFL course. They might be preparing for the Cambridge Certificate in Advanced English (CAE) exam or preparing for Cambridge Proficiency (CPE) over a two-year period (during the second year they would use *Progress to Proficiency* by Leo Jones). On the other hand, they might have no paper qualifications at all in mind and simply want to improve all aspects of their English in order to be able to communicate better in their work, studies or social life.

The material in this course is very flexible and can be used successfully with all the types of students described above. Throughout the book, there is an emphasis on the acquisition of skills that students will find useful in their everyday lives.

## How much time will it take to complete the course?

At this level it is impossible to predict exactly how long each section in a coursebook will take. As a rough guide, it is expected that the material in the book with its accompanying cassettes will provide approximately 80 hours of classroom work, plus further work to be done outside class. Each of the 24 units is likely to take two or three 90-minute sessions.

If you decide to devote a lot of time to the discussion activities the units will take longer to complete. Every class is likely to have its own strengths and weaknesses, which will lead you to spending more or less time on particular sections in a unit. Moreover, some topics may interest your students more than others and consequently there will be more discussion on these than on the ones that are of less interest to them.

The sections in each unit are designed to be used SELECTIVELY. Some sections that deal with aspects of English which your students are already confident in, or which are less relevant for them, may be omitted. You may also like to use supplementary materials and give your students an opportunity to contribute their own input to the course (in the form of discussions about current affairs, texts clipped from magazines or newspapers or student talks, for example).

## What are the aims of the course?

The aims of *Cambridge Advanced English* are:

- to build on the vocabulary that students already know and increase their range of expression
- to improve students' reading skills so that they can read more effectively and appreciate the implications and style of a text
- to improve students' listening skills so that they can understand a wide range of spoken texts and are able to participate actively in discussions and conversations with native and non-native English speakers from all parts of the world
- to improve students' writing skills and encourage them to develop useful practical techniques which will enable them to communicate effectively in writing
- to revise the 'problem areas' of English grammar in a stimulating, helpful and entertaining way
- to improve students' command of spoken English, by examining a full range of functions and providing frequent opportunities for discussion, so that they will be able to participate appropriately and confidently in a wide range of interactions with English speakers
- to increase students' awareness of and sensitivity to degrees of appropriateness in their use of English
- to give students a chance to use their English in class in interesting communicative activities and produce meaningful written work, not just to practise speaking or writing in controlled exercises
- to integrate different language skills in the practice activities, so that each skill is not practised in isolation
- to encourage students to improve their English outside class by reading widely and taking every opportunity to practise their English with native speakers and with each other

# What does the course contain?

There are 24 units in *Cambridge Advanced English*, each based on a different topic. There are two types of unit:

The odd-numbered units are '**Theme units**', which contain:

- informative Reading texts from a variety of authentic sources, with tasks, exercises and activities to improve students' reading skills – many of these can be prepared in advance at home
- Listening exercises with tasks and activities to help students to improve their listening skills
- Effective writing exercises to help students to develop useful techniques they can use in their writing
- realistic Creative writing tasks which give students an opportunity to express themselves in writing

The even-numbered units are '**Language units**' and they contain:

- shorter Reading texts and/or Listening exercises
- work on Grammar revision: the 'problem areas' of English grammar are dealt with in a thought-provoking and interesting way
- Word-study exercises to help students to develop their vocabulary skills
- Functions sections to help students to practise the functional language needed in different situations (in Units 14, 20, 22 and 24 there is work on Pronunciation instead)

Both the odd- and even-numbered units (i.e. all the units) contain:

- exercises on the vocabulary connected with the topic of the unit
- opportunities for discussion
- work on idiomatic expressions and phrasal verbs
- integrated activities where, for example, a listening task leads on to discussion, which in turn leads on to a reading task, which may then lead on to a writing task

Activities shown with this symbol ▐▓▌ are Communication activities, where individual students are given different information that they have to communicate to each other. These are printed at the end of the Student's Book in random order so that students can't see each other's information. There is a complete 'guide' to these on page 13 in the Teacher's Book and in the teaching notes for each unit. Most of the units contain Communication activities.

▐▭▌ indicates that there is recorded material on the cassettes. Every unit has accompanying recorded material.

|ht ✎| indicates that students should use a fluorescent highlighter for an activity. (A pencil may be used instead, if preferred, to <u>underline</u> or put rings round the words.)

The **Teacher's Book** of *Cambridge Advanced English* contains:

- correct or suggested answers to all the exercises in the Student's Book
- transcripts of all the material recorded on the cassettes
- teaching notes on every section of the Student's Book

## Different types of sections

### Reading

*Cambridge Advanced English* contains a wide variety of interesting authentic texts taken from newspapers, magazines and from fiction or non-fiction books. These are accompanied by exercises and tasks which will help students to develop their skills in: skimming a text to get the gist of the passage, scanning a text to find specific information, note-taking, summarising, coping with unfamiliar vocabulary, distinguishing the main idea from supporting ideas, using the information acquired from a text in a subsequent activity, etc. The passages are all chosen as springboards for discussion.

Before the reading comprehension tasks there are pre-reading tasks, preliminary discussion questions or questions about the theme that students may be able to answer from their own previous knowledge. These tasks help students to approach the text with more interest and curiosity than if they merely had to 'Read the text and answer the questions'.

It is essential for students to realise that they don't have to be able to understand every single word in a passage to perform the tasks. They should concentrate on what the writers are trying to say and the information they are communicating. Unfamiliar words in a reading text may be distracting but students should not assume that every single one is important and 'worth learning'.

There are many exercises where students have to `HIGHLIGHT` certain vocabulary items in a passage. This encourages them to deduce meanings from the context and also to notice how particular words are used.

After the reading comprehension questions there are further discussion questions, to encourage students to use some of the new words they have encountered in the text and share their reactions to its content with each other. In some cases there is a Communication activity or a writing task, arising from the content of the passage.

The first reading section is on page 4 of the Student's Book and pages 25–6 of the Teacher's Book.

## Listening

The cassettes contain a variety of recordings: broadcasts, discussions, lectures, talks, interviews and conversations. There are exercises and tasks designed to develop skills in finding the important information in the recording, note-taking, performing another task (in writing or speech) using the information acquired from a text, interpreting a speaker's attitude, etc.

Before the listening comprehension questions there are pre-listening tasks, preliminary discussion questions or questions about the theme which students may be able to answer from their own previous knowledge. These tasks help students to approach the recording with more interest than if they merely had to 'Listen to the cassette and answer the questions'.

Try to 'set the scene' for students before they hear the recording by explaining where the speakers are and what their relationship is (colleagues, good friends, etc.). Remember that students will be trying to understand disembodied voices coming out of a loudspeaker without the aid of a transcript, and this is much more difficult than being in the same room as a real person who is speaking.

In some of the listening exercises, students may need help with vocabulary. It is a good idea to read through the transcript in your copy of the Teacher's Book before the lesson, and highlight any vocabulary that you wish to draw your students' attention to.

Most classes will need to hear each recording at least twice to extract all the required information. In some classes, where students are weak at listening, you may need to pause the tape frequently and play certain sections again to help them to understand more easily. However, it is essential for students to realise that they don't have to be able to understand every single word to answer the questions. They should concentrate on what the speakers are trying to say and the information they are communicating, NOT the actual words they are using.

After the listening comprehension task there are often further discussion questions, to encourage students to share their reactions with each other and discuss the implications of what they have heard. In some cases there is a complete Communication activity, related to the theme of the listening text.

The first listening section is on page 2 of the Student's Book and on pages 19–23 of the Teacher's Book.

## *Vocabulary*

Each unit has a vocabulary section, covering some of the vocabulary connected with the topic of the unit. There are various types of exercises and activities in these sections, including warm-up discussion questions and a follow-up activity. While doing these activities and exercises, students should be encouraged to ask questions about vocabulary, and to use the relevant vocabulary they already know to discuss the topic.

There are two big problems about introducing new vocabulary. One is the difficulty of helping students to remember vocabulary items – giving them a large amount of controlled oral practice in class is no guarantee that they will remember everything a week later! The other is helping students to develop a sensitivity towards the kinds of contexts and situations in which each vocabulary item can be used: which words are formal or informal, which are used jokingly or seriously, which are used in a derogatory or complimentary sense, etc. Students also need to develop an awareness of the connotations of different vocabulary items, since many broadly synonymous expressions may have quite different connotations.

Unfortunately, there are no easy solutions. What will certainly help is:

- DISCUSSION of the meanings, connotations and usage of vocabulary introduced in class.
- Encouraging students to use a DICTIONARY intelligently, particularly studying the examples given after the definitions.
- Encouraging students to HIGHLIGHT vocabulary items they don't know and want to remember.
- Making sure that students get plenty of EXPERIENCE in reading – not just reading the texts in this book, but popular fiction and journalism.
- A REALISTIC approach to the problems: it's the students who have to do the remembering – all the teacher can be expected to do is introduce regular revision sessions throughout the course to help them not to forget (this may be described, perhaps disparagingly, as 'testing').
- Systematic use of NOTEBOOKS to store useful new vocabulary items, preferably devoting separate pages to each topic. It is recommended that students should discuss which system of vocabulary storage they consider most effective.

The first vocabulary section is on page 4 of the Student's Book and on pages 24–5 of the Teacher's Book.

## Effective writing

These sections are designed to help students to develop their writing skills. The discussion activities and exercises focus on various aspects of planning and writing essays, reports, narratives, letters and other compositions.

The Effective writing sections deal with the following points:

1.4  Joining sentences – 1
3.5  Punctuation
5.5  Making notes
7.3  Using appropriate language
9.4  Building paragraphs
11.5  Style, tone and content
13.4  Joining sentences – 2
15.3  Sequencing ideas
17.5  Expressing feelings
19.3  Word order
21.4  Semantic markers
23.4  A good introduction and conclusion

In an advanced class, each individual student may to a greater or lesser degree be 'good at writing'. It is essential to regard the exercises in *Cambridge Advanced English* as a starting point. Further remedial work may be necessary for students whose writing skills are particularly weak, or who need to develop their writing skills to a very advanced level. In particular, the feedback you give to students when handing back their written work should take into account each individual student's strengths and weaknesses. See **Mistakes and correction** on pages 15–16 of the Teacher's Book.

The first Effective writing section is on page 6 of the Student's Book and on pages 26–8 of the Teacher's Book.

## Creative writing

In these sections discussion in class leads up to the actual writing, which would be done at home. Many of the Creative writing sections give students a choice of topics: often between writing a more serious discursive essay or writing a more light-hearted, personal one. You may prefer to preempt the choice by stipulating which of the topics your class should write about.

At this level it is important for students to feel that they are being given opportunities to communicate and not just being given 'compositions' to write, particularly if their creative writing takes a long time to prepare, write and receive feedback on. The tasks set in *Cambridge Advanced English* are very open-ended, so that students really can express their ideas at some length, though it is to be expected that individual students will find some tasks more stimulating than others.

Make sure you allow everyone time to read each other's written work: this is particularly important if creative writing is to be considered as more than 'just a routine exercise'. Any piece of writing should be an attempt to communicate ideas to a reader. If students know that their partners, as well as you, are going to read their work, they are more likely to try to make it interesting, informative and entertaining! If you, their teacher, are the only reader, the process of writing is much less motivating. Students can learn a lot from reading each other's work – and from each other's comments on their own work. A piece of written work should be regarded as a piece of communication, not simply an opportunity to spot the grammatical errors that students make. See **Mistakes and correction** on pages 15–16 of the Teacher's Book.

The Creative writing sections cover the following areas:

1.5 Your own ideas    (narrative or discursive essay/article)
3.6 Planning ahead . . .    (writing a film review)
5.7 Describing a process
7.7 Keeping in touch    (personal and business letters)
9.5 A discursive essay
11.6 Household names    (life and achievements)
13.6 What happened?    (short story or letter)
15.7 My advice is . . .    (using information from a reading passage in a writing task)
17.6 A wedding . . .    (describing a family event)
19.7 Applying for a job    (writing a CV and letter)
21.5 Reports and opinions    (newspaper article and editorial)
23.6 Just say no . . .    (reacting to a controversial text)

The first Creative writing section is on page 8 of the Student's Book and on page 28 of the Teacher's Book.

## Verbs and idioms

Every unit contains work on idioms or verbs and idioms. These sections, which come at the very end of each unit concern phrasal verbs and the collocations in which certain common verbs are used. These can be fitted in when there is a little spare time during the lesson, or set for homework and checked in class later.

These sections deal with the following idioms and phrasal verbs:

1.6 All in all . . .
2.7 *Lose*
3.7 *At* . . . and *by* . . .
4.7 *Bring* and *carry*
5.8 *High, middle* and *low*
6.5 *Make* and *do*
7.8 *In* . . . and *out of* . . .
8.7 *Get*
9.6 *Ages:* age, new, fresh, old, young
10.5 *Give* and *take*
11.7 *For, on* and *off*
12.6 *Look* and *see*
13.7 Colours: red, blue, green, black and white
14.5 *Say, call, speak, talk* and *think*
15.8 *Day* and *time*
16.7 *Come, go* and *run*
17.8 Head over heels . . .: head, brain, mind, hair, face, eyes, nose, ears and mouth
18.7 *Hearts, hands, legs* and *feet*
19.8 *Hard, soft, difficult* and *easy*
20.7 *Keep, hold, stand* and *turn*
21.6 *Back, front* and *side*
22.8 *Pick, pull, put* and *set*
23.7 *First, second, third* and *last*
24.3 *Lay, lead, leave, let* and *lie*

The first Idioms section is on page 9 of the Student's Book and on page 29 of the Teacher's Book.

## Grammar

The grammar sections in the even-numbered units are designed to REVISE the main problem areas of English grammar that cause difficulties for advanced students.

   These sections contain a variety of exercises: contrasted sentences where students have to explain the differences in meaning, error-correction exercises where students have to find the 'typical mistakes' and correct them, sentence-completion exercises and other more open-ended tasks.

The grammar sections cover the following areas:

2.3 Looking back (simple past, present perfect and past perfect)
4.3 Simple + Progressive aspect
6.3 Articles
8.3 In the past (past tenses)
10.2 Modal verbs
12.3 Conditional sentences
14.2 Indirect speech
16.4 Comparing and contrasting
18.2 Emphasis (includes pronunciation)
20.3 The future and degrees of certainty
22.2 *-ing* and *to* __
24.2 Special uses of the Past

Students should realise that the grammar sections are intended as
REVISION of points that they have covered in previous courses. If they
require more detailed rules or guidelines they should refer to a
reference grammar book, such as *Practical English Usage* by Michael
Swan (OUP). Students should be encouraged to ask questions if they
are unsure about any points in the Grammar sections.

The first Grammar section is on page 12 of the Student's Book and
on pages 36–9 of the Teacher's Book.

## Functions

These sections will help students to develop their sensitivity to
degrees of appropriateness and extend their range of expression. The
emphasis of these exercises is on speaking skills but wherever
relevant this is associated with equivalent writing skills. There is also
recorded material on the cassettes for some of these sections.

The Functions sections deal with the following areas:

2.5 Really? That's amazing!    (expressing reactions)
4.5 That doesn't sound right!    (appropriateness)
5.2 Giving a presentation
6.2 Do you see what I mean?    (giving your opinion)
7.4 Different styles
8.6 Spoken and written English
10.1 What do they look like?    (describing people)
12.4 Sharing opinions
16.6 Describing a place
18.5 Bad feelings: sincerity and sarcasm, unhappiness, anger and
boredom

The first Functions section is on page 15 of the Student's Book and on pages 39–42 of the Teacher's Book.

## Pronunciation

In some units there is a Pronunciation section instead of a Functions section, with accompanying recorded material on the cassettes. The relatively small number of pages devoted to pronunciation does not imply that phonology is of little importance. Indeed, it requires constant attention, particularly when you are giving students feedback on their performance in spoken activities. At this level, correction is likely to be the most effective method of dealing with phonology.

The Pronunciation sections deal with the following points:

14.3 Spelling and pronunciation 1 – Consonants
18.2 Emphasis (includes grammar)
20.6 Spelling and pronunciation 2 – Vowels
22.6 Using stress
24.4 Reading aloud

The first Pronunciation section is on page 122 of the Student's Book and on pages 154–5 of the Teacher's Book.

## Word study

Each even-numbered unit contains a section on word formation or an aspect of vocabulary building, in addition to the topic-based Vocabulary sections. One of the primary purposes of a course at this level is to encourage students to expand their active vocabulary, which involves them in DECIDING what to learn, according to their own needs and interests. In particular, students who need to concentrate on improving their writing skills will need to increase their range of expression. (See also the notes on Vocabulary on page 6 above.)

The following points are covered in the Word-study sections:

2.6 How would you feel?     (synonyms and their force)
4.4 Words easily confused
6.4 Using abbreviations
8.5 Forming adjectives
10.3 Personalities     (descriptive adjectives)
12.5 Using synonyms and opposites – 1
14.4 British and American English

16.5 Using synonyms and opposites – 2
18.4 Using prefixes
20.4 Compound words
22.5 Making an emphasis

The first Word-study section is on page 16 of the Student's Book and on pages 42–3 of the Teacher's Book.

## Discussion opportunities

Every unit contains a variety of questions for students to consider and then discuss in small groups. These should be regarded as 'discussion opportunities', and if your students have little to say about some of these questions, they may be omitted. Conversely, if they have a lot to say, these discussions may go on for quite a long time. In other words, the amount of time that should be devoted to these is unpredictable.

If a particular topic is particularly popular, you may decide to ask students to do some supplementary written work, outlining their own ideas or summarising the discussion they have been involved in. This option is not included in the Student's Book rubrics, and is left to the teacher's discretion.

## Communication activities

Most of the Communication activities involve an information gap, where each participant is given different information which has to be

shared with a partner. These are shown with the symbol in the Student's Book and the Teacher's Book. The information is printed on different pages in separate sections to make it more difficult for students to see each other's information and they have to find it out from each other.

The first Communication activity is on page 4 of the Student's Book and the activities themselves are 1, 32 and 50 on pages 217, 230 and 237 respectively, and on page 24 of the Teacher's Book.

## Guide to the Communication activities at the end of the Student's Book

| Section | Description | | Communication activities |
|---|---|---|---|
| 1.2C | Desert island stories | | 1 + 32 + 50 |
| 2.4A | 'Photon war' jigsaw reading | | 4 + 36 + 53 |
| 5.3B | Civil engineering projects | | 6 + 24 + 41 |
| 6.2D | 'Prince Charles' jigsaw reading | | 16 + 51 + 69 |
| 7.5D | Principles of graphology | | 10 + 28 |
| 8.1C | 'Charles Lindbergh' jigsaw reading | | 18 + 43 |
| 9.3C | Distribution of population bar charts | | 23 + 60 |
| 10.1E | Photos of people | | 38 + 61 |
| 11.4B | James Dean and Marilyn Monroe | | 25 + 47 |
| 12.1C | Billionaires | | 58 + 64 |
| 12.4C | Chairing a discussion | | 2 + 39 + 67 + 73 |
| 13.2D | Meeting at the airport role play | | 46 + 68 + 74 |
| 13.5D | Key to logos | | 12 |
| 14.2B | Reported speech activity | | 9 + 44 |
| 14.2F | New York and Australia texts | | 66 |
| 15.2E | Urban legends: picture stories | | 8 + 49 |
| 15.3D | Unusual pictures | | 34 + 45 |
| 15.4 | Magic tricks | | 17 + 70 |
| 15.5C | 'Jim Bakker' jigsaw reading | | 25 + 40 |
| 16.3A | Two accounts of a meeting | | 11 + 27 |
| 17.7C | Synopses of famous novels | | 5 + 19 + 75 |
| 18.2E | Contradicting people exercise | | 15 + 76 |
| 18.3 | 'Body Shop' jigsaw reading | | 7 + 22 + 33 |
| 18.5C | Expressing feelings | | 29 + 54 + 71 |
| 18.6A | Medical emergencies | | 13 + 48 + 57 |
| 19.4C | Telephone role play | Student A | 21→42→72 |
|  |  | Student B | 3→14→30 |
|  |  | Student C | 26→31→37 |
| 19.5B | Taking messages | | 35 + 59 |
| 20.1C | *Metamorphosis* and *Woof!* | | 55 + 63 |
| 23.3D | Movie pictures and soundtrack | | 56 + 62 |
| 24.4C | Brasilia article | | 52 + 65 |

# Working in pairs or groups

Many of the exercises in *Cambridge Advanced English* are designed to be done by students working together in pairs or in small groups of three or four. They are NOT designed to be quickly done 'round the class' with each student answering one question.

There are several advantages to this approach:
- Students get an opportunity to communicate their ideas to each other while they are discussing each exercise.
- Students are more likely to remember answers they have discovered or worked out by themselves than answers other students give – or answers the teacher announces to the class.
- Students working in groups are more active than if they are working as a class: they talk more and do more thinking too. If a class of, say, 20 were doing a 10-question exercise 'round the class' half of them wouldn't answer a single question.
- If an exercise is done 'round the class', the less confident or more sleepy students can simply answer 'I don't know' when their turn comes and go back to sleep the rest of the time. Moreover, weaker students can be lulled into a false sense of security by writing down all the correct answers and kidding themselves that they have 'done' the exercise. The exercises and activities in *Cambridge Advanced English* are designed to help students to LEARN, not to test their knowledge or catch them out, and the idea is NOT for students to say to themselves 'Another 44 pages/exercises to go and then we've finished'!

One drawback of doing exercises in pairs or groups is that it does take time. However, as many of the exercises can be done as homework, time can be saved by setting some exercises to be done at home. Then, back in class next time, students can begin the session by comparing their answers in pairs or groups, and discussing as a class any problems they encountered.

Another possible problem is that errors may go uncorrected and that students might even learn 'bad habits' from each other. This can be dealt with by vigilant monitoring of students as they are working together and encouraging students to correct each other's mistakes – which they should be able to do quite efficiently at this level. This is covered in more detail below.

# Mistakes and correction

Although work on improving students' accuracy is an essential aspect of a language course, particularly at an advanced level, it is far more important for learners to be able to communicate effectively. It is very difficult to develop confidence if one is afraid of making mistakes, and if students are corrected too frequently they may become 'mistake-conscious'. In real life, after all, people have to communicate with each other *in spite of* the mistakes they may be making and their less-than-complete command of English.

Students should certainly be corrected when they make serious errors, but it is usually best to point out any mistakes that were made *after* the groups have completed an activity, rather than interrupting during the activity. While students are working together in pairs or groups, and you are going from group to group listening in, you may be able to make the occasional discreet correction without interrupting the flow of the discussion, but normally it is better to make a note of some of the errors you overhear and point them out later.

You may hear your students making mistakes in pronunciation, grammar or style, but rather than mentioning every mistake you have heard, it is more helpful to be selective and to draw attention to specific points that you think your students should concentrate on improving. It may be less confusing to focus on just one type of error at a time by, for example, drawing attention to pronunciation errors after one activity and then vocabulary errors after another. Accuracy is something that takes a long time to develop and it cannot be achieved overnight!

In marking students' written work it is important to remember how discouraging it is to receive back a paper covered in red marks! It's better for students to locate and correct their own mistakes, rather than have corrections written out for them. This is particularly important when you believe that a student has made a careless mistake or a slip of the pen.

In many cases once mistakes are pointed out to students they can often correct themselves. A 'marking scheme' like the one shown overleaf is recommended, but whatever scheme you use make sure your students are conversant with the system you're using. The symbols shown here would appear on the side of the page in the margin – make sure your students do leave a wide enough margin for your comments!

**X** = 'Somewhere in this line there is a mistake of some kind that you should find and correct'

**XX** = 'Somewhere in this line there are two mistakes that you should find and correct'

<u>An incorrect word or phrase underlined</u> = 'This particular word or phrase is not correct and you should correct it'

**G** = 'Somewhere in this line there is a Grammatical mistake that you should find and correct'

**V** = 'Somewhere in this line there is a Vocabulary mistake that you should find and correct'

**Sp** = 'Somewhere in this line there is a Spelling mistake that you should find and correct'

**P** = 'Somewhere in this line there is a Punctuation mistake that you should find and correct'

**WO** = 'Some of the words in this sentence are in the Wrong Order, please rearrange them'

**?** = 'I don't quite understand what you mean'

And equally important, more positive or encouraging marks:

**√** = 'Good, you have expressed this idea well!' or 'This is an interesting or amusing point'

**√√** = 'Very good, you have expressed this idea very well!' or 'Very interesting or amusing point!'

Remember that all learners need encouragement and praise. Just as you might sometimes ignore mistakes when students are speaking, perhaps occasionally some mistakes should be overlooked in their written work?

## Other materials

Students at this level are likely to have specific needs and interests that a general coursebook can only partly cater for. You may need to find supplementary materials (particularly topical reading or listening texts) from other sources.

Further material that you may find useful can be found in *Use of English* and *Ideas*, both by Leo Jones (Cambridge University Press).

Advanced students can benefit greatly from doing SIMULATIONS regularly. It will help them to develop confidence by using their English in a purposeful way. The simulations in *Eight Simulations* by Leo Jones (Cambridge University Press) are particularly recommended.

Students should also possess a good English-to-English dictionary: the *Longman Dictionary of Contemporary English* (LDOCE), the *Oxford Advanced Learner's Dictionary* (OALD), the *Collins COBUILD Essential English Dictionary* and *The Penguin Wordmaster Dictionary* are all comprehensive and relatively portable.

Although *Cambridge Advanced English* revises the main problem areas of English grammar, students should also have access to a comprehensive reference book. *Practical English Usage* by Michael Swan (Oxford University Press) is easy to use and highly recommended.

## Examination preparation

*Cambridge Advanced English* is not an examination preparation course, but the level and the type of activities in it are entirely suitable for students preparing for the Cambridge Certificate in Advanced English (CAE). A certain amount of exam-directed practice, using Practice Tests is recommended during the weeks before the exam takes place. Students taking this exam should devote more time to the Effective writing and Creative writing sections than students who have no exam in mind.

### CERTIFICATE IN ADVANCED ENGLISH

The CAE examination, launched in December 1991, is available on a twice-yearly basis.

Certificates are awarded in three passing grades A, B and C and two failing grades D and E.

The five papers each receive an equal weighting of 20%.

PAPER 1 **Reading** (1 hour)

Approximately 50 multiple-choice questions of varying type based on four texts, designed to test a wide range of reading skills and strategies.

PAPER 2 **Writing** (2 hours)

Two writing tasks (letter, report, review, instructions, announcement, etc.) of approximately 250 words each.
A A compulsory task based on a substantial reading input.
B One task selected from a choice of four.
Assessment is based on achievement of task, accuracy of grammatical control, fluency and range of expression.

PAPER3   **English in Use** (2 hours)

A  Multiple-choice and open-completion items based on two short texts, designed to test control over formal elements of the language in context.
B  Questions requiring the revision or correction of two short texts, designed to test ability to refine and proof-read samples of written English.
C  Questions requiring the completion of a text and/or the expansion of notes, etc. into a fuller form, designed to test ability to recognise, produce and organise written English which is appropriate to both purpose and audience.

PAPER 4   **Listening** (approx. 35 minutes)

Questions of varying type (selection, re-ordering, blank-filling, etc.) to test accurate understanding of spoken English, based on recorded material.

PAPER 5   **Speaking** (approx. 15 minutes)

Based on visual stimuli and other material. Candidates will be examined in pairs. Assessment is based on fluency and grammatical accuracy, pronunciation (individual sounds, stress and linking of phrases), communicative ability and vocabulary.

Timing: The written papers are administered on the same day as the Certificate of Proficiency. Candidates are not able to enter for the Certificate in Advanced English and the Certificate of Proficiency in English at the same sitting.

# 1 Desert islands

This is the first 'Theme unit'. In common with the rest of the odd-numbered units, there is a special emphasis on reading and listening skills and on writing skills.

## 1.1   A year on a desert island                Listening

▶ See page 5 of the introduction for a detailed rationale of the Listening sections in the book.

**A**   This brief discussion is a warm-up for the listening exercise in **B**. Allow just a few minutes for everyone to give their views. If preferred, the questions can be discussed as a class. If it is done in pairs or small groups, allow a little time for feedback from the pairs or groups: ask each pair or group to 'report back' on their answers to the questions. Correct any misunderstandings, but don't take too long.

▶ Whenever the instruction 'Work in pairs' or 'Work in groups' is given in the Student's Book rubric, feel free to overrule this and do the activity as a class, particularly if you have a small class.

**B**   Allow time for everyone to read through the questions before playing the recording to them. Answer any questions about vocabulary that are raised. Encourage them to 'guess' some of the answers, basing their guesses on their ASSUMPTIONS about what is likely to have happened in the story. Then, when they listen to the recording, this can confirm or contradict the answers they anticipated and make the task of listening more realistic. This may help to simulate the real life situation, where a listener often has some previous knowledge of the subject matter.

Before playing the recording, read through the transcript and highlight any vocabulary items that you'd like to draw your students' attention to later.

Background note: Lucy Irvine's first book was *Castaway* (1983). She has subsequently written about her earlier life in *Runaway* (1986), as well as a novel: *One is One* (1989).

📼 To give everyone a chance to get used to the voices before they have to concentrate on answering the questions, play the first twenty seconds of the recording through first, then rewind the tape back to the beginning. Then play the whole recording, with perhaps a short break in the middle for everyone to compare their answers so far.

After the first playing, decide whether you need to play the whole recording through again. If everyone thinks they have every answer right this won't be necessary. If everyone is unsure about some answers or still has some gaps unfilled, then the whole tape should be played through again.

Get everyone to compare their answers in pairs before going through the correct answers. If there is much disagreement about any of these, play the relevant sections of the recording again.

## Answers

Was it Lucy (L) or Gerald (G) or both of them (L + G) who ...

| | |
|---|---|
| wrote *Castaway*   L | wrote *The Islander*   G |
| had lived on another tropical island   G | had worked in a tax office   L |
| was 24 years old   L | was 51 years old   G |
| caught fish   L + G | tried to grow vegetables   G |
| did the cooking   L | was going to write a novel   G |
| was bad-tempered   G | went off for long walks alone   L |
| fell in love with the island   L | wrote a diary   L |
| was bitten by insects   G | couldn't walk   G |
| lost a lot of weight   L + G | had an irritating voice   L |
| lost touch with reality   L + G | drank salty water   L + G |
| did repairs for local islanders   G | went to Badu for Christmas   L + G |
| wanted to stay longer on the islands   G | wrote a best-selling book   L |

## Transcript

Presenter: ... the film was directed by Nicholas Roeg and is called *Castaway*. Jane Brown's been reading *Castaway* by Lucy Irvine. Tim Craven's been reading *The Islander* by Gerald Kingsland. Jane, you first.

Jane: Well, um ... well, Lucy Irvine had a ... a really boring, dead-end job in an income tax office so ... um ... she was longing for an escape, you know, for a bit of adventure and she saw this advert in *Time Out*, which said: 'Writer wants "wife" for year on tropical island' and ...

Tim: Yes, but ...

Jane:      ... and then she responded.

Tim:      Yes, but it all started long before that ad. Gerald Kingsland wanted to experience life on a desert island. He tried to find a suitable island: first Cocos Island off the coast of Costa Rica – he spent some months with the local soldiers and a female companion, then his sons came and they all lived together for the summer. But it wasn't a deserted island. Then he wanted to go to Robinson Crusoe's original island where Alexander Selkirk had first been cast away off ... just off Chile. But his companion fell ill before they could get to the island. So, he went back to London and advertised in *Time Out*. And, of course, there were lots and lots of applicants but he chose Lucy Irvine. Her age was 24 and he was 51.

Jane:      Well, anyway, they ... they got permission finally to spend a year on Tuin island in ... er ... the Torres Strait, which is between North Australia and Papua New Guinea ... er ... on the one condition that they would have to be married. So they did, they got married just before they ... um ... arrived on the island, but ... um ... Lucy Irvine actually decided that she wouldn't sleep with him, she insisted that they would sleep apart.

Tim:      Right, well, the island – it wasn't very big and it had just one small creek of fresh water, plenty of fish, of course, being an island, er ... coconuts and some fruit. It was very dry, there wasn't any rain and ... er ... their survival rations were a few kilos of rice, a bit of cooking oil, tea and ... they'd depend on the island's resources for food.

Jane:      Yeah, they ... they established their ... um ... different roles, the division of labour, but th ... I mean they both caught fish, which was their only protein, um ... he planted seeds and grew vegetables, cut wood, and built the shelter and ... er ... she did the cooking, collected the fruit, um ... oh, while he was writing his novel, of course.

Tim:      Right, w ... um ... while Gerald tried to write and tried to make some sort of a garden grow, Lucy went off by herself all day. But the island wasn't as beautiful as Cocos Island.

Jane:      While he stayed in the camp ... um ... Lucy ... er ... had to get away, she went off for long walks on her own to escape from his ... his bad temper and she wrote a diary. Um ... the ... the island to her was absolutely beautiful, very attractive place and ... er ... full of mystery. Um ... and he ... he seemed to find the island boring, which she couldn't understand at all.

Tim:      Yeah, but Gerald didn't want to rush into anything. You know, they had a whole year ahead of them: there was no point in building a permanent shelter.

Jane:      Um ... this was a bone of contention between them. Gerald actually refused to build a proper shelter, saying that ... that it wasn't a ... a priority.

Tim:      Meanwhile, they both had to sleep in the same small tent – not

|        | |
|--------|--|
|        | touching, of course. Um ... and sandflies bit him in the night, you know, he got tropical ulcers, that were so painful he could hardly walk and, of course, the sea water made them worse. |
| Jane:  | They were, in fact, both suffering ... um ... they got thinner and thinner and very weak in spite of ... er ... eating fish they ... they weren't getting enough carbohydrates, no potatoes or bread, and not enough vitamins. There was no rain, and all the vegetables withered, so ... um ... the tension grew between them. |
| Tim:   | According to Gerald, Lucy talked much too much and always seemed to be telling him what to do. |
| Jane:  | Well, according to Lucy, Gerald spent too long doing nothing, not getting on with surviving and not enjoying or appreciating the island and its beauty. |
| Tim:   | The water supply was drying up. W ... they seemed to be losing touch with reality, going around in a sort of dream. Gerald was unable to walk. |
| Jane:  | Oh, then out of the blue two visitors arrived: two young men, Peter and Derek they were called, and they were on their way to Singapore in ... in catamarans. Um ... they gave them antibiotics to help cure the tropical ulcers. |
| Tim:   | And one of them asked him how he could stand her bossy tone of voice and constant talking. |
| Jane:  | Well, they actually tried to persuade Lucy to leave the bad-tempered, weak old man. They were very sympathetic to her about being stuck with him but, in fact, she refused to leave. |
| Tim:   | Then, some weeks later, Ronald Lui, who was a local Badu ... island fisherman, he arrived at the island and he was very friendly, very friendly chap and he gave them some food, discovered that their water supply was salty because ... it ... it happened gradually and they hadn't noticed and you go crazy if you drink salt water. So he returned later bringing them fresh water. Soon after that two Australian nurses came over and gave them more antibiotics. |
| Jane:  | Well, at last, Gerald built a proper house and Ronald, the local fisherman, um ... he brought an old sewing machine for Gerald to repair ... um ... Gerald realised that he was the only person on the island who could do this, so he was very soon repairing outboard motors and generators for other local islanders in exchange for rice and flour and food, and bit by bit Gerald's health and ... and self-respect restored, so ... um ... Lucy felt that now she would ... um ... she would sleep with him. |
|        | ★　★　★ |
| Tim:   | Then the rainy season came: enormous storms and very rough seas. So they left the island to visit Badu for Christmas. They had to stay till the sea was calm enough for them to return. Gerald told Lucy she should be the one who would write the book about their adventure, so both of them happily spent the last months of their time on the island. |

Jane:         Er ... when the time came to leave, he wanted her to stay with him and live on the islands ... um ... the idea would be, you know, he'd repair engines to ... to make a living, but she didn't want to. She felt that she was too young for him and ... um ... she wasn't in love with him. So she left to go home and ... and write the account of ... of their adventure together and ... um ... her book was a best-seller, called *Castaway.*

Presenter: And how did the film, which you've both seen, manage to capture the two versions of the story, do you think? Um ... Tim?

Tim:          Ah, well, you have to remember that ... er ... of course, any film has to entertain rather than . . .

(Time: 6 minutes 50 seconds)

**C**   For this exercise you'll need to rewind the tape to the place marked with stars ★ ★ ★ in the transcript above. This can be done while the class are working in pairs on the first part of the activity. Set the counter to zero so that you can find the place again later if necessary.

Follow the procedure outlined in the Student's Book before playing the tape.

Play the tape for everyone to check whether they guessed correctly or not. Allow time to discuss other possible words that weren't actually used by the speakers. For example, in 9 the sentence could end with *adventures, experiences, time together, stay on the island,* etc.

## Answers

1 *Example: make sure everyone understands what they are supposed to do.*
2 calm enough
3 the book about their adventure
4 the island
5 stay with him and live on the islands
6 a living
7 young for him
8 love with him
9 adventure together
10 *Castaway*

**D**   This group discussion gives everyone a chance to air their views. Ask each group to report back on their discussion at the end. The amount of time you allow for this will depend on how much time you have available and how interested or involved everyone gets in their discussion.

# 1.2 **Islands and adventures** Vocabulary

▶ See page 6 of the introduction for more information about the Vocabulary sections.

**A** The opening discussion is intended to give students a chance to find out what vocabulary they need to discuss the topic. Encourage everyone to ask questions about any vocabulary they were searching for during this discussion.

**B** This is a straightforward gap-filling exercise – it can be done in pairs or by students working alone in class or as homework. It revises some of the vocabulary introduced in 1.1 and anticipates some literary references that are made in 1.3 later. Discuss any other answers that are suggested.

*Answers*

1 resources    fresh
2 survival rations
3 division of labour    shelter
4 tension    nerves
5 shipwrecked
6 rescued
7 surviving    circumstances
8 disaster    first

**C** ▐✦▌ In this Communication activity each student has different information which must be shared with a partner and there is an information gap to bridge.

Draw everyone's attention to the instructions in the Student's Book: this is NOT a reading aloud exercise but a chance to share information with each other.
Student A looks at Activity 1, which tells the story of *The Blue Lagoon*.
Student B looks at Activity 32, which tells the story of *The Swiss Family Robinson*.
Student C looks at Activity 50, which tells the story of *Robinson Crusoe*.

▶ If it's necessary to form a group of four, two students could 'share' the *Blue Lagoon* story in Activity 1.

At the end of the activity, when each group member has told his or her story, ask for feedback from the class:
- Do they have any questions?
- What did they find easy/difficult about the activity?
- If they could do it again, what would they do differently?

# 1.3 The Castaways                                        Reading

▶ See page 4 of the introduction for a description of the Reading sections in the book.

▶ If possible, get everyone to prepare this text as homework before the lesson and highlight the unfamiliar words.

The poet Adrian Mitchell was born in 1932. His poems are simple and topical, and easily accessible. He is committed to poetry as performance and much of his work contains social comment. His collected verse is published in *For Beauty Douglas: Collected Poems 1953–1979.*

**A** 🔲 A reading of the poem is recorded – play the tape as the class follow the text in their books. It lasts 3 minutes 40 seconds.

🔲 Before they do the task in **B**, ask everyone to highlight any unfamiliar words in the poem using a fluorescent highlighter. This symbol is used throughout the book whenever this has to be done.

Useful vocabulary is also to be found in other places in the Student's Book, of course – for example, in the rubrics and exercises. Point this out to everyone. Looking back at 1.2 **B**, for example, students might have highlighted *vicariously* in 8 and *bone of contention* in 3.

**B** To save time, perhaps each member of the group could concentrate on a different character and make notes on that one first. There are no 'correct answers' here: even what is 'useful' or 'pointless' may be a matter of opinion.

**C** This discussion will encourage students to think about the implications of the poem. Make sure there is time for feedback afterwards and make it clear that there are no 'right answers' when it comes to interpreting a poem.

The groups should compose their sentences together as a team OR could split up at this point to work alone.

▶ If you anticipate that your students will have difficulty with this discussion, do this section as a whole-class activity.

**D** This follow-up discussion gives students a chance to express their ideas and use the vocabulary introduced in the unit so far.

---

# 1.4 Joining sentences – 1 Effective writing

▶ See page 7 of the introduction for more information about the Effective writing sections.

The exercises in this section are intended as revision of work your students are likely to have done in previous courses. They will also help you to diagnose what kind of mistakes your students make in their writing.

**A** Ask the class to comment on the styles used in the six examples. The handwritten examples reflect spoken style while the typed ones reflect a more formal written style. In an informal personal letter, a style halfway between the two might be more appropriate.

**B** This should be done in pairs but if it is more convenient to set this as homework, make sure pairs of students have a chance to compare their ideas together in class at some stage.

   Notice that the past perfect has to be used in some of these sentences.

*Suggested answers* (many variations possible)

1 *Example: make sure everyone sees what they're supposed to do.*
2 As it was a cold, damp morning, I couldn't get my car to start, so I knew that I would have to push it down the hill. As the car gathered speed, I jumped in and managed to start the engine, but by the time I arrived at work I was late.
3 Her interest in politics made her decide to stand for parliament. Although she won the by-election with a large majority, she lost at the next general election and subsequently gave up politics for good.
4 After they had been dancing together, they went to a café. And as they had spent such a long time drinking coffee and talking, they got home very late.
5 Since the airport was closed because of fog, many flights were delayed and this caused inconvenience to hundreds of passengers.

Our plane didn't take off and, finally, we had to spend the night in the departure lounge.
6 After the ransom money had been paid, the hostages were released. However, when the kidnappers were trying to get out of the country, all ports and airports were being watched so that eventually they were caught by the police.

**C**   Let the class decide whether they'll do the straightforward exercise or whether they'd prefer to change the ending of each little story.

## Suggested answers

2 I arrived late for work because I hadn't been able to get the car to start one cold, damp morning. I decided to push the car down the hill and managed to start the engine after I had jumped in as it gathered speed.
3 Her interest in politics made her decide to stand for parliament and she won the by-election with a large majority, but she gave up politics for good after she had lost at the general election.
4 They got home very late because they had spent a long time drinking coffee and talking after they had been dancing together and then gone on to a café.
5 Our plane didn't take off as the airport was closed because of fog and many flights were delayed, which caused inconvenience to hundreds of passengers, including us: we had to spend the night in the departure lounge.
6 The kidnappers were caught by the police as all ports and airports were being watched while they were trying to get out of the country. They had eventually released the hostages when the ransom money had been paid.

**D**   Perhaps point out that there are no hard-and-fast rules about what is appropriate in formal or informal styles. The aim of this exercise is to help students to develop an awareness and 'feeling' for what is appropriate.

## Suggested answers

2 Once they had found some driftwood and built a bonfire on the beach, they caught some fish and grilled them over the fire.
3 After they had gathered palm leaves, they built themselves a rough shelter.
4 After suffering a sleepless night because of all the insects, they began to lose heart.

5 They made mosquito nets because they wanted to protect themselves the following night.
6 They were very glad when they found wild bananas growing on a hillside and, after eating them, they started to look for a supply of drinking water.
7 As they were unable to find any fresh water, they were afraid they would not be able to survive on the island.
8 Although they hoped to collect some rainwater to drink, there was so little rain that they were in despair.
9 After they had built a raft from the remaining driftwood, they set sail across the ocean.
10 In the end, as the raft started to sink, man-eating sharks began to circle ominously round them.

Finally, ask the class what they found most difficult in this section and, if necessary, do some remedial work. There are suitable exercises in *Use of English* by Leo Jones (CUP) Units 35 to 37.

▶ There is more practice on using past tenses in section 2.3. Joining sentences – 2 is in section 13.4.

---

# 1.5 Your own ideas

## Creative writing

▶ See page 7 of the introduction for more information about the Creative writing sections, and page 15 for more information about mistakes and correction.

**A** In this, as in many of the Creative writing sections, students are given a choice between a lighter and a more serious topic to write about. Depending on your students' interests and long-term objectives (using English in their academic studies, their work, for an exam, etc.) you may decide to recommend or even stipulate which one they should choose.

Encourage everyone to make notes before they start writing. This can be done by students working together in pairs or groups.

**B** Make sure everyone follows the instructions, so that the activity in C is set up suitably.

**C** After the group work, collect everyone's work and mark it. Treat this exercise as a way of diagnosing your students' writing skills. Try to make comments on each person's work and help them to be aware of their strengths and weaknesses in writing.

# 1.6   All in all . . . Idioms

▶ See page 8 of the introduction for more information about the Idioms and Verbs and idioms sections.

Although the Idioms and Verbs and idioms sections are printed at the end of each unit, they can all be done at ANY stage, depending on the time available. They can, for example, fill a convenient 10–15 minutes at the end of a lesson and be completed as homework.

▶ Point out to the class that just doing these exercises is not going to 'teach' them the expressions. The exercises revise expressions they may already know and introduce new ones – learning the idioms they consider to be useful is up to them and it will take time for such idioms to be incorporated into their active vocabulary.

**A**  *Answers*

| | |
|---|---|
| 2  overall | 10  All being well |
| 3  overalls | 11  all important |
| 4  all over | 12  all right |
| 5  was all over | 13  all right |
| 6  it's all the same to | 14  all the same |
| 7  all in | 15  all told      all at once |
| 8  all in | 16  above all |
| 9  All at once      all but | |

**B**  *Answers*

1  in all
2  being well
3  the same to
4  the same
5  over
6  the same to
7  Above all

**C**  ▨ As pointed out above, students should make their own decisions about what vocabulary is useful for them to learn. Highlighting will help to draw attention to vocabulary when they are reviewing a unit.

# Finally . . .

▶ Recommend to everyone that they should spend twenty minutes reading through the whole of this unit at home before going on to the next one. In this way, new vocabulary is more likely to 'sink in' and be remembered permanently.

# 2 Around the world

This is the first of the 'Language units'. In common with the rest of the even-numbered units, there is a special emphasis on grammar revision, word study and functions. But there is also some listening and/or reading in these units too.

## 2.1 United nations                                    Vocabulary

▶ If possible, take a large map of the world, a globe or perhaps an atlas into class for this section.

**A** These exercises contain a number of tricky nationality words, even for students whose geographical knowledge is good. Some of the countries are included because they will be referred to later in this unit.

1 Note that we are concerned with nationality words, not the word for a native or resident of the cities (e.g. *Muscovite, Viennese, Roman*, etc.) in this exercise.

### Answers

Baghdad – an Iraqi      Bamako – a Malian
Bangkok – a Thai        Belgrade – a Yugoslav / a Yugoslavian
Bogotá – a Colombian      Brussels – a Belgian
Bucharest – a Romanian      Budapest – a Hungarian
Cairo – an Egyptian      Caracas – a Venezuelan
Dakar – a Senegalese      Delhi – an Indian
Dublin – an Irishman/woman      Havana – a Cuban
Jakarta – an Indonesian      Karachi – a Pakistani
Khartoum – a Sudanese      Kuala Lumpur – a Malaysian
Lagos – a Nigerian      Lima – a Peruvian
Manila – a Filipino      Moscow – a Russian
Oslo – a Norwegian      Prague – a Czech
Pretoria – a South African      Riyadh – a Saudi Arabian
Rome – an Italian      São Paulo – a Brazilian
Seoul – a South Korean      Sofia – a Bulgarian
Tehran – an Iranian      Vienna – an Austrian

## 2 *Answers*

Switzerland    Canada    Denmark    Greece    Ireland
the Netherlands / Holland    Portugal    Poland    Sweden
Finland    CD = diplomatic corps(!)

Swiss    Canadian    Danish    Greek    Irish
Dutch    Portuguese    Polish    Swedish    Finnish
a foreign diplomat

## 3 *Suggested answers*

some Asian countries:
  Vietnam, Cambodia, Afghanistan, Burma, Laos, North Korea,
  etc.

some Latin American countries:
  Uruguay, Bolivia, Mexico, Nicaragua, Brazil, Honduras, Cuba,
  etc.

some Middle Eastern countries:
  Lebanon, Oman, Jordan, Egypt, Dubai, Saudi Arabia, etc.

some members of NATO:
  Canada, Norway, Belgium, Italy, Turkey, Greece, etc.

some members of the European Community:
  Spain, Greece, Denmark, Luxembourg, Ireland, etc.

some African countries:
  Zaïre, Gabon, Botswana, Zambia, Zimbabwe, Malawi, etc.
  Algeria, Morocco, Libya, Sudan, Tunisia, etc.

**B**   Make sure everyone makes notes and asks about any vocabulary
they need during this discussion.

**C**   This could be started on the board and then completed for
homework. Make sure students don't include any items that are
already well-known to them (e.g. *China, Japan, USA,* etc.).

# 2.2 **World Music** Listening

▶ If you listen carefully to the recording between each listening exercise you may notice a very low-pitched 'hum'. If you're playing the tape as you fast forward it (CUE) or rewind it (REVIEW) this 'hum' is heard as a distinctive 'beep' tone, making it easy to find your place on the tape. If your cassette player does not have CUE or REVIEW controls, this will not be possible.

**A + B + C** 🖭 Follow the procedure suggested in the Student's Book. Perhaps pause the recording at the place marked with ★ ★ ★ in the transcript for everyone to compare their answers thus far.

*Answers*

## A

| | |
|---|---|
| Algeria | Cheb Khaled |
| Cuba | Elio Revé and his Orquesta Revé |
| Hungary (Transylvania) | Márta Sebestyén |
| Mali | Toumani Diabate |
| | Salif Keïta |
| Pakistan | Nusrat Fateh Ali Khan |
| Senegal | Youssou N'dour |
| South Africa | General M.D. Shirinda and the Gaza Sisters |
| | Ladysmith Black Mambazo |
| Sudan | Abdel Aziz El Mubarak |

## B

1 popular     cultures
2 nineteenth     crazes
3 West Africa     rhythm and blues     the Congo
4 album     South African
5 creative/alive/fresh/imaginative     big business     marketing
6 traditions     centuries/generations
7 Cuba     dance
8 category     Bulgaria     Hungary
9 record producers     section
10 studios     Paris     London     high-tech and handmade

**C** The adjectives used are <u>underlined</u> in the transcript below.

**D**   This follow-up discussion gives students a chance to find out about each other's tastes in music – 'foreign countries' include the USA and the UK in this case.

## Transcript

Presenter:   . . . back with us at the same time tomorrow. Now, have you heard of World Music? It's a term that may be unfamiliar to you. Pat Brown's been finding out for us. Pat.

Pat:   What is World Music? I asked record producers Jim Spring and Lucy Charlton.

Jim:   Well, it's ... it's popular music that comes from cultures other than Britain and the USA.

Lucy:   Basically, it's music that's popular in Africa, Latin America and other parts of the world. Um ... it's been referred to as 'living traditional music', which means that it's <u>real</u> and it's still being played and enjoyed – it's not being revived or rediscovered.

Pat:   So is this a new trend: discovering music from other cultures?

Jim:   Oh no, not at all, no. Er ... since the nineteenth century all popular dance crazes – er ... the polka, waltz, tango – they've all originated i ... in other parts of the world. Th ... the dances and their rhythms were taken by middle-class people who wanted to be shocked by sexy new rhythms. The ideas were imported from other cultures or from ... from their own under-classes – w ... for example, th ... the blues: that came from the poor black people of North America. W ... most of what we consider to be purely American popular music: rock 'n' roll, jazz, it's all rooted i ... in West Africa. The slaves took their traditional music and rhythms with them when they went to America. Historically and ... er ... and musically too, rock 'n' roll is a development of rhythm and blues, which itself developed originally from the music of the Congo.

Pat:   There was an upsurge of interest in African music after Paul Simon released his *Graceland* album in 1987.

Lucy:   It's true that Paul Simon did increase public awareness of *South* African music: bands and groups from the townships like Soweto. Er ... Ladyship (*sic*) Black Mambazo, for example, are an <u>extraordinary</u> group of singers who sing unaccompanied, using their voices as instruments. And ... um ... General M.D. Shirinda and the Gaza Sisters are great too. But ... ah ... I'm sorry, Paul Simon didn't start the whole thing. Actually, there had been a growing interest dating from the mid-eighties among enthusiasts and musicians who were, well, a lot of them were finding Anglo-American popular music increasingly <u>unimaginative</u> – sterile.

Pat:   Where is this more <u>imaginative</u> music coming from? Jim Spring again.

Jim:   Well, er ... ah ... from all over the world: anywhere where people

are still creating music and improvising, wh ... where the music is
still <u>alive</u> and <u>fresh</u> and *not* organised and managed by ... er ... big
business interests and marketing. If we just look at West Africa,
where music-making is still very much alive, there are all sorts of
different traditional styles and ... er ... unusual instruments –
different kinds of percussion instruments a ... and string
instruments too, like ... er ... like the kora: w ... that's a
<u>wonderful</u> 21-stringed West African harp-lute. It ... it has a quite
<u>magical</u> sound – Toumani Diabate from Mali is ... is a great
virtuoso. Many of the people who are becoming well-known
in the West now are already superstars in their own countries
– their music's based on local traditions dating back hundreds
and hundreds of years wh ... where particular families have
carried on the tradition of music-making for generation after
generation. Two of the biggest names are ... um ... Youssou
N'dour from Senegal and ... er ... Salif Keïta from Mali: both of
them belong to families of musicians. Often they've combined
their traditional instruments from Africa with Western
instruments, like ... er ... electric guitars, in strikingly <u>unique</u>,
<u>original</u> ways. Th ... their melodies are quite remarkable too.

★ ★ ★

Pat: And where else in Africa does this World Music come from?

Jim: Well, the music of North Africa is becoming much better known:
Algeria has its own special popular music it's called Rai: Cheb
Khaled, for example. Er ... and Abdel Aziz El Mubarak from
Sudan. Their music is ... it's quite <u>wonderful</u>. Er ... there's also ...
there's a wide range of ... of Latin American music, mostly getting
its basic rhythms from West Africa. Er ... for example, on the
island of Cuba: it has its characteristic salsa and son-changüi
bands: Elio Revé and his Orquesta Revé – <u>marvellous</u> music, it
really makes you want to dance.

Pat: What about Europe and Asia?

Lucy: For some reason, the ... er traditional folk music of Western
Europe falls outside the category of World Music but, to confuse
you, not the popular music of Bulgaria and Hungary, for
example, which uses instruments and sounds and voices with
some wonderfully <u>haunting</u> songs: Márta Sebestyén's songs from
Transylvania – amazing. Now Asian music is still little known
but that's changing. The melodies and rhythms of Nusrat Fateh
Ali Khan from Pakistan: devotional Muslim songs, they're
<u>fascinating</u>.

Pat: The term 'World Music' was actually invented by a group of
record producers a few years ago, so that record shops would
have a convenient special section where customers could find this
kind of music. Record buyers didn't even know where to find it
in the few shops that did stock it! This kind of music tended to
be only available as imports and was hard to come by anyway.

Jim: These days World Music tends to be recorded in modern studios

in Paris or London, or ... or of course, in Peter Gabriel's new ... er
... Real World Studio down in Wiltshire.

Pat: Peter Gabriel invested £5 million in a studio in the heart of the
English countryside – his motto is 'high-tech and handmade' –
where musicians from all over the world can make music and
record it using the latest recording techniques.

Lucy: You can find all kinds of World Music on labels like
EarthWorks, Hannibal Records, Stern's Africa, World Circuit,
Real World Records – there are lots of them. You just have to
browse around in your local record shop to see the range that's
available (it's filed under World Music) – all you have to do is
discover it for yourself!

(Time: 6 minutes 15 seconds)

# 2.3   Looking back                         Grammar

▶ See page 9 of the introduction for more information about the
Grammar revision sections in this book.

This section revises the basic uses of the simple past, present perfect
and past perfect. There is more work on tenses in 4.3 and 8.3.

**A**   This type of exercise occurs in most Grammar sections – the
idea is to make students aware of shades of meaning expressed
through grammatical structures and to give them a chance to
discover what they already know, what they are unsure of, and what
they don't know.

The suggested answers below can be amplified by referring to a
grammar reference book, such as *Practical English Usage* by Michael
Swan (OUP).

*Suggested answers*

1 When they heard the song everyone started singing.
   *– the song hadn't finished, they heard the beginning and then joined in
   with the rest of it*
   When they had heard the song everyone started singing.
   *– they listened to the whole of the song and then began to sing (maybe
   a different song)*

2 Did you enjoy your holiday?
   *– your holiday is probably over now and you're back at work/home now*
   Have you enjoyed your holiday?
   *– you are still technically on holiday but it's nearly over*

3 I never enjoyed travelling alone.
   *– this was the situation at the time in the past I'm talking about*
   I've never enjoyed travelling alone.
   *– this is true now and it always has been*
   I had never enjoyed travelling alone.
   *– this was the situation before an event that happened in the past which perhaps changed my mind*

4 She lived abroad for several years.
   *– in the past but now she's probably living in this country*
   She has lived abroad for several years.
   *– she's still living abroad now*
   She had lived abroad for several years.
   *– this was the situation before another event occurred*

## B  *Suggested answers*

### Simple past

1 She **was born** (e) in India and **came** (e) to Britain when she **was** (e) eighteen.
   She **began** learning English six years ago when she **was** twelve years old.
   **Did you see** that programme about Japan on TV last night?
2 Look over there: someone has broken a window. I wonder who **did** (a) it?
   What a lovely photograph! **Did** you **take** it yourself?

### Present perfect

3 She **has worked** (d) hard all her life.
   I **haven't seen** (d) her recently.
   **Have** you ever **been** to the USA?
   **Have you read** Lucy Irvine's new book?
4 I've just **returned** (c) from a long trip, so I don't feel like travelling anywhere.
   I heard on the news today that there **has been** a terrible earthquake in China and thousands of people **have been** killed.

### Past perfect

5 It was very cold when he got to Moscow because winter **had** (already) **arrived** (b).
6 My car wouldn't start this morning because I **had left** (b) the lights on all night.
   He **wasn't able to / wasn't allowed to** get on the plane because he **had forgotten** his passport.

7 She said she **had been** (f) in Burma in 1988 but that she **had** (f) never **been** to India.
We asked him why **he hadn't come** to the party the previous weekend.

Discuss any problems before doing C below.

**C** This exercise can be done by students in pairs, or to save time, set as homework and discussed in class later.

## Suggested answers (some of these are debatable)

already – 2, 4      a few minutes ago – 1
a little while earlier – 4      a long time ago – 1
a moment ago – 1      all my life – 2      always – 3, 4
at midnight – 1, 4      by midnight – 4      by now – 2
by the end of the year – 1, 4      by four o'clock yesterday – 1, 4
for two months – 3, 4      in the morning – 1, 4
in 1990 – 1, 4      just now – 1      last year – 1
never – 1, 3, 4      not long ago – 1      not long before that – 4
recently – 3      so far – 2      still – 2
some time previously – 4      this afternoon – 2
this week – 2      this year – 2      till now – 2
till midnight – 1, 4      two years ago – 1      until today – 2
up to the present – 2      when I was at school – 1
yesterday – 1, 4      yet – 2

**D** Note that there are two ways of doing this exercise. Decide which one you'd prefer the class to do.

**E** *Suggested answers*

2 It's six years since their eldest son **was** born.
3 What a delicious Indian meal that was – **did you cook** it yourself?
4 Where **did you get** that marvellous Persian rug?
5 I couldn't look up the word because I **had** lost my dictionary.
6 That is the funniest story I **have** ever heard.
7 It **has been** a long time since I wrote to my friends in Mexico.
8 I **haven't finished** yet, can I have a few more minutes, please?
9 He **had had** three cups of tea by the time I arrived.
10 By 1965 most African countries **had** become independent from colonial rule.

Point out that errors like the ones in this exercise may well be the kinds of mistakes that members of the class make in their own writing.

**F**   This is an 'activation' exercise to give you and your students a chance to see how well they can use the structures they have been studying. Go round the class listening to each group and correcting any relevant errors, i.e. mistakes in using past tenses.

## 2.4   Other people, other customs

**A**   🎭   In this Communication activity, Student A looks at Activity 4, student B at 36 and C at 53. Each person has a different part of the same article about 'Photon' – a craze that's sweeping Japan and which may become popular in other countries too. The idea is to exchange information and not to read the texts aloud word-for-word. Make sure, therefore, that everyone has a few minutes to study their text before they start sharing its contents.

**B**   The discussion on 'national stereotypes' may be done as a class, rather than in groups, if time is short.

## 2.5   Really? That's amazing!

▶ See page 10 for more information about the Functions sections in this book.

**A**   ▭   Play the tape, perhaps pausing momentarily after each extract for students to think for a moment before they note down each answer.

| | | | | |
|---|---|---|---|---|
| surprised: | 8 | 12 | not surprised: | 9 |
| annoyed: | 4 | | relieved: | 6 |
| disappointed: | 11 | | uninterested: | 1 14 |
| pleased: | 5 | | sympathetic: | 3 15 |
| interested: | 7 | 13 | excited: | 2 10 |

*Transcript*

| | | |
|---|---|---|
| 1 Man: | There's a party on Saturday night! | |
| Woman: | Oh, wonderful. | *(lack of interest)* |
| 2 Man: | There's a party on Saturday night! | |
| Other man: | Oh, wonderful! | *(excited)* |

| | | |
|---|---|---|
| 3 | Man: | I think I've lost the front door key. |
| | Woman: | Oh. *(sympathetic)* |
| 4 | Man: | I think I've lost the front door key. |
| | Other man: | Oh. *(annoyed)* |
| 5 | Man: | It's all right, I've found the key in my bag. |
| | Woman: | Oh, good. *(pleased)* |
| 6 | Man: | It's all right, I've found the key in my bag. |
| | Other man: | Thank goodness. *(relieved)* |
| 7 | Woman: | Did you know that Great Britain is the world's eighth largest island? |
| | Man: | Really? *(interested)* |
| 8 | Woman: | Did you know that Great Britain is the world's eighth largest island? |
| | Other woman: | Really? *(surprised)* |
| 9 | Woman: | Did you know that Great Britain is the world's eighth largest island? |
| | Man: | Really? *(not surprised)* |
| 10 | Man: | The show is on tomorrow. |
| | Woman: | Really?! *(excited)* |
| 11 | Man: | The show is on tomorrow. |
| | Other man: | Ohh! *(disappointed)* |
| 12 | Woman: | It's his forty-second birthday tomorrow. |
| | Man: | Fancy that! *(surprised)* |
| 13 | Man: | That film I wanted to see was on TV last Saturday. |
| | Woman: | I see. *(interested)* |
| 14 | Man: | That film I wanted to see was on TV last Saturday. |
| | Woman: | I see. *(not interested)* |
| 15 | Man: | That film I wanted to see was on TV last Saturday. |
| | Woman: | How annoying! *(sympathetic)* |

(Time: 1 minute 35 seconds)

## B  Suggested answers

SURPRISE  That's amazing!     Good lord!     Really!
Fancy that!     *Good heavens!*

EXCITEMENT  Fantastic!!     That's wonderful!     How exciting!
*Great!     How thrilling!*

DISAPPOINTMENT  What     a     pity!     What a shame!
What a nuisance!     Oh dear!     *I'd been looking forward to …*

INTEREST  Really!     How interesting!     *That's interesting!*

PLEASURE  I *am* pleased!     Fantastic!!     That's wonderful!
*Oh, good!*

SYMPATHY  What a pity!     What a shame!     Oh dear!
*I'm sorry to hear that.*

ANNOYANCE  How     annoying!     How     infuriating!
What a nuisance!     *That's typical!*

RELIEF  Thank  goodness!  Phew!  That *is* good news!
Thank heavens!  That's a relief!  *Thank goodness for that!*

Some other expressions are given in italics above.

**C** 📼  Play the second part of the recording and pause the tape after each remark (shown with a ★ in the transcript). Ask members of the class to suggest various ways in which they might react to what they have heard, using the expressions they've studied in **B**.

*Transcript*

Narrator: Imagine that the people you're talking to are friends of yours and reply to them appropriately.

Man: Did you know that there's an underwater mountain in the Pacific Ocean that's the same height as Mount Everest?
★

Woman: You know that job I applied for teaching in China? Well, I've been accepted and I start in September!
★

Man: I've got to babysit tonight, so I'm afraid we won't be able to go out together.
★

Man: You know those notes you lent me? Well, I'm afraid I've lost them. You'll have to write them out again.
★

Woman: I've got us all tickets for that show – you know, the one we thought was sold out.
★

Man: I've already made arrangements for that evening, so I won't be able to come with you to the show.
★

Man: You know Bill and Maria? Well, I've just found out that they're getting married in April!
★

Woman: Did you know that the book *Robinson Crusoe* is based on a true story?
★

Man: As it's your birthday next week, we've all decided to take you out for a meal. Our treat!
★

Man: Remember I told you I'd lost your notes? Well, I've just remembered where I put them – they're in my briefcase.
★

(Time: 1 minute 25 seconds)

**D**  Finally, a chance for everyone to practise using the expressions. Make sure the class is divided into pairs of pairs, so that they can recombine into groups of four later. If necessary, some 'pairs' can be groups of three to start with.

---

## 2.6  How would you feel? Word study

▶ See page 11 of the introduction for more information about the Word-study sections in this book.

**A**  Make sure everyone understands the way the chart works before beginning **B**.

**B**  To save time, different pairs could be assigned different groups of words to cover, or the work could be begun in class and completed as homework.

Make it clear that the purpose of this exercise is to increase students' awareness and sensitivity – there are no fixed rules about the meanings of words like these.

*Suggested answers* (many of these are open to discussion or argument)

| *slightly* | *'normal'* | *very* | *extremely* |
|---|---|---|---|
| dissatisfied | ANNOYED | angry | furious |
| irritated | cross | indignant | livid |
| resentful | discontented | | wild |
| | grumpy | | |
| | upset | | |
| taken aback | SURPRISED | amazed | astonished |
| | | shocked | thunderstruck |
| | | | horrified |
| | | | stunned |
| unworried | CALM | impassive | serene |
| | composed | indifferent | |
| | detached | self-controlled | |
| | relaxed | unemotional | |
| | | unmoved | |
| | | unruffled | |

| *slightly* | *'normal'* | *very* | *extremely* |
|---|---|---|---|
| amused | HAPPY | delighted | overjoyed |
| glad | cheerful | exhilarated | thrilled |
| pleased | light-hearted | jubilant | |
| satisfied | | on top of the world | |
| | | | |
| disappointed | UNHAPPY | dejected | depressed |
| disgruntled | discontented | gloomy | desperate |
| dissatisfied | down | miserable | heartbroken |
| fed up | feeling low | wretched | inconsolable |
| glum | upset | | |
| sorry | | | |

**C**  Perhaps give everyone a little help with this by starting the activity as a class and calling for suggestions, before starting the pair work.

---

## 2.7  *Lose*                    Verbs and idioms

This section can be done at any stage, not necessarily at the very end of the unit. The exercises can be done in pairs in class or as homework.

**A**  *Answers*

  2 lost my head      was at a loss
  3 losing myself in      have lost interest
  4 were lost without
  5 lost face      lose any sleep over
  6 lose my balance
  7 lost their lives
  8 lose weight      lose heart
  9 lost my nerve
 10 have lost touch (with each other)
 11 is (such) a bad loser      have lost count of
 12 lost patience      lost my temper with

>>>→

## B  *Answers*

| | |
|---|---|
| 1 interest | 5 your head |
| 2 touch (with each other) | 6 my way |
| 3 heart | 7 his nerve / his balance |
| 4 face | 8 patience with them |

**C** Make sure everyone does highlight some of the expressions in this section – and in the rest of the unit too.

# 3 That's show business!

## 3.1 Films, shows and concerts    Vocabulary

**A**  The discussion prepares students for the exercise in **B** and leads them gently into the theme of the unit. If preferred, this can be done with the whole class, rather than in groups.

**B**  This exercise can be done in pairs, or begun in class and completed for homework.

*Answers*

1  series
2  feature     cartoon     produced
3  special     storyline/plot/screenplay
4  directed     sequel     screenplay/script
5  camerawork     editing     scene/shot     stunts
6  soundtrack     equipment/facilities
7  titles     dubbed
8  part     co-     stole/dominated
9  co-production     location     praise/awards     overrated
10  plot/story     flashbacks
11  director/producer/composer/director of photography/writer of the screenplay, etc.     credits cast/list     played     crew     extras
12  Western/horror/comedy/documentary/cartoon, etc. Westerns/horror films/comedies/documentaries/thrillers/cartoons, etc.
13  production     sets/costumes
14  electric guitar, synthesiser, bass guitar, drums, keyboard, saxophone, etc.
15  cellos, clarinets, timpani, double basses, harps, oboes, French horns, bassoons, etc.

**C**  Encourage questions on vocabulary during the follow-up discussion.

## 3.2 One of my favourite films . . .      Listen and discuss

**A** 🔲 Set the counter to zero before playing the tape, so that you find the beginning again easily.

### Answers

*A Fish Called Wanda* starring John Cleese, Jamie Lee Curtis, Kevin Kline, Michael Palin; directed by Charles Crichton

*Trading Places* starring Dan Ackroyd, Jamie Lee Curtis, Eddie Murphy, Denholm Elliott; directed by John Landis

*Some Like It Hot* starring Marilyn Monroe, Tony Curtis, Jack Lemmon; directed by Billy Wilder

*Robocop* starring Ronnie Cox, Peter Weller; directed by Paul Verhoeven

*Moonstruck* starring Cher, Nicolas Cage; directed by Norman Jewison

*Local Hero* starring Peter Riegert, Burt Lancaster, Denis Lawson; directed by Bill Forsyth

**B** 🔲 Rewind the recording to the beginning and play the first speaker's contribution again. Pause the tape as necessary so that everyone has enough time to note down the relevant information.

Note that the 'transcript' in the Student's Book does not contain all the hesitations that the speaker makes. Perhaps point out to everyone that they don't have to write down every time he says 'sort of'.

In the transcript below, the missing words are <u>underlined</u>.

**C** 🔲 As this is quite a demanding task, it may be best for students to work on the plot summaries in pairs OR for different pairs to do the summaries of different films.

**D** It may help to jog everyone's memories if you make a list of some well-known films on the board, taking suggestions from the class.

### Transcript

Kerry:     A film I really enjoyed that I saw recently was … er … *Robocop*, which … er … didn't have a well-known <u>cast</u>. There was an actor named Ronnie Cox who played the <u>villain</u> and I think the guy who played Robocop was called Peter Weller, and it was directed by a Dutch director, Paul Verhoeven, or something like that, it was his first American film. And ... er ... it's basically set in the near future, where um ... the law enforcement agency of ... er ... the city of ... er ... Detroit, I think it is, has been privatised. And it's actually quite a ... political film and a very funny film, um ... what would happen if ... if th ... the police were privatised and basically ... um ... they ... they wanted to cut down on the ... their manpower ... er ... so it would be more cost-effective. And this thing called Robocop is built from a guy who's been ... um ... virtually killed by a ... a vicious gang of thugs and all that's left is sort of his torso and his brain and he's sort of put together into this sort of half-man half-machine and he goes around after the bad guys, which is not usually the sort of film I like because I don't usually like sort of violent films about cops, but it was actually *very* funny, hilarious, and it had a lot of sort of ... er ... pastiches o ... of TV commercials that were going on at the time because the whole ... it's a very TV sort of oriented society. And ... um ... I just thought it was really funny and the audience was just sort of screaming with laughter, which really suprised me. And ... er ... I think it was a much better film that ... er ... than, say, *Batman* or something that's attempting to do the same sort of thing.

Richard: One of my favourite films is *Local Hero*, which stars ... um ... Peter Riegert, Burt Lancaster and Denis Lawson, amongst others and it's directed by Bill Forsyth and it's the story of ... um ... an American ... big American international oil firm that decide to buy up an entire Scottish village ... er ... on the Scottish coast to make an oil refinery there and they send this American trouble-shooter over to soften up the locals and to make them an offer. Er ... and there's a lot of humour to be extracted out of the way he finds the locals: totally different cultures that meet, and the way he's gradually seduced into their way of looking at things and forgets what his job is meant to be and just enjoys ... um ... the community there. Um ... so the things I like about it really are the humour and the sort of warmth of the characters and the wonderful landscape.

Blain: A film that I have enjoyed in the past twelve months was *A Fish Called Wanda*. In the current way things are done in the cinema it was a combination of good American actors and good British actors: the main British actors being John Cleese and Michael Palin and the Americans, the very beautiful Jamie Lee Curtis and the extremely funny Kevin Kline. It was directed by a man who was famous for doing the old British Ealing comedies, Charles Crichton. It was an extremely good film, slightly overrated I suppose: had a lot of good, funny moments. In the film, John Cleese plays a lawyer who falls in love with the much younger Jamie Lee Curtis. The very funny romance is paired with another storyline which has to do with a heist, a robbery, and it has a very surprising conclusion too.

Enzo:    A film which I enjoyed in the last ... er ... two years was a film called *Moonstruck* which starred Cher and Nicolas Cage. And it's all about an Italian family and ... um ... er ... Cher plays this woman who is in love with this Italian guy and he ... er ... he's forty and they haven't decided to marry yet. He goes away to Europe and ... um ... in the meantime she falls in love with his brother who's this kind of rough and tough ... er ... baker, Italian baker and they have an affair and Cher's boyfriend comes back from Europe and she tells him all about it ... about the affair and they end up getting married: Cher and Nick C ... Nicolas Cage end up getting married. And ... er ... *Moonstruck* was directed by Norman Jewison.

Anne:    Er ... well, one of my favourite films is *Some Like It Hot* ... er ... it stars Tony Curtis, Jack Lemmon and Marilyn Monroe and it was directed by Billy Wilder. Er ... now, it's set in the twenties and the story's all about ... um ... the characters played by Jack Lemmon and Tony Curtis ... er ... they're a couple of very hard-up jazz musicians and accidentally they witness the St Valentine's Day Massacre in Chicago and so, of course, they have to escape from the gangsters who are ... who are after them ... um ... because they've seen the massacre. Well, the only way they can actually get out of town is by dressing up as women and joining this girls' band who are going off to Florida to play in a ... a big hotel there, and the singer in the band is played by Marilyn Monroe. Well ... um ... one of these chaps falls in love with her, but he can't let her know who he really is – you know, that he's a man – because the gangsters are still after them. So if he wants to have a date with her, he has to dress up as a short-sighted millionaire. Now, a real millionaire falls in love with the other one, played by Jack Lemmon, thinking he's a woman, and of course that causes even more problems. A ... and then the gangsters have their annual convention at the same hotel in Florida that they're all playing in, so of course the situation gets even more complicated. But in the end it all ends very happily, and it's a very funny film.

David:    I've ... er ... seen *Trading Places* and thoroughly enjoyed it a couple of times but never at the cinema, both times on television. But ... um ... the two stars are Dan Ackroyd and Eddie Murphy. Eddie Murphy of course went on to do *Beverly Hills Cop* and things like that, Jamie Lee Curtis, who went on to do *A Fish Called Wanda* and Denholm Elliott, who plays a wonderful English butler. Basically the story's very simple ... er ... two elderly gentlemen who work in the American stock exchange decide on a bet whereby one of their very rich employees, played by Dan Ackroyd, they bet that he won't be able to swap places, or trade places, with Eddie Murphy who is a down-and-out tramp living in New York. John Landis directed the film absolutely superbly and of course he went on to bigger and better things. What eventually happens, just to outline the story very briefly, is that ... er ... Eddie Murphy and

Dan Ackroyd decide to get their own back on the two people who have sought to swap their places and ... er ... decide to take them for all they've got, and it all ends very happily.

(Time: 7 minutes)

# 3.3  For adults only?                         Reading

**A**  This is a preliminary discussion to prepare students for the topic of the reading passage in **B**. Ask for reactions to the 'Attempt to ban Rambo' article.

**B**  ![ht] To save time in class, perhaps get everyone to read the article at home and do this exercise for homework. Remind everyone that highlighting words in this way will help them to remember them.

*Answers*

*articulated* – expressed     *articulate* – speaking clearly
*oafish* – idiotic     *garrulous* – very talkative
*preposterous* – ridiculous-looking     *perpetrated* – committed
*inexhaustible* – never-ending     *brief* – instructions
*gleefully* – joyfully

**C**  The questions can be answered in writing, or discussed in pairs.

*Suggested answers*

1 Everything: the lack of dialogue, the female assistant not being played by an Oriental, the violence, the way the audience's worst instincts are played upon, etc.
2 Nothing
3 His body and his preoccupation with exposing it, his voice, etc.
4 Difficult: this is a matter of opinion; probably the arrow shot through a guard's head impaling him to a tree (ugh!)
5 They enjoyed the film and cheered and howled their approval
6 According to the writer, Americans who feel that America is the greatest country in the world and have strong patriotic/nationalistic feelings about the nation's defeat in Vietnam
7 It boosts the American self-image

8 The deliberate mistakes make the concept of 'Rambo' the all-powerful warrior seem more ridiculous

**D** 📼 Play the whole tape through or, perhaps, pause it between each speaker, and get the groups to discuss their reactions. It may be necessary for everyone to make notes to help them to remember what was said.

Perhaps play the tape a second time to give everyone a chance to note down any useful vocabulary that is used.

## *Transcript*

Ann: Well, it's something that we accept really, isn't it. We read about it every day. It's ... um ... become a way of life. We just seem to accept it these days rather than be shocked by anything that's violent.

Andrew: W ... I think all the killing and the violence you get o ... on television now a ... and in films, not only in the ... in the drama but in ... on the news bulletins as well could have a very devastating effect on ... on children who see it. We've no idea how it affects them or ... or how they might be upset by it or even it may affect their behaviour.

Kate: I was ... er ... watching the Geraldo Rivera Show ... um ... an ... and I just turned it on because I heard it was pornographic and I didn't know what that meant and I was curious and he was doing this show about massacres in schoolyards and it was like reading the National Enquirer, it gave me chills an ... and I ... b ... – I'm from Stockton, California, that's my hometown – I left and a week later over the news I heard that a guy had taken a rifle and shot five Vietnamese children dead in a schoolyard about ten blocks from my dad's house and I'm sure he was watching that ... the same show. I'm sure that's what put it in his head.

Karen: Well, I don't think it's surprising that there's so much crime because I mean just look at all these ads and all the television programmes – they promote such a lifestyle that everybody envies it and just wants to copy it.

Melinda: Well, I don't let my children watch television. Um ... you know, you can't even watch the news without seeing terrible scenes of violence and I just don't think it's very good for them.

Enzo: Um ... television is very informative and educational. In particular, I mean the news, we have an extensive ... er ... coverage of news all the time on TV on all the channels and in particular my ... my favourite programmes are ... are programmes like Horizon which are very informative ...

Juliet: Well, I think once you're over sixteen you should be ... you should be able to see any film that you want to really.

Tim:     Well, the basic problem about ... er ... television in general is that ...
         er ... it destroys family life, there's no conversation, nobody ever
         talks to each other, nobody communicates, all they do is sit and
         vegetate.
Ishia:   Well, I mean, I think the thing is that people are really too ... too
         sensible to be taken in by everything that they see on the
         television – I mean, they know it's only ... the violence is only
         pretend, anyway.

                                          (Time: 2 minutes 30 seconds)

## 3.4  Evaluating and emphasising    Word study

**A**  The idea of this exercise, which should be treated flexibly, is to
enrich students' *active* vocabulary (explain this to the ones who say
'We know all these expressions already'). The chart should be drawn
in students' own notebooks.

*Suggested answers* (some of these are debatable)

TERRIBLE: boring   dreadful   forgettable   frightful   horrible
    lousy   rotten
TERRIFIC: exceptional   extraordinary   fabulous   fantastic
    first-rate   great   impressive   magnificent   marvellous
    memorable   out of this world   outstanding   remarkable
    sensational   special   splendid   superb   tremendous
    wonderful
NOT MUCH GOOD: mediocre   not bad   nothing special
    nothing to write home about   passable   reasonable
    run-of-the-mill   satisfactory   second-rate

The expressions that would not normally be used in the second
sentence are:
    not bad   nothing special   nothing to write home about
    out of this world

**B**  Students should be encouraged to experiment with the various
combinations and develop a feeling for good collocations. Begin by
discussing with the class which of the intensifiers can be used with
*good* or *bad*.

*Suggested answers* (many of these may be controversial)

very + awfully: *These lists are complete in the Student's Book.*
absolutely: *As listed* + extraordinary    fabulous    fantastic
  first-rate    frightful    great    horrible    lousy    magnificent
  marvellous    out of this world    outstanding    reasonable
  remarkable    rotten    sensational    splendid    superb
  tremendous    wonderful
extremely: *As listed* + impressive    mediocre    satisfactory
  second-rate
really: good    bad    appalling    astonishing    awful    boring
  dreadful    excellent    exceptional    extraordinary    fabulous
  fantastic    first-rate    forgettable    frightful    great
  horrible    impressive    lousy    magnificent    marvellous
  mediocre    memorable    not bad    nothing special
  out of this world    nothing to write home about
  outstanding    reasonable    remarkable    rotten
  run-of-the-mill    satisfactory    second-rate    sensational
  special    splendid    superb    tremendous    wonderful
dreadfully: bad    boring    mediocre
exceptionally: good    bad    awful    boring    dreadful
  horrible    impressive    mediocre    rotten    run-of-the-mill
extraordinarily: good    bad    awful    boring
incredibly: good    bad    awful    boring    impressive    mediocre
perfectly: adequate    appalling    astonishing    awful    dreadful
  excellent    frightful    marvellous    remarkable    satisfactory
  splendid
remarkably: good    bad    impressive    satisfactory(?)
terribly: good    bad    boring    forgettable    impressive
  mediocre    run-of-the-mill    second-rate
thoroughly: appalling    astonishing    boring    forgettable
  mediocre    run-of-the-mill    satisfactory    splendid
totally: appalling    astonishing    awful    boring    dreadful
  exceptional    extraordinary    first-rate    forgettable
  marvellous    mediocre    rotten    run-of-the-mill    sensational
unbelievably: good    bad    appalling    astonishing    awful
  boring    dreadful    frightful    horrible    impressive    mediocre
  run-of-the-mill    second-rate    special    splendid    superb

**C**   Perhaps start things off with a short round-the-class exercise:

Teacher: Here's a book with lots of long academic reading passages in it.
Class:   : It sounds absolutely appalling / pretty boring, etc.
Teacher: I'm going to talk to you about how to entertain your friends.
Class:    That sounds really great / absolutely sensational, etc.

For the pair work exercise, divide the class into an EVEN number of pairs, so that pairs of pairs can be formed later. Some 'pairs' can be groups of three.

---

# 3.5   Punctuation                    Effective writing

## A   *Suggested answers*

1  his sister's friends and colleagues
   *– the friends and colleagues of his (one) sister*
   his sisters' friends and colleagues
   *– the friends and colleagues of his (several) sisters*
   his sisters, friends and colleagues
   *– his (several) sisters and his own friends and colleagues*

2  Her sister, who works ...
   *– she has only one sister*
   Her sister who works ...
   *– she has more than one sister and only the one who works in America is a film star*

3  Roger Rabbit
   *– the character was wonderful*
   "Roger Rabbit"
   *– the film was wonderful*

4  I don't watch television – much!
   *– probably ironic or self-mocking, the speaker probably watches more than he or she should*
   I don't watch television much.
   *– straightforward statement*

5  They said it was entertaining.
   *– straightforward statement*
   They said it was entertaining!!
   *– I think that's amazing*
   They said it was "entertaining".
   *– that was the word they used, but that seems a strange word to use in the circumstances*
   They said it was entertaining?
   *– I find that hard to believe*
   They said it was entertaining . . .
   *– but they probably had some reservations OR I'm about to tell you more*

## B  *Suggested answers*

### Apostrophes ( ' ' ' )
mother's sister      father's sister
'89
it's      its
Don't      they're

### Commas ( , , , )
commas      understand/follow
Michael Douglas, Mel Gibson, William Hurt, Jeff Bridges,
Harrison Ford, Denholm Elliott, Woody Allen, Gérard Depardieu,
Sigourney Weaver, Greta Scacchi, Jamie Lee Curtis, Kathleen Turner,
Barbara Hershey, Isabelle Adjani, etc., etc.!!
When the film was over, we stayed sitting in our seats to watch the
final credits.

### Colons ( : : : )
There are four members of my family: my father and mother, my
sister and me.

### Quotation marks ( " " ' ' ) either double or single
"Well, that's all I have to say, thank you for listening, ladies and
gentlemen," the lecturer said at the end of the lecture, "Does anyone
have any questions?"

### Semi-colons ( ; ; ; )
'Trading Places' was a wonderful film; the director was John Landis.

### Dashes ( – – – )
'Roger Rabbit' was a great film – we all enjoyed it.

## C  *Complete text with punctuation* (as used in the original
article – a few more commas are possible)

'A Nightmare on Elm Street' made one experienced journalist scream
with terror at the preview screening I went to. The noise frightened me
more than the film itself, written and directed by Wes Craven, an ex-
professor of humanities.

  "It's all very spooky but not at all bloody," says Wes of this teen-
orientated horror film, which has a ghostly and ghastly murderer
attacking the children of Elm Street not in their waking hours but in
their dreams.

  John Saxon and Ronee Blakley don't believe all this, and he, a
policeman, goes looking for a real madman. But we know better, and
so does Heather Langenkamp as their daughter. Langenkamp,
apparently known in America as the world's most promising Scream
Queen, screams louder than the journalist. I just cringed.

I think Craven has done better, though one has to admit that it's a good idea followed through with efficiency and state of the art special effects. Perhaps my trouble was that I wanted the Evil One to win. I can't stand those awful kids.

---

# 3.6  Planning ahead . . . Creative writing

The activities in this section give students a chance to exchange views on the need for planning and methods of planning. We aren't dictating to them what they should do, but leaving it to them to decide.

**A** 🎞️ Play the tape, perhaps pausing after each speaker. Then get the groups to decide which of the advice they approve of. Remind them that writing in a foreign language is more difficult than the situation the speakers are envisaging and is likely to require much more careful planning.

*Transcript*

| | |
|---|---|
| Coralyn: | I never plan what I'm going to write – I just start writing and hope for the best. |
| Nigel: | When I don't plan ahead I usually find that I write far too much and my writing lacks structure, which makes it difficult and boring for someone else to read. |
| David: | I don't plan very thoroughly: I just make a few rough notes on the back of an envelope or ... um ... a piece of scrap paper. |
| Nicolette: | I like to use a large, clean sheet of paper and I put down all my ideas in note form. And I like to leave plenty of room between the lines for any extra ideas I have. |
| Richard: | If I spend a short time planning before I write I can decide on the best order for the various points I want to make. |
| Kerry: | Well, when I ... when I don't plan ahead, I ... I just tend to forget what I wanted to say right in the middle of writing. |
| Janenne: | Planning helps me to weed out the irrelevant points and decide which are the most important points. |
| Carole: | Planning's a waste of time, it stops you being creative. |
| Nick: | A few minutes spent planning before I write saves me a great deal of time when I'm writing. |

(Time: 1 minute 10 seconds)

**B**  Again, it's up to students to accept or reject these guidelines. But, of course, they may want to ask your advice.

**C + D + E**  Follow the procedure in the Student's Book.

# 3.7 *At . . .* and *by . . .*                    Idioms

## A   *Answers*

| | |
|---|---|
| 1 at a loss | 11 at our expense |
| 2 at a loss | 12 at a glance |
| 3 at cross purposes | 13 At long last |
| 4 at short notice      at least | 14 by all means |
| 5 at the expense of | 15 by means of |
| 6 at all times | 16 By the way |
| 7 at random | 17 by any chance |
| 8 at least / at any rate | 18 by the thousand |
| 9 at the last minute | 19 by sight      by name |
| 10 at any moment | 20 by myself |
|     at any rate / at least | |

# 4 Food and drink

## 4.1 To whet your appetite . . . Vocabulary

**B** *Answers*

1 carbohydrates    protein    vitamins
2 recipe    dish    ingredients
3 vegetarians    principles    butter/yogurt/milk/ice cream
4 loaf    slices
5 Wholemeal    fibre/goodness
6 sell by    keep/last    additives
7 eggs, flour and milk    spatula    tossing
8 set    menu
9 proper/cooked/full/big    grab
10 water    rumble

**C** *Suggested answers*

pancake batter: beaten    mixed    stirred    + fried
cake mixture: beaten    stirred    + baked
carrots: chopped    grated    peeled    sliced    washed
    + boiled    eaten raw    served    steamed
cheese: grated    sliced    + eaten raw    served
cream: beaten    whipped    + served
dough: kneaded    mixed    + baked
a lemon: grated    sliced    squeezed    + baked    served
a lettuce: tossed    washed    + eaten raw    served
liver: chopped    sliced    + baked    fried    grilled/broiled
    roasted    served    stewed
potatoes: chopped    grated    peeled    sliced    + baked
    boiled    fried    roasted    steamed
rice: washed    + boiled    fried    steamed
walnuts:    chopped    grated    ground    + baked    eaten raw

**D**  Encourage questions on vocabulary during this discussion.

# 4.2  Good food?                    Listen and discuss

**B**   Give everyone a chance to look at the questions and guess some
of the answers (from their previous knowledge of the subject) before
playing the recording.

🔲   Play the recording, perhaps with a short break in the middle.

## *Answers*

 1  fish and chips      450
 2  hamburgers      380
 3  200      Chinese      Indian
 4  chicken      140      pizzas      80
 5  20
 6  £36      year
 7  ingredients
 8  fat      sugar      additives
 9  percentage      lean      25%      830
10  four
11  fresh milk      ice cream      flavours      wood pulp
12  colouring      browner      beef fat
13  Latin America      tropical rainforests      five
14  greenhouse effect

## *Transcript*

Presenter:      Fish and chips is the traditional British takeaway meal – it's
a complete hot meal that can be taken home to eat or eaten
in the street, and it's still the most popular, isn't it, Peter
Stanton?

Peter Stanton:  It certainly is, yes. Er ... the figures speak for themselves. For
instance, the fish and chip market represents 450 million
portions of fish and chips sold per year. This compares with
only 380 million takeaway hamburgers a year. Um ... also
looking at the ethnic takeaway meal, specially ... um ...
Chinese and Indian, that accounts for 200 million meals per
year. The fried chicken market, Kentucky and otherwise,
that's 140 million meals a year – 80 million takeaway pizzas
per year. And that means that in Britain 20 million takeaway
meals are sold per week and as a total the British spend £1.8
billion per year on takeaway meals and that works out at
£36 per head.

Presenter:      But takeaway meals may not be very good for our health,
according to Dr Janet Marshall.

Dr Marshall:    One of the major problems around takeaway food is that restaurants and fast food outlets are not actually required by law to disclose the ingredients in their dishes – unlike for instance supermarkets – and ... er ... takeaway meal are stuffed full of fat and sugar and additives. And of course high fat means a large amount of calories. If we look at some of the ... er ... th ... the calorific c ... er ... quantities in some of these takeaway foods, for instance hamburgers, which only contain a small percentage of *lean* meat – the rest being fat and other parts of the animal – well, a half-pounder hamburger contains 25% pure fat, which works out at 830 calories – which is in fact half a typical woman's daily requirement. And ... um ... if we look at ... er ... a typical portion of Chinese sweet and sour chicken for instance, that would contain four ounces of pure fat, which works out at 2,052 calories! Milk shakes ... um ... very rarely contain fresh milk or ice cream and their flavours are generally artificial. And their thickness is attributable to ... er ... additives like emulsifiers and wood pulp. And then the chip, which ... er ... we all know and love, is often made to look browner through colouring and ... er ... chips are often fried in beef fat, which ... er ... is something vegetarians perhaps should be aware of as well.

Presenter: Terry Green of Friends of The Earth also has misgivings about takeaway food.

Terry Green: Well ... er ... the meat that they use in these hamburgers is often beef that they get from Latin America and ... er ... the beef that they export to the United States and Japan and Europe is produced by cutting down tropical rainforests to make room for the cattle. OK, to produce a single hamburger, five square metres of rainforest have to be destroyed. Now the problem with this is that people all over the world are being encouraged to eat more and more beef and the only way they can raise this beef is by cutting down more rainforests. Now the packaging of the hamburgers has got CFCs [chlorofluorocarbons] in it, and we all know ... er ... that those contribute to the greenhouse effect. But I guess the most noticeable thing about these fast food places is the huge mountains of rubbish ... er ... from the packaging and the ... parts of uneaten hamburgers thrown all over the street. It's really disgusting.

Presenter: But is this a typically British phenomenon? Is it just the British way of eating that is becoming more and more dominated by takeaways? Peter Stanton again.

Peter Stanton: No, every country seems to have its own 'typical' fast foods. For example, if we look at the various . . .

(Time: 3 minutes 55 seconds)

# 4.3   Simple + Progressive aspect   Grammar

The work in this section is intended as revision. Refer to *Practical English Usage* for more information on the simple and progressive aspect.

## A   *Suggested answers*

1 ... the train had just left.
   *– we were too late: the train had departed a short time before we got to the station*
   ... the train was just leaving
   *– we were late: the train was departing so we had to jump on at the last minute, OR we missed it*

2 She stood up when ...
   *– he came in and she stood up*
   She was standing up when ...
   *– she stood up, he came in and she continued standing*

3 He usually prepares ...
   *– he waits till she returns and then starts cooking*
   He is usually preparing ...
   *– he starts cooking before she returns and when she comes in he hasn't finished*
   He has usually prepared ...
   *– he starts cooking before she returns and is no longer cooking when she comes in*

4 I have been reading ...
   *– reading only some of it, probably not all*
   I have read ...
   *– all the book and now I have finished*

5 I'm not having dinner ...
   *– I don't intend/plan to have dinner till 8 o'clock this evening*
   I don't have dinner ...
   *– I never have dinner till then, as a general rule*

6 They always ask ...
   *– straightforward statement*
   They're always asking ...
   *– and I feel amused/surprised/annoyed by this*

7 I think you are being silly.
   *– what you are doing now is not sensible*

I think you are silly.
*– nothing you do is sensible: you are a silly person*

8 Will you join us ...
*– I'm inviting you*
Will you be joining us ...
*– I'm asking about your plans/intentions*

9 We'll be having ...
*– This is our plan OR we'll be in the middle of breakfast at that time*
We'll have ...
*– We'll start breakfast at that time*

**B** This exercise consists of three stages: (a) developing a feeling for what is correct, (b) filling the gaps, and (c) writing examples. There is no need to 'explain the rules' for each example as long as everyone agrees that a different form is either wrong or has a different meaning.

*Suggested answers*

**Present simple or present progressive: *does* or *is doing***
2 Most days she **has** lunch at her desk but today she's **eating** out.
    NOT   is having ✗     eats ✗
have/eat/serve    I'm having/eating/serving them
3 I **hear** that you had a Chinese meal last night.
    NOT    am hearing ✗
has just become
4 When the sketch **begins**, a man **arrives** at a restaurant and **starts** eating.
    NOT   is beginning ✗     is arriving ✗     is starting to eat ✗
eats / has eaten    explodes / is ill / feels sick
5 When **are** you **having** dinner this evening?
    NOT   do you have ✗
are    arriving/coming

**Past simple or past progressive: *did* or *was doing***
6 I **didn't want** to phone her while she **was having** dinner.
    NOT   wasn't wanting ✗   had ✗
was eating / was drinking    choked
7 He **was** just **finishing** dinner when his wife **got** home from work.
    NOT   finished ✗    was getting ✗
arrived    was still having
8 He **didn't start** preparing dinner until his wife **got** home.
    NOT   wasn't starting to ✗   was getting ✗
didn't find out / didn't receive

9 Traffic **was diverted** because a new bridge **was being built.**
    NOT   was being diverted ✗     was built ✗
  was being     was
10 I **was wondering** if you could tell me why you don't like her.
    NOT   wondered ✗
  wasn't expecting

## Present perfect simple or progressive: *has done* or *has been doing*

11 I **have been reading** this book for a week but I've only **read** 23 pages so far.
    NOT   have read ✗     have only been reading ✗
  been learning     learnt
12 They **have been living** / they **have lived** in London for two years.
  *– no difference in this case*
  has lived / has been living
13 The restaurant is closed because the cook **has been taken** to hospital.
    NOT   has been being taken ✗
  they been

## *will do* or *will be doing*

14 What **will** you **be doing** tomorrow evening? **Will** you **be waiting** for your guests to arrive? What **will** you **do** if they're late?
  *– The meaning changes if the verbs are different:* What **will** you **do** tomorrow evening? **Will** you **wait** for your guests to arrive? What **will** you **be doing** if they're late?
  I'll be having dinner     I'll watch TV
15 **Will** you **be coming** with us or are you busy tonight?   *FUTURE*
  *– The meaning changes if the verbs are different:*
  **Will** you **come** with us …
  will be arriving
16 **Will** you **come** with us? We'd love you to be there.   *INVITATION*
  *– The meaning changes if the verbs are different:* **Will** you **be coming** with us …
  Will

## C  *Corrected sentences*

1 We usually **have** lunch out on Sundays.
2 We can take a picnic but what will we **do** if it starts to rain?
3 She stayed at home because she **had** a cold.
4 While I **was driving** along I suddenly remembered that I had left the freezer door open.

5 *no errors*
6 Breakfast is normally **served** in the dining room but today it is **being served** in the coffee shop.
7 Who **does** this recipe book that's lying on the table **belong** to?
8 She **disliked** vegetarian food at first but now she **enjoys** it whenever she **has** it.

**D + E**   These discussions will help students to use the forms more freely. Listen in to each group and correct or make notes of any relevant errors you overhear.

# 4.4   **Words easily confused**          Word study

**A + B + C**   It will save a great deal of time if some of this section can be prepared as homework.
  Make sure everyone understands what to do. If possible, take a few English–English dictionaries into class for this activity, then students can refer to them instead of relying too much on you.
  No correct answers are suggested here – use a dictionary to check any you may be unsure of!

# 4.5   **That doesn't sound right!**          Functions

This section revises some aspects of English usage that are probably fairly well-known to your students. As pointed out in the Student's Book, deciding whether a particular remark is appropriate or inappropriate depends on the WHOLE situation and, indeed, there are degrees of appropriateness. Encourage everyone to discuss what 'feels' appropriate. It's naive to expect there to be easily-learnt 'rules' about this in English – or in any language, for that matter.

**A**   Some suggested appropriate answers are recorded on the cassette. Play this after everyone has completed the exercise.

*Transcript*

| Narrator: | These are improved versions of the conversations. Notice the tone of voice used, as well as the words the people say. |
| 8 year-old: | Hello. |
| Adult: | Hello. Is your mummy at home? |

63

| Narrator: | OR |
|---|---|
| Adult: | Can I speak to your mummy? |

1 Assistant: Can I help you?
  Customer: No, it's all right thanks, I'm just looking.

2 Patient: Good morning, doctor.
  Doctor: Hello, what seems to be the trouble?

3 Your boss: Yes, come in.
  You: Is it all right if I come in half an hour late tomorrow?

4 Boss: Do you see what I mean?
  New employee: Yes, but I'm not sure I quite agree.

5 Friend: Sorry, I must just make a phone call.
  You: Fine.

6 Student: Have you had time to mark my composition?
  Teacher: Yes, it was quite good and I've underlined the mistakes you've made.

7 Waiter: Are you ready to order now?
  Customer: Not quite, we'd just like a little longer to study the menu.

8 Wife: Oh, can you give me a hand with the washing-up, please?
  Husband: Sure, just a minute.

9 Waiter: Did you enjoy your meal?
  Customer: Yes, thanks it was very good.

10 Guest: The meal was absolutely delicious.
   Hostess: Oh, good. I'm so glad you enjoyed it.

(Time: 1 minute 30 seconds)

**B** *Suggested answers* (some of these may be debatable)

1 A lot of people like fish and chips. NEUTRAL
  Loads of people like fried chicken. FAMILIAR
  Lots of people like curry. INFORMAL
  Many people enjoy hot dogs. FORMAL
  A significant number of people prefer sandwiches. VERY FORMAL

2 Good to see you. FORMAL/NEUTRAL
  Hello. INFORMAL
  Hi there. FAMILIAR
  It's a pleasure to make your acquaintance. VERY FORMAL
  Pleased to meet you. FORMAL

3 I'd like to introduce myself. My name's . . .   FORMAL/NEUTRAL
I'm . . . – what's your name?   INFORMAL/FAMILIAR
May I introduce myself, I'm . . .   NEUTRAL
My name's . . . – who are you?   INFORMAL/FAMILIAR

4 Do you feel like a drink?   NEUTRAL
Like a drink?   INFORMAL
Want a drink?   FAMILIAR
May I offer you a drink?   FORMAL
Would you like me to get you a drink?   FORMAL

5 Can I have tea, please?   NEUTRAL
I want tea, please.   FAMILIAR
Tea, please.   FAMILIAR
I'd like a cup of tea, please.   NEUTRAL
Would it be possible for me to have some
tea?   VERY FORMAL

6 One should always try to be polite.   FORMAL
You should always try to be polite.   NEUTRAL

7 Give my best wishes to your parents.   FORMAL
Give my love to Jan, won't you?   INFORMAL
Oh, love to Jim, by the way.   FAMILIAR
Remember me to your husband.   FORMAL
Please give my best regards to your wife.   FORMAL

**C** Encourage everyone to come up with examples of actual situations they might really find themselves in.

To give a complete list of all the possible situations in which each term might be used would take up a lot of space and be pretty boring to read! So, trust your own feelings here. To save time, pick out the more 'extreme' items in each list and give an example of when you might use it – or explain why you would never use it.

In the suggested answers below the expressions have ONLY been rearranged very roughly according to their formality – for more information consult LDOCE, OALD or *Collins* COBUILD.

## Suggested answers

1 children    youngsters    boys and girls    kids
2 human beings    population    citizens    persons    people
ladies and gentlemen    men and women    everyone
3 male    person    gentleman    man    chap    fellow
guy    boy    bloke
4 female    person    lady    woman    girl

5 nutrition   cuisine   cooking   banquet   food   feast
  meal   something to eat
6 appetising   delicious   wonderful   superb   tasty
  nice   quite nice   yummy

► Students should be aware of the need for appropriateness in their conversation and writing. Look out for inappropriate language in their next piece of written work and draw their attention to it. This point is taken up in 7.3.

# Extra activity      "How nice to meet you" ➡

This might be a suitable time for a role play 'cocktail party' to practise using appropriate small talk. The instructions on the next page are addressed to students and may be photocopied if wished.

► To add realism and help the activity go well perhaps play a tape of soft music during the 'party'.

# 4.6   Let's eat!                                   Reading

**A + B**   This is a straightforward discussion leading to a role play.
    If you have any other authentic menus available for photocopying they would make the role play that much more realistic.

# 4.7   *Bring* and *carry*              Verbs and idioms

## A   *Answers*

2 it down        5 them round      8 them round/over
3 them back      6 off/away        9 it through/out
4 it up          7 it off/away

## B   *Answers*

1 brings back      5 bring   up          9 got carried away
2 brought up       6 brought   about/on  10 carry on
3 brought out      7 brought on/about    11 carrying on with
4 brought   round  8 bring   forward     12 carried out

# "How nice to meet you"

Imagine that you and the other members of the class have been
invited to a formal buffet dinner – but that you DON'T know each
other. You should spend a few moments talking to each of the other
'guests' and then move on and talk to another, as shown below.
First, look at the useful gambits you can use.

▶ Imagine that you are wearing your best suit or your best dress.

1 Greet each other, comment on the party and introduce yourselves:

> Hello, are you enjoying yourself?
> It's a great/lovely/nice party, isn't it?
> These... are really delicious, aren't they?
> This really is a lovely/nice/magnificent house/flat/room, isn't it?
> Haven't we met before somewhere?
> May I introduce myself, I'm...
> I don't think we've been introduced. My name's...
> Hi/Hello, I'm... How nice to meet you. Pleased to meet you.

2 Talk for a few moments:

> How well do you know our hostess/host?
> Do you know that lady/man/girl/fellow over there?
> What do you do (for a living)?
> Do you come from this part of the country?

3 Make an excuse, take your leave and find another
   guest to talk to:

> Well, it's been very nice/enjoyable/interesting talking to you.
> Well, I suppose I'd better circulate.
> I've just seen someone I haven't talked to for ages, will you
>   excuse me?
> Excuse me, I must just go and have a word with our host/hostess.
> I think I'll just go and get another drink / some more to eat –
>   can I get you something?
> Well, see you later, I hope.

# 5 Crossing the Channel

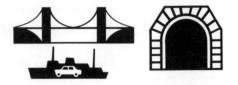

## 5.1 Inside the Channel Tunnel

Reading

**A** This pre-reading discussion can be done as a class, if preferred.

**B** This pre-reading task will encourage students to approach the task with a clear purpose. It is up to them to decide on what they want to find out. Of course, many likely questions are not answered in the article (e.g. what the fare is), but that's what often happens when one reads an article in a newspaper or magazine in the real world!

**C** *Suggested answers*

1 On special freight shuttles with 25 wagons, each carrying one lorry
2 On normal freight trains, presumably
3 On special tourist shuttles running in a loop between the Chunnel's terminals
4 On special trains from London (Waterloo or King's Cross), Swanley in Kent or a northern town
5 35 minutes from Folkestone to Calais
6 This is a matter of opinion: the speed, perhaps, or the convenience

**D** *Answers*

1 toll          4 boarded
2 submit     5 symbolise
3 loop        6 routine

**E** 〔▭〕 *Answers*

EuroRoute (illustration **b**)
1 By road: lorries drive through
2 On high-speed freight trains
3 They drive through
4 On high-speed passenger trains
5 *not stated*
6 Lower running costs than Chunnel; no queueing for motorists waiting for trains – people will prefer to drive across

Channel Expressway (illustration **a**)
1 By road: lorries drive through
2 On freight trains, mostly at night
3 They drive through
4 On trains every half hour
5 *not stated*
6 *not stated* (But presumably this offers the best of both worlds: road and rail)

Flexilink (illustration **c**)
1 On ferries
2 It isn't
3 On ferries
4 They have to get on a ferry
5 About 90 minutes
6 Cheapest, most reliable, safest, most flexible, most environment-friendly, most pleasurable scheme

## Transcript

First speaker: EuroRoute is a scheme that operates at much lower running costs than the Channel Tunnel. Er ... what happens is this: motorway bridges go from each coast ... er ... ten kilometres out from the coast and connect up with a twenty kilometre submerged concrete tube tunnel made on two man-made islands in the English Channel. Er ... the ... roadways spiral gently down to the level of the tunnel. It's the same principle as the Chesapeake Bay Bridge-Tunnel in the USA and it ... it's well-researched technology. Thinking ahead to the twenty-first century, er ... I believe that people will prefer, w ... will want to drive across, not queue up waiting for trains.
And finally, there are also two separate supplementary rail-only tunnels, and they can take up to 30 high-speed passenger and freight trains in each direction per hour.

Second speaker: The Channel Expressway is a scheme consisting of two tunnels which carry both road and train traffic. The rails are laid flush with the road surface like tram tracks in the fast lane which is closed to traffic once every half hour for the trains to pass through. Er ... really, both the passenger trains and the freight trains are able to use the tunnel, but the freight trains'll mostly run during the night when there's less road traffic. There will be special pumps at regular intervals along the tunnel to clean the air and remove the exhaust fumes from it.

Third speaker: Flexilink is the cheapest and most reliable scheme of them all, really. Ferries, especially the new giant super-ferries are more economical, safer and a lot more flexible than building a tunnel. And they're also friendlier to the environment. For the motorist and the lorry driver, the pleasurable experience of strolling on the deck with time to enjoy a meal and take a relaxing break during the journey is much more pleasant than the claustrophobic sensation of being underground for an hour – and the idea of, you know, being trapped. Time saved for cars and road freight by building the Channel Tunnel is less than an hour: insignificant saving on journeys of twelve hours or more. There's no doubt that ferries will continue operating in competition with the tunnel, both on the short Channel crossing and on the longer crossings from Southern England to France and England to Holland, Belgium, Germany and Scandinavia.

(Time: 2 minutes 20 seconds)

**F** Each group should be asked to report on its findings after the discussion.

## 5.2 Giving a presentation Functions

As in 3.6, students are expected to make their own decisions here. Those with more experience will have more authority. Point out that by 'presentation' we mean any short talk given to a group of people.

## 5.3 Connecting or protecting Listening

**A** Make sure everyone has enough time to do the pre-listening task before playing the recording.

Play the recording, with a short pause between each of the presentations. The task is very straightforward so as to give everyone a chance to concentrate on the way each speaker gives his or her presentation.

Perhaps play the recording a second time through so that everyone can just sit back and listen (perhaps with eyes closed).

*Answers*

```
Name of project: PANAMA CANAL

Date completed: 1914          Length: 82 km

Reason for its construction:
   To save voyage of 8,000 km round southern tip of South America
Engineer or client: John F. Stevens
```

Most surprising or interesting fact:
Medical officer eradicated yellow fever and reduced malaria
Water supply threatened by jungles being cut down

---

Name of project: GREAT WALL OF CHINA

Date completed: 221 BC        Length: 3,460 km

Reason for its construction:
   To protect northern frontier of China and keep out hostile tribes
Engineer or client: The Emperor of China

Most surprising or interesting fact:
   500,000 labourers built it and many died
   Shi Huang Ti also had mausoleum built containing 6,000 terracotta soldiers

---

Name of project: GOLDEN GATE BRIDGE

Date completed: 1937        Length: main span is 1,280 metres

Reason for its construction: To connect San Francisco with Marin County,
   previously only connected by ferry or road all round San Francisco Bay
Engineer or client: Joseph B. Strauss

Most surprising or interesting fact:
   Earthquake-proof bridge
   A ship collided with it during construction

## Transcript

Helena:  Well, I'd like to tell you about the building of the Panama Canal.
The ... there were three other important ship canals: the Suez
Canal, the Kiel Canal and the Houston Canals. Now, they're all
at sea level, but the Panama Canal is different, it ... it rises to 26
metres and has huge locks. It's 82 kilometres long. Now, it ... it
takes between 24 to 30 hours for a ship to pass through the canal,
but it does save 8,000 nautical miles of journeying round Cape
Horn.
   The ... the project was ... was first started by a French company
under a ... a man called Fredinand de Lesseps in 189 ... er ... 18 ... er
... 79, but thousands of men died of yellow fever and malaria,
which at the time were thought to be caused by the climate, not
mosquitoes, which is quite interesting. And this led to work being

abandoned in 1889, so they did ten years of working on it before abandoning it. Then the United States of America bought part of the Republic of Panama and began construction in 1906. The chief engineer at the time was a man called John F. Stevens but however ... the ... the ... the main contributor to the success of the scheme was not the chief engineer but the medical officer ... er ... a man called Colonel William C. Gorgas, who eradicated yellow fever and reduced the incidence of ... of malaria. The ... the total cost of the Canal was $380 million, with 43,000 labourers, who were mostly black West Indians.

The Canal was first opened in 1914 and consists of a ... a series of lakes connected by canals and locks with specially built locomotives to pull ships through the locks. Lake Gatun at the top supplies the water for the canals and they had to cut down a lot of jungles ... um ... and that has affected the climate of the area, and there is a lack of water at some times of ... of ... of the year. Now, this unfortunately is likely to get worse as the lake fills up with silt and ... and earth.

The ... the Canal Zone itself was politically part of the United States of America un ... until it was given back to the Panamanian Republic in 1977, but the Canal will revert to Panamanian control in ... in the year 2000.

Carole: Did you know that the Great Wall of China is the only human structure that can be seen from space? It's 3,460 kilometres long and it's wide enough for chariots and carts to travel along the top. Um ... it was built around 221 BC ... um ... on the orders of Shi Huang Ti, the first great emperor of China, and it was to protect the northern frontier of China and keep out hostile tribes. Er ... half a million labourers were needed to build it and its nickname was 'the longest cemetery in the world', because so many died building it. And this emperor Shi Huang Ti was the first Chin emperor and he united China for the first time, giving it its name.

As well as that he introduced a standard form of the Chinese written language throughout the empire, and he also had a mausoleum built for himself containing 6,000 soldiers made of pottery: 'the terracotta army'. This took 700,000 labourers 36 years to build and is actually larger than the Pyramids of Egypt. Um . . . in addition to that he also burned all the books in his empire and he buried his political opponents alive.

Michael: Er ... the Golden Gate Bridge in San Francisco opened in 1937 – cost $35 million. It's still the world's tallest bridge, it's high enough for the largest ships in the world to pass underneath, it's about 80 metres above the sea. And the main span of 1,280 metres has three lanes in each direction and it connects San Francisco with ... er ... Marin County, er ... replacing all the ferries that used to cross over or ... er ... otherwise you'd have to make a ... a journey completely around San Francisco Bay.

Now, the chief engineer was … er … a guy called Joseph B. Strauss and … er … the building of the bridge was a … really a tremendous technical achievement because they had … er … they blasted rock … er … under the water, really deep water because … er … of course in San Francisco there's lots of earthquakes and they had to make it earthquake-proof. And there were storms all the time and fog and even a ship collided with the bridge and it caused some really serious damage.

(Time: 5 minutes)

**B**    In this Communication activity, student A looks at Activity 6, B at 24 and C at 41. Make sure everyone spends a few moments studying the information there before exchanging information with each other.

**C**    Perhaps remind students of some impressive local buildings or public works that they might know about.

**D**    Discuss this as a class if your students lack inspiration. Less technically-minded students should avoid technical subjects.

---

# 5.4    Let's blow up the Channel Tunnel        Reading

**A**    If possible, students should prepare this article at home before the lesson, noting down their answers so that they are ready to discuss them with a partner in class.

## Suggested answers

1 Ironic/facetious/not serious
2 Probably meaning (a) cause to explode
3 Meaning (d) fill with air
4 The way in which the Earth isn't rigid but flexible, like a rubber ball
5 He's being ironic and really means 'a spectacular disaster'.
6 The technology is experimental and there could be many setbacks that would delay completion and increase the cost. The possibility of any kind of disaster would not be acceptable.

**B**   *Answers*

2   why coalmine tunnels have to be supported
11   consequences of escaping hot liquid
3   conventional tunnelling
1   cost of building Channel Tunnel
9   dissolving rock
8   how to heat rock
5   techniques of boring oil wells
4   plasticity of the Earth
7   problems with hard rock
6   pumping up
10   sealing holes
12   shape of final tunnel

**C**   *Answers*

1 encountered      ultimate
2 elaborate      appeals
3 mishap
4 snag
5 consequence      techniques

**D**   This exercise draws attention to cohesive features, both lexical and grammatical. Students should look again at the text AFTER they have done this exercise.

# 5.5   **Making notes**   Effective writing

**A**   This again encourages students to make their own decisions.

**B**   Ask the pairs to report on the extra points they have added.

**C**   Get the pairs to show another pair the notes they have made and ask for comments. These notes could form the basis for some extra written work, perhaps.

# 5.6   **Building bridges . . .**   Communication activity

**A**   The title of this section is ambiguous: communicating your ideas with other people also involves 'building bridges'.
   This problem-solving activity may seem slightly childish to some

students, but doing it will provoke a lot of lively discussion, which makes it well worth while trying.

There is no best possible solution to this problem but you'll find that paper that has been folded into a tube or into a channel is stronger than unfolded paper.

There is another, more complex, version of this activity in *Ideas* by Leo Jones (CUP) Unit 15.

**B** Each group gives a short presentation/demonstration of its project.

---

## 5.7 Describing a process        Creative writing

▶ If anyone was absent for 5.6, they should carry out the experiment at home (with members of their family, perhaps) and write it up, if they are going to choose the first topic.

Spend some time in class discussing how everyone will approach the task and which one they'll be doing. They should submit the NOTES as well as the report, so that you have some feedback on what they may have learnt from the work they did in 5.5.

---

## 5.8 *High, middle* and *low* Idioms and compounds

**A** *Answers*

1 highlight
2 high season
3 highlights
4 highbrow  lowbrow  middlebrow
5 it's high time you did it (NB a verb in the past is needed here)
6 high and low
7 high-rise  low-rise
8 high tech
9 in high spirits
10 at high tide   at low tide
11 feeling low
12 keep a low profile
13 middle-aged
14 middle class
15 higher education
16 hi-fi   high street
17 UPPER CASE   lower case
18 Middle Ages

# 6 Buildings and homes

## 6.1 **Where do you live?** Vocabulary and listening

**A** Make sure that everyone makes notes of vocabulary that comes up, or that they want to ask you about, during this discussion.

**B** ▭ Play the recording, perhaps pausing after each speaker.

*Transcript*

Kate: I like my present home because it's ... in the suburbs, in that there are a lot of trees around it but it's only about half an hour's ride from the centre of town. And it's got this ridiculous patch at the end of the garden that's owned by my next-door neighbour that has ducks and ... er ... chickens and ... and geese, w ... who are like guard geese and who quack in the night if there are strangers about. I like that.

Nick: I like my present home because it's a flat near the City ... er ... about ten minutes out of the City and that's very convenient for getting in, for cycling in, which is what I do. Er ... and it's also got a lot of amenities close to it: there's a swimming pool, cinema, library, theatres. Er ... it's ... er ... some very good markets as well: fruit and vegetable and clothes and that's why I like the present flat that I've got.
    If I had a lot of money, I'd keep the flat that I've got in London and I'd buy one out in the country, probably up North, which is where I came from originally. Er ... in fact, I could probably buy a house up there if I had a *lot* of money. So that's what I'd do, I'd have the two places: one for a 'pied à terre' in London and one for going up to at the weekends.

Melinda: I wouldn't mind moving home if I had enough money to move into the country and live in the sort of house I'd really like to live in ... um ... something really old, with lots of land ... um ... preferably a beach to wander on in the mornings. Er ... yes, I'd move home for that!

Blain: The main differences between homes in North America and Britain are really two: size and height. Er ... homes in North America tend to be a little bigger, I suppose because they don't cost quite so much in most places, and secondly they don't go 'up'

76

quite so frequently, they spread out, whereas homes in Britain tend to be built on one, two, three storeys perhaps.

Kate: The main differences between homes in North America and Britain are ... you've got screen doors in North America to keep the flies out and it's not warm enough in Britain usually to have flies. Um ... the heating in Britain is terribly important – it's less so in America, we use underfloor heating there.

Richard: Um ... I like my present home because ... because it's in the country to start with and surrounded by fields and because it's sort of the end of a no-through-road so very few people drive past, it's on an old dirt track. Mind you, you hear them when they do. And because it's an old cottage and I like ... it's got an open fire and things like that and I'm a bit of a romantic.

If I had a lot of money I'd keep the house I've got but I'd get a nice flat in the middle of London, another one in the middle of Cardiff, because I work in those two places, and I think a small chalet in the Alps – that'd do me.

Karen: My ideal living room would contain absolutely everything that you need for everyday life. In fact it would even have the bed in it because I cannot stand having to go upstairs and downstairs having left something that I needed upstairs to bring back down. So I'd have all mod cons and every single thing you could imagine that you n ... you might need throughout the day there.

(Time: 3 minutes 20 seconds)

# 6.2 Do you see what I mean? Functions

**A** This can be discussed with the whole class.

**B** 🔲 Play the recording, pausing after each conversation for students to catch up with their notes.

▶ Play the recording again and get everyone to note down how strongly the last speaker in each conversation agrees or disagrees with what has just been said (*as shown in italics in the transcript below*).

*Transcript* (the exponents used are underlined)

1
Ann: <u>What do you think about</u> modern architecture?
Ken: <u>Well, in my view</u> it totally fails to take into account the human scale of things – it's almost as if people don't count any more. <u>Do you see what I mean?</u>

77

Ann: Mm. *(= yes)*

Ken: I think architects should be made to consider what it's like to live or work in the building that they design. In fact, I think they should actually have to live in their own buildings. Don't you think?

Andrew: Yes, I couldn't agree with you more. *(= complete agreement)*

2

Karen: W ... what are your views on living in the country, a ... as opposed to living in the city?

Melinda: Well, I'd say that for most people it's just not practical. Um ... I think it'd be awful to be living in the middle of nowhere. Do you see what I mean?

Karen: No, I'm sorry could you explain why?

Melinda: Well, you'd be cut off from all the amenities of urban life: supermarkets and cinemas, shops, theatres, things like that. Part of your life would be missing, don't you agree?

Blain: Um ... that's one way of looking at it, I suppose. *(= not really)*

3

Ishia: What are your feelings about living with your parents?

Juliet: Well, it seems to me that for most young people it's something they have to do and, well, they just have to come to terms with it. People have to adjust to, you know, living together, if you see what I mean.

Ishia: Oh yes, yes, I see.

Juliet: Would you agree that even if you don't get on with your parents, you've just got to put up with it while you're young?

Tim: Well, no, no, not entirely. *(= partial disagreement)*

4

Andrew: So ... so what are your feelings about the building of the Channel Tunnel?

Kate: Well, the way I see it the whole project is ridiculous, OK?

Andrew: No, I don't quite follow ... I mean, er ... do you mean the cost is too high?

Kate: No, I just mean it's ... it's dangerous. Er ... what if there's a fire and you're there trapped under tons of water? No, you'll never persuade me to go in a train under the ocean.

Ken: Mm, I think I see what you mean, but if we don't have . . .
*(= sceptical)*

5

Blain: What do you think about nuclear power?

Enzo: Well, if you ask me it's the only sensible ecological solution to the world's energy problems. Right?

Blain: No, I'm not quite with you. Are you saying that nuclear power is safe? Now, you can't mean that!

Enzo: Oh, but I do – burning fossil fuels produces carbon dioxide which is contributing to the greenhouse effect. It's both safer and cheaper to generate electricity in nuclear power stations.

Ishia:  That's true in a way, I suppose.  *( = sceptical)*

6

Tim:  Hey, what do you think of ... er ... John and Mary's new flat?

Michael:  Well, you know, I can't help thinking they ... they kind of made a mess of the decoration. You know what I mean?

Tim:  Yeah, I know: all those rainbow colours in the living room – oh!

Michael:  I mean, if you're decorating a room it's supposed to be relaxing and calm – bright red and yellow and blue, it just makes you feel restless and uncomfortable.

Janenne:  That's true!  *( = complete agreement)*

(Time: 3 minutes 15 seconds)

**C**  This discussion could be started off by everyone in the class adding more topics for discussion on the board in the classroom.

**D**  [■] In this 'jigsaw reading' activity, student A sees the first part of the article in Activity 16, student B sees the second part in 51 and C sees the last part in 69. Each person finds out some information about Prince Charles's views on architecture, which he or she must share with the others.

It may be necessary to remind students that this is not a 'reading aloud' exercise: students should study their part of the text and then find out the main points of information that the others have gleaned from their parts of it.

**E**  If you have any large photos showing controversial buildings, bring them to class so that they can be discussed too.

# 6.3  Articles                              Grammar

**A**  *Suggested answers*

1 I'm going to buy a paper.
  *– a newspaper*
  I'm going to buy some paper.
  *– writing, typing or wrapping paper*
  I'm going to buy the paper.
  *– the newspaper I usually take, or the writing paper that was mentioned earlier*

I'm going to buy paper.
 – *writing, typing or wrapping paper not another product*

2 There's a hair in my soup!
 – *one hair*
There's hair in my soup!
 – *quite a lot of hair*
There's the hair – in my soup!
 – *the hair that was mentioned earlier*
There's some hair in my soup!
 – *one hair or several hairs*

3 Ask a teacher if you have a question.
 – *it doesn't have to be a particular teacher*
Ask the teacher if you have a question.
 – *your own teacher, or a particular one we have in mind*
Ask any teacher if you have a question.
 – *every teacher will be willing and able to answer the question*

4 She has some grey hairs.
 – *just a few grey hairs*
She has some grey hair.
 – *more than just a few*
She has grey hair.
 – *all her hair is grey*
She has a grey hair.
 – *just one grey hair*

5 After leaving school he went to sea.
 – *he worked as a seaman after finishing his education*
After leaving the school he went to the sea.
 – *he went out of the school building and down to the sea shore,
 perhaps for a swim*

**B** *Brief comments on the uses shown in the examples* (for
more information, consult *PEU* or a similar reference book)

### The *or Ø (zero article)*
 4 I don't really like towns but I do like **the** towns in this region.
 – *in general – the particular towns here*
 5 Modern architecture is impressive, but **the** architecture of the
 1970s was terrible.
 – *in general – in particular*
 6 They enjoy living in **the** city but they often spend (**the**) weekends
 in **the** country.
 – *a particular city, or a city in general – (optional) – in general*

7 She's looking forward to going to **the** Philippines / **the** Odeon /
  **the** Atlantic / **the** Middle East / **the** Nile / **the** Sahara / **the** Royal
  Hotel.
  *– These are examples of place names that take the definite article.*
8 He's looking forward to seeing France / Asia / Oxford Street /
  Trafalgar Square / Lake Superior / Westminster Abbey / Gatwick
  Airport / Waterloo Station.
  *These are examples of place names that take the zero article.*
9 There are twenty students in **the** class, but only ten are in class
  today.
  *– this particular class – at school, not absent*

## A *or* Ø

10 They're both public employees: she's **a** tax inspector and he's **a**
   teacher.
   *– jobs or professions: plural and singular*
11 They have **a** dog called Rover and **a** cat, but they haven't got any
   children.
   *– not two dogs or two cats*
12 I'd like **a** glass of milk and **a** cheese sandwich.
   *– one of each*
13 Windows are made of glass. Cheese is made from milk.
   *– materials or origins of products*

## Some *or* Ø

14 There are **some** amazing new buildings in the city.
   *– more than one, several*
15 Would you like **some** tea?     Would you like tea or coffee?
   *– a cup of tea – which will you choose?*
16 People are funny, aren't they?     **Some** people are funny, **some**
   aren't.
   *– all people, in general – not all, just a certain proportion*

## C   *Answers*

air U – breath C
architecture U – plan C
behaviour U – reaction C
bridge C – engineering U
cash U – coin C
clothing U – garment C
cooking U – kitchen C
experiment C – research U

fact C – information U
flu U – cough C
gadget C – equipment U
harm U – injury C
job C – work U
joke C – fun U
journey C – travel U
laughter U – smile C

| | |
|---|---|
| luck U – accident C | safety U – guard C |
| luggage U – suitcase C | thunderstorm C – lightning U |
| peace U – ceasefire C | traffic U – vehicle C |
| permit C – permission U | tune C – music U |
| poetry U – poem C | university C – education U |
| progress U – exam C | water U – drop C |
| report C – news U | weather U – shower C |

**D**  Refer to a dictionary for examples of the two uses of these words if necessary.

**E**  *Corrected sentences*

1 If there has been **a** robbery you should call **the** police.
2 Her brothers were all in bed asleep when she left home in **the** morning.
3 Most houses in **the** South of England are built of brick.
4 He's in hospital having **an** operation.
5 *no errors*
6 What wonderful news about Henry's sister getting **a/the** scholarship!
7 How much luggage are you going to take on **the** plane?
8 I'd like **some** information on holidays in **the** USA. Can you give me **some** advice?
9 What **a** magnificent view of **the** mountains in **the** distance!
10 He has brown eyes and **a** moustache.

**F**  *Suggested answers*

2 First of all make sure you disconnect the computer from the mains before you lift the cover. Then to replace the battery you have to use a screwdriver to loosen the screws shown as A and B on the diagram and then lift the cover. Take out the old battery from the socket labelled Z and replace it with a fresh battery.
3 Could you send us the instruction manual for the machine we ordered at the end of the month? The Production Manager would also like a copy of the specification sheet, please.
4 When you're in the supermarket, could you get a kilo of potatoes, some ketchup, a loaf of bread, a bottle of wine, and some food for the cat – she only eats the sort with the blue label, remember.
5 Is a building like a work of art or is it a piece of engineering? Should it be designed for the people in the street and also for the people inside? Is a building a 'machine for living in' where every part of it has a function? Or can some of the parts be for decoration, so that it is a 'pleasure to the eye'?

## G   *Complete passage*

60% of families in the UK own **their** own homes after borrowing money (known as a mortgage) from a building society or bank. They have to make Ø monthly repayments of **the** total sum (plus interest) for 20–25 years. Borrowers can usually borrow a sum equivalent to three times **their** annual salary, but need to put down a cash deposit of 10% of **the** purchase price. Ø people in Britain tend to move Ø home several times in **their** lives. **The** typical pattern is for a young couple to start as 'first-time buyers' in a small flat or house, then move to a larger house when they have a family and, when **the** children have left Ø home, to move into a smaller house or bungalow. Usually they move into Ø other people's houses or into a new home that has been built on a new estate by a builder. Families in Ø/**the** lower income groups are more likely to live in Ø rented accommodation, for example in a council house or flat.

Moving home can be a stressful experience, only slightly less traumatic than a bereavement or divorce. Often **the** buyer and seller of a house are part of a 'chain', where **the** sale of one house depends on a whole series of strangers doing **the** same thing at **the** same time. If one deal falls through at **the** last moment, **the** whole chain breaks down and no one is able to move.

---

# 6.4   Using abbreviations                Word study

## A   *Answers*

i.e. – that is      e.g. – for example      fig. – figure
•pp. – pages      qv – see another entry      cf – compare
ch. – chapter      ed. – edited by      para. – paragraph
NB – important note      intro. – introduction      cont'd – continued

## B   *Answers*

2  personal assistant
3  £15,000 per annum
4  not applicable
5  enclosed curriculum vitae and photograph
6  as soon as possible
7  reference number
8  15 packs at £19.99 (including Value Added Tax) per dozen, with the usual 15 per cent discount
9  Limited      public limited company
10  telephone number      extension
11  on behalf of      Department

## C Answers

1 Dr Brown doesn't live at 43 St Albans Ave any more – she's moved to no. 120, hasn't she?
2 LPs don't sound as good as CDs.
3 The USSR is over 22 million sq. km. in area: it's 70 times larger than the UK.
4 This equipment operates at 240 v. AC, not DC.
5 At the end of the talk there wasn't time for a Q & A session.

**D** This section contains four separate activities. If you can bring copies of some English-language newspapers to class the first one could be done right away without preparation.

Find out from the class which international abbreviations are different in their language(s) and in English, e.g. USSR.

Some more common abbreviations:

EC/EEC   NATO   UNO   P.S.   PC   ASAP   Rd   Sq.
PTO   km.   RSVP

---

# 6.5 *Make* and *do*   Verbs and idioms

## A Answers

MAKE collocations:
 the most/best of a situation, a cake, mistakes, a plan, a habit of, arrangements, a suggestion, improvements, a decision, an effort, an excuse
DO collocations:
 the shopping, your best, some painting, someone a good turn, someone a favour, an exam (also take), some cooking, harm, some reading, good

## B Answers

1 make way
2 make out
3 make up
4 made it up
5 make do with
6 make out
7 make it up to you
8 makes out
9 make
10 making up to
11 do-it-yourself (DIY)
12 over and done with
13 dos and don'ts
14 do without
15 **did** away with
16 has something to do with
17 had nothing to do with
18 do up

# 7 Put it in writing

---

## 7.1 The unstoppable Albert Sukoff    Reading

**A**  To save time in class, the text and the questions in **A** should be prepared as homework.

*Answers*

 1  1,286 words; in the New York Times; about his recollections of various people in previous administrations (governments)
 2  Details of futile feats (and world records)
 3  One rainy Wednesday in February 1985 while looking at the calendar; he had nothing planned for that day
 4  Mr Stein is an economist, working for the US government; Mr Sukoff is a freelance writer and city planner
 5  Mr Stein did, Mr Sukoff didn't
 6  Using a personal computer, rather than an old manual typewriter
 7  Mr Stein's
 8  1,404 words; the San Francisco Chronicle; how he found out about Mr Stein's record and explaining how he set about writing the sentence
 9  Requoting Mr Stein's sentence; quoting names from a phone book
10  They feel restricted by unwritten rules about sentence length and having to fit their ideas into a short article. (They often get paid by the number of words they write too, by the way!)
11  By editing their work and inserting some full stops
12  A mere 500 or so

**B**  The 'synonyms' given here show the approximate meaning of the words in the contexts: they are not full-scale dictionary definitions. There is other vocabulary in the text that may cause problems, but this exercise picks out the more useful words.

*Answers*

*respectively* = separately in the order mentioned
*emulated* = copy    *futile* = pointless    *feats* = achievements
*entry* = piece of information in a reference book

*alerting* = make aware of   *profounder* = more serious
*ramble* = write/speak at great length   *banal* = unoriginal
*ploy* = tactic   *superseded* = replace   *constrained* = limit
*invariably* = always

1 futile    feats
2 superseded    entries    respectively
3 rambled
4 invariably    rambling
5 profound/banal    banal/profound
6 ploy
7 constrained    alert

**C** 🔲 This section is intended to draw attention to some features of the article that students can use in their own writing.

Other examples of participles in the article:
   ... a 1985 calender **detailing** Guinness records on the date they were set ...
   ... but instead **peppering** it with dashes ...
   ... such as **stating** that the longest sentence ...
   ... especially when, as **expected**, it appears in the next Guinness Book ...

**D**   *Original paragraphs* (the second one would probably be clearer if it was divided into shorter sentences)

1 Why does language provide such a fascinating object of study? Perhaps because of its unique role in capturing the breadth of human thought and endeavour. We look around us, and are awed by the variety of several thousand languages and dialects, expressing a multiplicity of world views, literatures and ways of life. We look back at the thoughts of our predecessors, and find we can see only as far as language lets us see. We look forward in time, and find we can plan only through language. We look outward in space, and send symbols of communication along with our spacecraft, to explain who we are, in case there is anyone there who wants to know.

(from *The Cambridge Encyclopedia of Language* by David Crystal)

2 This book has been specially prepared to make it enjoyable reading for people to whom English is a second or foreign language. An English writer never thinks of avoiding unusual words, so that the learner, trying to read the book in its original form, has to turn frequently to the dictionary and so loses much of the pleasure that the book ought to give.

(from the preface to a book in the Longman Simplified English Series)

# 7.2 **Spoken and written English – 1** Listening

**A** This could be done as a class, making notes of suggestions on the board.

**B** 🎞 This is the first part of a lecture. The second part will be heard in 8.4. Although the silent language used by the lecturer in his talk would only be perceptible on video, the listener can easily imagine what he is doing as he demonstrates.

Places where you can pause the tape for students to catch up with their notes and compare notes with each other are shown with ★ ★ ★ in the transcript.

Students could be asked to write up their notes as homework as an essay on Spoken and Written English – or this could be saved till they've heard the rest of the lecture in 8.6.

## *Model notes*

```
Speech: 'rapid conversational English' face-to-face,
     unplanned, spontaneous
Writing: 'formal written English' happens alone, unplanned

Main features of speech missing in writing:
1 Hesitation - in writing hesitation not visible because
   writer stops to think, resting pen or stopping typing
2 Listener contact - e.g. question tags (like a tennis
   match??) + eye contact + questions at end of lecture
3 Silent language - gestures + body language - e.g.
   scratching head
   Not used in writing + on the phone - but watch people in
   phone boxes!
```

© Cambridge University Press 1991

## *Transcript*

Lecturer: . . . OK, so what I'm going to do is to compare two very common styles of English: first of all, 'rapid conversational style' – that is the kind of English that's used when you're having a conversation with some friends or with some colleagues – and on the other hand I want to talk about 'formal written style' – that is the kind of English that's used in business letters, reports, textbooks, things like that. And I'm going to refer to the former as 'Speech' in this lecture (of course there are other kinds of speech as well, obviously) and the latter as 'Writing' (though obviously there are other kinds of writing as well, many other styles).

So, various points I want to make: first of all, Speech. Now, rapid conversational English is face-to-face, it happens when you can see someone and that is part of what go ... go ... is going on, the way that you can see what's happening, and the other person can see what's happening. It's unplanned: you don't know what you're going to say until you say it, and it's spontaneous.

Secondly, Writing is different because formal written English happens alone, if you could actually see someone you wouldn't bother to write to them. It happens alone and it's planned: you don't write something until you've thought what you're going to write.

★  ★  ★

Now, what I want to do now is to look at the main features of Speech that you don't get in Writing. Um ... well, let me just first ... well, first of all, let me just ... er ... um ... explain that ... um ... one of the things that doesn't happen in ... at all in ... in writing but actually when you ... when you're ... um ... when you're listening to someone you may not always notice it. You can probably notice ... notice what I'm doing now ... er ... because I'm ... I'm sort of trying to exaggerate this particular ... er ... this particular phenomenon that ... that happens i ... i ... in conversation and I'm sure you can all fill in the gap in this sentence: 'What I'm doing now a lot is ... um ... hesitating.' Now, hesitation is something which happens all the time in conversation but in writing it doesn't happen. That doesn't mean to say that when you're writing you write and write and write, of course not because when you're writing if you need to stop and think, if you need to ... um ... find the right word or if you need to ... um ... er ... look something up, or find out some information, you stop writing, you put the pen down, you stop typing or whatever it is. In other words, hesitation in Writing is invisible but hesitation in conversation is audible, you can always hear it and some people hesitate more than others: what I was doing just now was hesitating more than I would normally do!

★  ★  ★

Second feature: the second feature is what I could call 'listener contact'. Now, listener contact is the way in which in a conversation the people involved are always ... somehow communicating with each other during the ... er ... during the interaction. Er ... a typical example of this is ... um ... the use of what are called 'question tags' – er ... questions as well actually – you know question tags, those things like *isn't it?* and *don't you?* and *can't you?* Um ... I often think this is something like a sort of tennis match where someone is serving the ball to the other one, you know:

'It's a lovely day today, *isn't it?*'
'Oh, yes, it's wonderful too. It was nice yesterday too, *wasn't it?*'
'Oh, yes, and I think it's going to be nice tomorrow, *don't you?*
And so the 'ball' goes backwards and forwards in the
conversation. In other words, people are 'throwing' the
conversation over to each other.

Now, listener contact goes on in other ways as well, obviously.
Um ... in this lecture that I'm giving now ... er ... I'm keeping in
contact with you while I'm lecturing, I'm not looking at my notes
reading word-for-word what it says here, I'm looking at the
reactions I'm getting ... er ... we're keeping in touch with our eyes.
In a lecture you can't sort of talk back to me and involve yourself
in a conversation but when I've finished at the end, you'll
probably have some questions and that's your way of contacting
me about the communication that's gone ... gone on between us.
And the eye contact, as I said, is very important there.

★ ★ ★

Now, eye contact is something which we could also describe as
'silent language' and this is the next point really. Er ... an
important part of Speech is the stuff that you can't actually hear.
If you're listening to a recording of something, if ... if ... say if you
listen to a recording of this lecture, there are various things going
on that you can *see*, but a listener wouldn't be able to notice. I
mean things like me doing this – well, you know I'm scratching
my head but the listener wouldn't have a clue and wouldn't know
that I meant 'I'm puzzled' or 'I can't think what to do next.' And
if I point at something and say 'Look at this!' then you can see
what I'm pointing at, you know what it is but someone just
hearing it wouldn't have a clue. In other words, the kind of thing
that's going on in a conversation, even the kind of thing that's
going on in a lecture like this, is essentially not just sounds
happening but vision as well. And you don't get that in Writing.
And it's also missing on the phone, isn't it, of course? When
you're on the phone to someone ... er ... if you want to draw
attention to something ... er ... it's no good pointing at it and
saying 'Look at this' ... er ... it's no good sort of waving your arms
about and saying 'This is very important' because the person on
the other end of the line can't see ... can't see what you're doing.
If you look at people in telephone boxes you often see them
waving their arms about and pointing at things because they can't
help it, it's part of what you're doing when you're talking.

(Time: 5 minutes 40 seconds)

# 7.3 Using appropriate language

Effective writing

Although this section involves reading skills, it is subtitled *Effective writing* because it emphasises the need for students to avoid the inappropriate style of the computer in their own writing.

**B** *Suggested answers*

1 A short story and some poems written by a computer
2 Only the introduction, which was written by Mr Chamberlain
3 It's faultless
4 Because the women have inferior roles in the story – one is a maid and they both have to do all the cooking
5 The ending of the story is left to the reader's imagination

**C** *Suggested answers* (though what is incongruous is a matter of opinion here)

2 The butcher is weary <u>and tired</u> because he has cut meat and steak <u>and lamb</u> for hours <u>and weeks</u>.
3 He does not <u>desire</u> to <u>chant</u> about anything with <u>raving</u> psychiatrists but he <u>sings about his dentist</u>, he dreams about a <u>single</u> astronomer, he thinks about his dog.
4 (Mathew), who <u>yearned</u> to look into Helene's nightgown (was) walking for an hour in <u>his</u> immense <u>boudoir</u>.
5 (The maid Helene was) slowly <u>ironing her brassiere</u>.

# 7.4 Different styles

Functions

**A** *Answers*

1 Introduction to a 'simplified edition' of a novel (a Longman Simplified English Series Reader) – as seen before in 7.1 D
2 Description of a book and its plot (the blurb of *Empire of the Sun* by J.G. Ballard)
3 Weather forecast – printed in a newspaper or, perhaps, read aloud on the radio
4 Part of a guidebook to Japan
5 Instructions packed with personal stereo headphones
6 Part of an advertisement persuading people to go by train
7 Part of a personal description of a place, perhaps in a personal letter

8 Part of a book about running (*The Book of Running* by James Fixx)

9 Directions for use, from the back of a bottle of tablets

10 The small print on an insurance form

**B**   Discuss this with the class when they have highlighted the 'clues'.

**C**   This can be set as a homework task.

---

# 7.5   Writing letters                          Listening

**B**   [cassette]   *Answers*

### Number of private letters sent in UK per year

| | |
|---|---|
| 1900 | *1,000 million* |
| 1930 | *3,000 million* |
| 1980 | *650 million* |
| now | *700 million* |

### Letters written by 16- to 24-year-olds in UK

| | |
|---|---|
| 22% | *Thank you* letters |
| *19* % | sent to addresses abroad |
| *12* % | fan letters |
| *29* % | love letters |
| 5% | letters to *grandparents* |

Women write *20* personal letters per year, men write *10* per year.

70% of all letters are connected with *business*

Worldwide, more *faxes* are sent than *telexes*

## Transcript

Presenter: When did you last write a personal letter? Do you write lots of letters or are you one of those people who prefer to pick up the phone? Sally James has some thoughts about letter writing.

Sally: In Britain the number of private letters sent, that is letters sent from one private address to another was 1,000 million in 1900 – this had risen to 3,000 million in 1930, but in 1980 dropped to an all-time low of 650 million. Now, the good news is that this figure has been rising every year since then, so that now 700 million personal letters are written every year.

So, people do still write letters, even though it's easy to pick up the phone to get in touch with someone, it's much cheaper to write a letter. Many people prefer to compose their thoughts and ideas in writing. People look forward to receiving letters, they often reread them and keep them to read again later.

The results of a survey among 16 to 24 year-olds have just been published. Now, according to this: 22% of the letters they write are thankyou letters, 19% are sent to addresses abroad, 12% are fan letters sent to pop stars or film stars, 5% are letters to grandparents and 29% are love letters! Among the people surveyed, it was discovered that the women wrote twice as many letters as men. Among the whole population of all age groups, women write twenty letters per year and men only ten letters per year.

Most of the letters that are sent are business letters. In the UK, 70% of all letters delivered in the UK are connected with business in some way: circulars or bills or straightforward business letters. Between companies, business letters *are* still being written, in spite of the new technology of fax and electronic mail. Business people tend to prefer letters because they enable them to keep a permanent record of transactions, positions, and a good-looking well-written letter is appreciated by clients and a useful part of marketing strategy in many companies. Quite simply, people like receiving letters.

In business, the number of fax messages has overtaken the number of telex messages, generally a fax is cheaper to send and much quicker to write and reply to, and you can handwrite a fax message if you're in a hurry. The main advantage of fax and telex is of course speed: even if you send a letter airmail, it may not arrive for several days – or even several weeks in some countries. So, for communication between continents, it makes sense for businesses to fax or telex each other. And a high-quality fax can look attractive just like a letter anyway and contain illustrations or diagrams and even photos: much more impressive than a scruffy telex.

One day, the experts say, everyone'll probably have a fax machine connected to their phone, and they'll be able to fax letters to each other instantaneously instead of posting them and waiting for the postman to deliver them. We'll probably write far more personal letters in future, but we won't be popping them in the postbox, we'll be faxing them to each other. Love letters by fax? Mm, I hope not, because it's so nice to find a handwritten envelope addressed to you among all the bills and circulars, or to receive a postcard with an exciting foreign stamp on it, and know that someone cares enough about you to want to write to you. *(doorbell rings)* Oh, that's the postman now, excuse me, I'm expecting a letter!

(Time: 3 minutes 45 seconds)

**C**  Ask each group to report back on their discussion.

**D**  ![icon] In this Communication activity, student A looks at Activity 10, while B looks at 28. Each has different information about graphology. Follow the procedure suggested in the Student's Book.

---

# 7.6  **Writing business letters** Reading

**B**  ![icon] The idea of this exercise is to encourage students not to depend on dictionaries or the teacher – or despair – when they come across unfamiliar words. All the meanings can be deduced from their context.

*Suggested answers*

*remorse* = regret
*whodunit* = who is responsible (a whodunit is a detective story)
*suspect* = not to be trusted
*deadwood* = unnecessary/superfluous text
*sap the strength* = take away the force
*credibility* = being believed and trusted
*wimpy* = weak and timid
*coverup* = attempt to conceal a problem
*vented his fury* = expressed his anger
*upbeat* = positive, hopeful      *tenfold* = ten times
*regimen* = plan or system      *heavy-duty* = large and complicated (in this context – a word processor here refers to a computer program or application, not a dedicated word processor)

**C**  The ad appeared in an American computer magazine (it could have been a business magazine) and the intended reader is a business person who has to write a lot of routine letters.

# 7.7 Keeping in touch

Creative writing

**B**   The first letterhead is suitable for a personal letter and the third
is suitable for a business letter – this should be well-known to
everyone, but it's probably a good idea to remind everyone of the
standard formats shown here. The second letterhead is unsuitable for
either type of letter.

**C**   *Suggested answers* (P = suitable in a personal letter
B = suitable in a business letter      P + B = suitable in both)

```
Dear Ms Hartman,      B
Dear Julie Hartman,   B(?)
Darling Julie,        P (!)
Dear Madam,           B (if you don't know her name)
Julie!                neither
Dear Julie,           P+B
Dear Friend,          neither
```

```
It's a very long time since I last wrote to you and I feel
   quite ...                              P
I'm pleased to inform you that ...  B
I'm sorry not to have written earlier, but I've been
   very busy with ...                     P
I hope your new job is going well ...   P+B
How are you? I'm fine.                  P(?)
Thank you for your enquiry about ...  B
The reason I'm writing this letter is to let you know that ... P+B
I hope you enjoyed your visit to ...    P+B
```

**D**   *Answers*

```
Good luck with your new job.                      P+B
I'm off to lunch now, so I'll post this on the way.    P
I have to stop now because lunch will be ready in a few
   minutes.                                          P
I hope you enjoy your holiday.                     P+B
I look forward to meeting you next month.           B
Well, I must stop now so as to catch the post.      P

Give my regards to your husband and the family.  B
Again, thank you for doing business with us.  neither–see 7.6A
Remember me to Ted and the kids.                  P+B
Assuring you of our best attention at all times. B(?)
```

```
Yours,                 P
Best,                  B (US style)
All the best,          P+B
Kind regards,          B
Your loving friend,    P(?)
Yours faithfully,      B
Yours sincerely,       B (GB style)
Best wishes,           B
Sincerely,             B (US style)
```

**E**  Follow the procedure outlined in the Student's Book. You may prefer to recommend or even stipulate which one of the suggested topics students should choose, though.

# 7.8  *In* . . . and *out of* . . .   Idioms

## A  *Answers*

1 in pencil     in ink
2 in doubt
3 In comparison with
4 in public     in the circumstances     in private
5 in tears     in a whisper
6 in writing     in cash
7 In view of     in addition to
8 in difficulty/trouble     in   trouble/difficulty
9 in   detail     in brief
10 in return     in fun

## B  *Answers*

1 out of fashion     in love
2 in   danger     in control
3 in contact/touch     out of touch
4 in   pain     out of hospital
5 out of focus     out of practice
6 in season     in stock
7 out of luck     out of work     in debt     in prison
8 out of tune     out of doors

# 8 Those were the days!

## 8.1 The 20th century Reading

**A** The correct sequence of paragraphs was: C F B E D A – but other arrangements are possible.

### Suggested answers

1 Events are reported 'as they happened' as if they are today's news
2 German, French and American editions
3 It reflects a British perspective on world events – presumably including events that affected Britain but not other countries

▶ Perhaps ask the class this extra question about the *Chronicle* blurb:

4 How many women are mentioned in the blurb?

The answer is 'None at all, apart from Queen Victoria' (see 8.3 **D**). Perhaps this is because female achievements are not considered newsworthy in the same way as male achievements: women are rarely responsible for starting wars, for example. Moreover, female historical figures are often less well-known internationally than they are within their own countries.

Ask the members of the class to name some female historical figures who are well-known in their country – e.g. Emmeline Pankhurst in Britain, La Pasionaria in Spain, Joan of Arc in France, Susan B. Anthony in the USA, etc.

**B** *Suggested answers*

1 Cinema, fashion, design, the media, advertising, popular music and dance, sport, leisure activities
2 Politics, wars, power struggles, etc.
3 to 5 *are a matter of opinion*

**C** 🖤 Student A reads the story of Charles Lindbergh, the famous aviator, as told in *Chronicle of the 20th Century* in Activity 18, student B sees the story as told in *Dreams for Sale* in 43. They then have to find out about the other's version of the story.

# 8.2 Talking about history    Vocabulary

**A** *Suggested answers*

1 hindsight      consequences      impact
2 historical      short-term      analyse      interpret      long-term
3 objective      subjective
4 outbreak      historic/momentous      powers      conflict

**B + C** Encourage students to ask questions about vocabulary during these discussions.

# 8.3 In the past    Grammar

The ideas in this section are intended as revision, but as this is a notorious 'problem area' of English grammar, there may be some unexpected difficulties.

**A** *Suggested answers and continuations*

1 ... we would spend ...
– *we used to do so, this happened usually or repeatedly*
      ... play on the sand every day.
  ... we spent ...
– *straightforward narrative*
      ... stayed in an old-fashioned seafront hotel.
  ... we had to spend our holidays at the coast and ...
– *we were obliged to do it*
      ... were sorry we couldn't stay at home.

2 ... I didn't use to stay ...
– *this didn't usually happen*
      ... the first time I went to a hotel as an adult was quite a treat.
  ... I wasn't used to staying ...
– *I wasn't accustomed to it*
      ... I didn't know how to behave.
  ... I wouldn't stay ...
– *I refused to stay*
      ... my parents had to go on holiday without me.

3 I was going to tell her what had happened but ...
– *I intended to tell her but something stopped me*
      ... I didn't have the nerve.

I was telling her what had happened but ...
 – *I was in the middle of telling her*
    ... she stopped me and said she already knew.
I told her what had happened but ...
 – *straightforward narrative or report*
    ... she didn't believe me.
I had told her what had happened but ...
 – *I told her earlier*
    ... she said she didn't remember me telling her.
I was about to tell her what had happened but ...
 – *I was on the point of telling her*
    ... then I realised that she already knew.

4 ... they had been doing ...
 – *they had done some of it and they still had more to do*
    ... their books were open on the desk.
 ... they had done ...
 – *they had completed all of it*
    ... they had already finished their report.
 ... they were doing ...
 – *they were in the middle of doing it*
    ... they were busily looking things up.
 ... they were going to do ...
 – *they hadn't started but they were planning to start soon*
    ... they had a long list of books they were going to consult.

5 I used to be interested in ...
 – *a habit or activity that I have now dropped or grown out of*
    ... but I've gone off it now.
I was interested in ...
 – *straightforward report or narrative*
    ... because it was my favourite subject at school.
I was used to ...
 – *I was accustomed to it*
    ... so reading another one was easy for me.

## B  Suggested answers

b) I <u>didn't recognise</u>[1] Sally at first because she <u>used to be</u>[3] much thinner. She <u>had put on</u>[2] a lot of weight and her hair <u>was going</u>[3] grey. When I <u>had last seen</u>[2] her she <u>was</u>[3] slimmer and her hair <u>was</u>[3] black. She <u>used to exercise</u>[3] regularly but for the past few years she <u>hadn't had</u>[2] time to continue since she <u>had moved</u>[2] to London. It <u>took</u>[1] me some time to get used to seeing her looking so different.

c) The boss <u>arrived</u>[1] late that day and <u>was told</u>[1] that everyone <u>had been reading</u>[2] newspapers and making paper aeroplanes all morning. Apparently, no one <u>had done</u>[2] any work: they <u>had taken</u>[2] the phone off the hook and <u>hadn't opened</u>[2] any of the mail. She <u>was about to lose</u>[5] her temper and <u>was going to sack</u>[5] them all when someone <u>pointed out</u>[1] that it <u>was</u>[1] April 1 and that they <u>had been pulling</u>[2] her leg.

d) Father <u>had gone</u>[2] up the ladder without securing it and, sure enough, the ladder <u>had slipped</u>[2] and he <u>was stuck</u>[1] on the roof. Well, no sooner <u>had</u> the ladder <u>fallen</u>[2] to the ground than it <u>started</u>[1] to pour with rain, so there <u>was</u>[1] no one in the street to hear his cries for help. By the time the rain <u>stopped</u>[1] it <u>had got</u>[2] dark and although he <u>went on</u>[1] shouting all evening, no one <u>heard</u>[1] him and he <u>had to spend</u>[1] the whole night on the roof. The next morning, by the time I <u>got</u>[1] there, he <u>had been rescued</u>[2] (by the window cleaner). It <u>was</u>[1] the first time I <u>had seen</u>[1 or 2] him look embarrassed – it <u>was</u>[1] one of the funniest sights I <u>had ever seen</u>.[1 or 2]

## C  Corrected sentences

1 I didn't **know** that you **were coming** to stay with me next weekend.
2 In the 1970s people **used to be/were** less well-off than they are now.
3 In the nineteenth century people **didn't (use to) watch** TV – they **had to** make their own entertainment.
4 I **had just written/was just writing** a letter to her when she **phoned** me.
5 *no errors*
6 He **studied / has studied / has been studying** history for three years.
7 It was the first time I **had been/gone** abroad and I was feeling very excited.
8 He arrived late because he had **forgotten** what time the train **would be leaving / left.**

## D  Answers

VICTORIAN BRITAIN
When Queen Victoria **died** in 1901 she **had reigned** for 63 years. During her reign many great scientific discoveries **were made** and the population of Britain **rose / had risen** from 18 million to 40 million. The British Empire **had grown** to become the largest empire the

world **had** ever **known** and by then it **included** a quarter of the world's people. During her reign Britain **enjoyed** a time of peace and prosperity and **had** not **fought** in any major war since the battle of Waterloo in 1815. No one **suspected** that the First World War, in which so many young men **would be killed, was going to / would break out** some 13 years later.

THE DARKER SIDE

During the reign of Queen Victoria (1837–1901) life for the middle classes and the aristocracy **had** never **been** better: the Industrial Revolution and the Empire **provided** them with undreamed-of luxury, convenience and wealth – but at the expense of the lower classes. Although slavery **had been abolished** in the British Empire in 1834, the working classes in the slums of Britain's industrial cities **were treated** almost as badly as slaves, and even young children **were forced / were being forced** to work long hours in factories and coal mines. During this period over 10 million people **escaped** from these appalling conditions and **emigrated** to America and Australia. The magnificent Empire which **brought** vast profits to Britain's manufacturers **exploited** the people of the colonies, who **produced** cheap raw materials for British factories, and **created** nations of customers who **came** to depend on a supply of British products.

## E  Answers

1 lay       had stung
2 rewound
3 awoke/awakened
4 flown     clung
5 laid      swept
6 arose     chose
7 wept      shrunk
8 foresaw   rewritten
9 rode      led
10 swore    trod

▶ Some other verbs with tricky past simple and past participle forms are:

*bind    deal    draw    forego    grind    mistake
overcome    overhear    overthrow    seek    spread
stride    swing    weave    withhold*

**F** Here is the correct arrangement of people, events and dates, in case you need to settle any arguments:

| | | |
|---|---|---|
| William the Conqueror | Battle of Hastings | 1066 |
| Christopher Columbus | Atlantic Ocean | 1492 |
| Ferdinand Magellan | Pacific Ocean | 1521 |
| Napoleon | Waterloo | 1815 |
| Wilbur and Orville Wright | Dayton, Ohio | 1903 |
| Archduke Franz Ferdinand | Sarajevo | 1914 |
| October Revolution | Russia | 1917 |
| John F. Kennedy | Dallas, Texas | 1963 |
| Neil Armstrong | Moon | 1969 |

---

# 8.4   Fourteen ninety-nine                    Listening

**A** 🔲 To answer some of the questions it's necessary to realise that the year being referred to as 'this year' is 1499.

*Answers*

**Vasco da Gama** left Lisbon on **July 8** 1497 with 170 men and provisions for three years. Out of sight of land for 93 days between Cape Verde Islands and **Cape of Good Hope** (**6,000** km). Finally arrived at Calicut in **India** on **22** May 1498 after 23 day voyage across **Arabian** Sea.
Left India in August 1498 with cargo of **spices, drugs, silk** and jewels.
Arrived back in September 1499 with only **55** survivors – the rest died of scurvy (a disease caused by lack of vitamin C).
His voyage opened up **an important new trading route** to Asia.

**Christopher Columbus**'s first voyage was financed by King Ferdinand and **Queen Isabella** of **Spain**. Left Spain on **2** August 1492 with **three** ships and **90** men to travel west via the **Canary** Islands. Out of sight of land for **36** days (**4,000** km). Reached other side of Atlantic Ocean (presumably islands off the coast of **China** or **Japan**) on **12 October** 1492.
Returned to Spain in **March** 1493 with cargo of a small amount of **gold**, six 'Indians' and some **parrots**.
His second voyage began in **September** 1493 with **1,200** men: set up first **permanent** European **settlement** on other side of Atlantic.
His third voyage began on **30 May 1498**: didn't find **a through route** to the Indies.

## *Transcript*

| Presenter: | Good evening, we have with us in the studio two people who have recently come back from Asia: Mr Vasco da Gama ... |
|---|---|
| Vasco da Gama: | Hello. |
| Presenter: | ... who has just returned from India and Mr Christopher Columbus ... |
| Columbus: | Hello, everyone. |
| Presenter: | ... who has just returned from his third voyage to the east coast of Asia. Mr da Gama, you set off from Lisbon in July 1497, didn't you? |
| Vasco da Gama: | Yes, July 8th it was, July 8th, if I remember rightly. Now, I set off and I took with me 170 crew and also provisions for approximately three years, just to make sure, you see. Now, the longest leg of the journey was a 6,000 km stretch between Cape ... the Cape Verde Islands and the Cape of Good Hope. We were out of sight of land for 93 days – a long time! Anyway, now on the way I managed to deal with some rather unfriendly Muslim rulers on the East coast of Africa and then another long sea voyage of about 23 days across the Arabian Sea. Well, we arrived in India on May 22 last year, and thanks to my skills as a diplomat we got on good terms with the ruler of Calicut. |
| Columbus: | Er ... could I just come in here for a minute, Robyn? |
| Presenter: | Oh yes, certainly, Mr Columbus, yes. |
| Columbus: | Isn't it true, Vasco, that Bartolomeu Dias first sailed round the southern tip of the African continent in 1488, ten years earlier than you – and if his crew hadn't refused to carry on further a ... a ... across the Indian Ocean that he'd have got there first? |
| Vasco da Gama: | But he didn't and that's the point. Anyway, we left Calicut late August 1498, loaded with lots of spices, drugs, silk and precious stones, ah ... |
| Presenter: | You didn't get back till this September, did you? Er ... why did it take so long? |
| Vasco da Gama: | Well ... um ... in fact we were delayed by contrary winds and difficulties en route, you see. Unfortunately, only 55 members of my crew survived. |
| Presenter: | Oh! Why was that? |
| Vasco da Gama: | B ... because of scurvy. |
| Presenter: | Oh. Still, it is a fantastic achievement and it looks as though you have opened up an important new trading route with the Orient. Now, Christopher Columbus, you've just returned from your third voyage, I think? |
| Columbus: | Yes, that's right, Rob ... er ... and I think in the long run ... er ... my discovery of the east coast of Asia will be more significant than Vasco's little trip. |

| Presenter: | Perhaps you could remind our listeners about your previous trips. |
|---|---|
| Columbus: | Yes, certainly Robyn, well, most educated people believe the earth is round, of course. You do too, don't you, Vasco? Haha. And ... er ... so you just have to keep going west to reach Japan and the Indies. Well, I couldn't persuade the King of Portugal to finance the trip in 1484, so in the end I had to go next door to ... er ... Spain and ... er ... get the money from King Ferdinand and Queen Isabella. That was eight years later and I have to tell you that I had to do a big selling job on them because they hesitated quite a lot before deciding they would finance my incredible voyage. So I left Spain on 2nd August ... er ... 1492. Er ... a lot of people were leaving Spain that day, you may remember it was the same time that all the Jews were driven out of Spain. Anyway, we left ... 2nd August ... er ... in 92, we had three ships and 90 men. Well, I decided to go ... er ... via the Canary Islands so that I could pick up the winds to carry us off to the west. Now, on this first voyage we were out of sight of land for 36 days from the Canary Islands to the Indieth ... to the Indies, sorry. That ... that's a distance of 4,000 kilometres, Robyn. Er ... we reached the other side of the Ocean on October 12th of that year and ... er ... we explored one or two of the islands. Obviously these are islands off the coast of China or Japan. |
| Presenter: | Now, you arrived back in Spain on ... in March 1493, yes? With a small amount of gold, six local residents from the island – um ... er ... you call them 'Indians', yes? |
| Columbus: | Indians is ... is right, Robyn, yes. |
| Presenter: | Yes, and some parrots. Not quite the gold mine you had promised, uh? |
| Columbus: | Er ... n ... not ... that ... that may be true. Maybe not, but that was early days, remember. I ... I'd proved it could be done, and that is the main point, if I may say so, Robyn. Now, my ... my second voyage began six months later. This time I had 1,200 men and I set up the first permanent European settlement on the other side of the Atlantic, do not forget that! My third voyage began on 30th May last year ... |
| Presenter: | Yeah, and what was the purpose of this third voyage? |
| Columbus: | To discover a sea passage through to the Indies. |
| Presenter: | And did you? |
| Columbus: | W ... well, to be quite frank with you, no, no. But we did discover a huge river and we sailed all along the coast of Asia looking for a route through it or around it. Now, the ... the trouble is that land appears t ... to block the through |

route to the Indies but I am convinced that if we can find
a route then it's only a few days' sailing to ... er ... to get to
the Indies.

Presenter: So what are your plans for the future?

Columbus: Well, of course, I've already started organising a ... a
fourth voyage and this time I'll sail through to India. I'll
see you there, Vasco!

Vasco da Gama: I rather doubt it, Chris.

Presenter: Mr Da Gama, Mr Columbus, thank you.

Columbus: Yeah, thank you, Rob.

Vasco da Gama: Thank you.

(Time: 3 minutes 25 seconds)

**B** If the last question catches your students' imaginations, they
might perhaps role play some historical interviews.

## 8.5 Forming adjectives                     Word study

**A** *Answers*

-ous    ambitious    courageous    dangerous    mountainous
        synonymous

-ic     artistic    catastrophic    dramatic    energetic
       Islamic    magnetic    metallic    optimistic
       pessimistic    sarcastic    scientific    symbolic
       sympathetic    systematic    tragic

-ical   ecological    grammatical    logical    philosophical
       political    theatrical    theoretical

-al     commercial    emotional    financial    functional
       intentional    national    professional    regional
       sensational    social    traditional

**B** *Answers*

-able   enjoyable    forgettable    obtainable    preferable
       regrettable    reliable    knowledgeable    memorable
       reasonable

-ive    communicative    competitive    decorative
       descriptive    destructive    explosive    informative
       possessive    productive    repetitive

-ly     daily    fortnightly    monthly    neighbourly
       quarterly    yearly

-y      itchy    jumpy    satisfactory    shiny    slippery
       supplementary    sweaty    dusty    gloomy    guilty
       hasty    lucky    moody    sandy    stripy    tasty

**D** It may be necessary to show a couple of examples on the board for this exercise:

Because of turbulence we had a very ............... flight.
She was very ............... after dropping the vase.

# 8.6 Spoken and written English – 2 Functions

This section is in four distinct parts, two of which involve listening. They can be done on separate occasions.

## A Suggested answers

These sentences could be used in 'rapid conversational style':
1, 2, 3, 4, 6, 7, 9, 12, 13, 14, 16, 18, 19
These sentences could be used in 'formal written style':
3, 5, 8, 10, 11, 13, 15, 17, 18, 20

**B** 📼 Perhaps pause the tape at the point marked ★ ★ ★.

## Model notes

```
1 Stress, intonation, pausing - help to make message
  clear
  In writing only punctuation and layout: bold type
  underlining, etc.
2 Feelings + attitude - tone of voice
  In writing you can't tell if writer is angry
  Use of special words in novels to show feelings:
  'whispered', 'sarcastically', etc.
3 Vocabulary - use of words like 'nice' - listener can
  ask questions
  Writing has to be less ambiguous than speech
4 Grammar and style - unfinished sentences, less
  complex style
  More hesitation and time taken to get to the point

Different paces:
- takes less long to speak but listener receives
  information slowly
- takes longer to write but reader receives
  information quickly
Reader can't ask questions - writing has to be
  unambiguous
Listener can ask questions!
```

## *Transcript*

Narrator: You'll hear the second part of a lecture – you heard the first part of this in Unit 7.

Lecturer: . . . look at people in telephone boxes you often see them waving their arms about and pointing at things because they can't help it, it's part of what you're doing when you're talking.

OK, next point is to do with stress and intonation and pausing. Now, when you're using language you're talking ... um ... to make the message clear, you sometimes emphasise things by saying, 'This is very *important*' or you may pause in order to perhaps also have the same effect, 'This is very ... (wait for it) ... important.' In Writing we have to do something different because you can't sort of make a long space before the next word, what you can do is something else though, you can perhaps print it boldly or underline it or print it in italics or in capitals: there are other techniques used for the same effect.

Um ... but one thing that is tricky I think about the ... th ... the way that it's sometimes difficult to ... to relate the two styles we're talking about is when we come to the question of feelings and attitude. Now, when people are talking, especially if they're talking in a conversation, especially if they're getting worked up about something, feeling emotional about something, then their voice carries not just information in the words they're using but also information in the *tone* that they're using, the way their voice sounds. Now in Writing the words that are used are just words on a page, there's no way of knowing if the read ... if the writer is angry at a particular time or timid at a particular time or nervous at a particular time, and so what we have to do and what ... I suppose is necessary, for example, in things like novels or stories is to somehow get over the idea that there is a tone involved in the way things are ... are actually spoken. I mean, let's say someone just says, 'Thank you.' In a novel that might be written as ' "Thank you," he said.' If someone says, 'Thank you!', in a novel it might say '... he said in an angry voice'; 'Thank you', in a novel it might say, ' "Thank you," he said timidly.' Would you say that was timidly? Or 'Thank you', in a novel that would be, ' "Thank you," he ... he whispered', wouldn't it? In a novel and in stories very often special words are used like 'whispered', 'shouted', 'in an angry voice', 'he yelled', 'he said sarcastically' in order to reflect the tone that is used in ... in Speech.

★ ★ ★

Right, there are just two more points I'd like to make. In ... in fact these are probably the two most important points of all. Anyway, first of all, let me just say a few words about vocabulary. Er ... let's just take some examples of vocabulary ... um ... for example, in Speech the use of things like phrasal verbs is very common ... um ... and the use of descriptive adjectives is not as common as it is in Writing. If I say to you it was ... 'I had a very nice meal' and you say, 'OK, that's interesting, fine' then I know I've got my message across, but if I say, 'I had a very nice meal' you say, 'What do you mean "nice"? Was it delicious, was it ... er ... interesting, was it ... er ... entertaining, were the people fun?' You can come back and ask me questions. In Writing you can't do that. Because it's a one-way thing, because the message goes across through the post or through the print or wherever it is, the people at the other end don't have a chance to ask questions back, and therefore the Writing somehow has to be much clearer, much less ambiguous than Speech can be.

Um ... let's take the final point which is to do with grammar and style. Now, if we listen to Speech, we hear that it's full of unfinished sentences, and the style and the kind of grammar that's used is much less complex generally than it is in Writing. Let's just take an example: if you ask me a question like, 'What's the point of studying history?' ... er ... I might reply, 'Well, that's an interesting question. Yes, I'm glad you asked me that ... um ... well, I think one of the ... you know ... one of the most valuable lessons we can learn from history is that it ... er ... it can help us to kind of underst ...' And so I might go on without actually getting to the point and then maybe get to the point and give my information. In Writing all that hesitation, all that time spent not finishing sentences and thinking about things is taken up by sitting down with a pen on the table or maybe ... er ... nothing happening until we're ready to go and then we'd write: 'Studying history can ...' and then think a bit longer, continue the sentence: 'help us to understand the causes of current events' and so we might then go on.

In other words, getting the message from something that's written can often be done much more quickly than getting the message from something that's spoken. In other words, from the hearer's point of view or from the reader's point of view, the kind of information you're getting comes at quite a different pace. And the paces are also different from the producer's point of view, from the writer's point of view or the speaker's point of view, except those are reversed. If you want to say something it doesn't take very long compared with the time it does ... takes to write it. If you want to read something it takes less long than the time it takes to listen to it. So there's an efficiency thing involved here. It's to do with the question of Writing being something which is thought about, planned and which is something that has to communicate with people in an unambiguous way, where the people haven't got a way of coming back to you and ... um ... asking questions. Well, in Writ ... in Speech normally they do have a chance to ask questions, so now's the time for you. Any questions?

(Time: 6 minutes)

## C   Suggested answers

| | |
|---|---|
| 1 enjoyable | 5 likeable |
| 2 complimentary | 6 pleasantly |
| 3 thoughtful | 7 friendly |
| 4 smart | 8 generous |

**D** 📼 Play the recording, pausing as necessary for students to note down their answers or to discuss them one by one. The tone of voice is all-important here.

## Transcript with ANSWERS

Narrator: You'll hear fifteen short extracts of spoken English. Follow the instructions in your book. The first is done for you as an example.

1 . . . I know it doesn't look very good but ... um ... I ... I mean, I spent literally hours on it honestly, and ... and then I ... I ... asked Mr Brown and he said it was all perfectly all right so . . .   LIE

2 . . . you know Tony? Well, listen to this: apparently he and Tracey are going on holiday together, which is incredible because everyone thinks he's about to get engaged to . . .   RUMOUR

3 . . . the deadline for handing in the assignments is July 7th – but if any of you want to give them in ... er ... ahead of that date, please don't hesitate. So has everyone got that?   ANNOUNCEMENT

4 . . . and so Ferdinand Magellan set sail in 1519 with a crew of 150 men, sailed round the world and was the first European to circumnavigate the earth . . .   LECTURE

5 . . . sorry, if ... if I could come in here, in fact Ferdinand Magellan didn't actually get all round the world, because he was killed by hostile natives in the Philippines. Er ... he *was* the first European to sail across the Pacific Ocean but it was his second-in-command ... er ... Delcano with just eighteen men out of the original 150 who were the first Europeans to actually sail all round the world, I think you'll find . . .
    CONTRADICTION

6 . . . you see the normal practice, when we refer to historical figures is to talk about the leader or ... or the captain or whatever. I mean if you're talking about Napoleon marching on Moscow, it's understood that he had thousands of anonymous soldiers under his command and . . .
    EXPLANATION

7 . . . if you get the facts wrong in an essay you're sure to lose marks, so you need to be especially careful about dates and so forth . . .
    WARNING

8 . . . might be a good idea to check your facts before you start writing, especially the dates. It's easy enough to look them up in a reference book . . .   FRIENDLY ADVICE

9 . . . so after waiting for a very long time I started to feel rather

uncomfortable so I knocked at the door and this strange young woman opened it! Well, you can imagine how embarrassed I felt! I mean there was I . . .     ANECDOTE

10 . . . but I'm sure I set it right. Anyway, that meant I got stuck in rush-hour traffic, so that's why I'm . . .     EXCUSE

11 . . . sure I said I'd do it but I just forgot. Er ... I know you were relying on me and all that but, sorry I just couldn't ... be helped. Still, I ... I'm really . . .     APOLOGY

12 . . . mm, well yeah, I thought it was a very good film. Oh, by the way, how's your work going? Last time we met you were feeling a bit fed up and thinking of leaving . . .     SMALL TALK

13 . . . and about your present job? Why are you thinking of leaving? Er, what are your reasons for leaving . . .     INTERVIEW

14 . . . happy about it. I think it'd be better for all of us if you spent a little less time . . .     COMPLAINT

15 . . . the fat man said to the thin man, 'Why did you jump so high?' And the thin man said to him, 'Well, if I hadn't done that, you'd be . . .'
     JOKE

(Time: 4 minutes)

# 8.7 *Get*                              Verbs and idioms

## A  *Answers*

| | |
|---|---|
| 1 have | 8 receive |
| 2 persuaded | 9 prepare |
| 3 become | 10 arrive |
| 4 fetch | 11 acquire/obtain |
| 5 earn | 12 acquire/obtain |
| 6 manage | 13 start |
| 7 understand | 14 annoys |

**B**  Two of these sentences need to be rewritten to show the change in word order.

## *Answers*

2 get through
3 It may be difficult to get these ideas over/across to everyone
4 getting at
5 Try not to let it get you down if someone gets at you.
6 get down
7 get out of
8 get over

109

 9  get together      got round to it
10  get into
11  get away
12  get ahead/on
13  get going       getting on for
14  get along/on with
15  getting nowhere
16  got her own back

▶ Some other idioms with GET are:
get at = reach
What's got into her? = What's the matter with her?
get on = become old
get over an illness = recover from
get through to = reach

# 9 The third age

---

## 9.1 'U3A'

According to the article, there are four ages of man. Shakespeare, rather more unkindly, chronicled seven ages of man in Jaques' famous speech in *As You Like It*:

> All the world's a stage,
> And all the men and women merely players:
> They have their exits and their entrances;
> And one man in his time plays many parts,
> His acts being seven ages. At first the infant,
> Mewing and puking in the nurse's arms.
> And then the whining school-boy, with his satchel,
> And shining morning face, creeping like a snail
> Unwillingly to school. And then the lover,
> Sighing like a furnace with a woeful ballad
> Made to his mistress' eyebrow. Then a soldier,
> Full of strange oaths and bearded like the pard,
> Jealous in honour, sudden and quick in quarrel,
> Seeking the bubble reputation
> Even in the cannon's mouth. And then the justice,
> In fair round belly with good capon lined,
> With eyes severe, and beard of formal cut,
> Full of saws and modern instances,
> And so he plays his part. The sixth age shifts
> Into the lean and slippered pantaloon
> With spectacles on nose and pouch on side,
> His youthful hose well saved, a world too wide
> For his shrunk shank; and his big manly voice,
> Turning again to childish treble, pipes
> And whistles in his sound. Last scene of all,
> That ends this strange eventful history,
> Is second childishness and mere oblivion,
> Sans teeth, sans eyes, sans taste, sans everything.

▶ Perhaps your class might like to see this speech – you might like to photocopy it.

**B**  As this is a very long text, it should be prepared at home before the lesson.

111

## Answers

1 To postpone the Fourth Age of weakness and death by filling the Third Age, which may last 30 years, with activities and stimulation
2 They are cooperative: everyone can contribute something
3 The first was founded in Toulouse in 1972
4 In Britain they are run *by* by the elderly not *for* them; in France they are run in, and by, existing educational institutions; in France there is a law requiring educational institutions to provide classes for elderly people
5 Because it was realised that people decline physically when they have no stimulation, no work to do and no interest in life around them – money could be saved on health care by improving/introducing education for older people
6 112 at the last count
7 1,200 to 1,500

## C   Answers

*chronicled* – recorded     *mutual interest* – interest shared in common
*founder member* – one of the group who started it
*adamant* – determined     *promote* – encourage
*followed suit* – did the same
*singsong* – party where everyone joins in singing
*like wildfire* – very rapidly     *thriving* – successful
*with strings attached* – with conditions that must be fulfilled
*resources of the area* – available talents and facilities
*fulfilment* – feeling of deep satisfaction

**D**   Even if you suspect that your students might find this 'stylistic analysis' beyond them, I suggest you let them try doing at least the first two questions together in pairs (or perhaps in groups) before deciding whether to do the rest as a whole-class activity.

## Suggested answers

1 a) By using short verbless clauses, repeating *the* at the beginning of each one
   b) By using *you* in the description: *your friends, you may not notice it*
   c) By using comparative forms in the second sentence: *cheerier, more intense, more avid, more grey hairs* and by prefacing these with an understated *little*
2 Paragraphs 4, 8 and 9, and *loneliness* in paragraph 12 – the effect is to emphasise the alternative to the stimulating U3A experience

3 These answers will be a matter of opinion – if possible, highlight
   your OWN examples of each aspect
4 Again, a matter of opinion

**E**  It might be worth pointing out that in many cultures there is no
'problem' of old people – they have a part to play in society and
remain active, valued members of the community. It may only be a
'Western' or 'Northern' problem, rather than a universal one.

## 9.2    Living to a ripe old age             Vocabulary

**A**  *Answers*

1 pension      pensioner      senior citizen      retiree
2 confidence      wisdom      adaptable      agile      energetic
3 health      welfare
4 life expectancy
5 ageism
6 nostalgically      good old days      Those were the days

**B + C**  Encourage questions on vocabulary during both these
discussions.

▶ There is more vocabulary work in 9.6.

## 9.3    Granny power                          Listening

**A** 🔲  *Answers*

1 41%      27%
2 10%
3 20%
4 Japan      USA      Germany
5 Brazil      Korea      Egypt
6 productive      adaptable      flexible
7 skill      judgement
8 20%
9 60      55      payroll
10 450,000      half/50%      68%
11 35      large family units      all four parents
12 widows      widowers      immoral

13 unproductive
14 competitive
15 health and welfare

## B   *Suggested summary* (many variations possible)

In the 21st century, Western countries will find it increasingly difficult to support their older populations and compete with 'younger' countries.

## *Transcript*

| | |
|---|---|
| Presenter: | . . . for both old people and young people. In the West old people are living longer and fewer babies are being born. According to Tracy Harris, this is having a drastic effect on the profile of the population. |
| Tracy Harris: | If we look ahead to the year 2025, we can see that the profile of the population in many countries will be very different from what it is today. In West Germany, for example, 41% of the population will be over 50 compared with the current figures of 27%. And one in ten people will be over 75 years old, and that will be true in Japan as well. By the year 2025 in most Western countries one in five people will be over 65. So today's 25 to 40 year-olds are tomorrow's over-sixties. |
| Presenter: | Why should this be regarded as a 'problem'? |
| Tracy Harris: | The major industrial nations like Japan, the USA and Germany will be elderly, whereas countries like Brazil, Korea and Egypt will have much younger populations. Now, the point is that younger workers are generally more productive, adaptable and flexible. While it is true that older workers have acquired skill and judgement, they do tend to lose speed and flexibility. In the future, with constantly changing technology, it's the more adaptable workers who will succeed, and they're more likely to be the younger ones. |
| Presenter: | It's not only in the West that this trend is visible, as Clive Manston reports from China. |
| Clive Manston: | Well, China has had a one-child policy for quite a long time now: married couples are only allowed to have one child. So this means that the population is getting older all the time, if you see what I mean. By the year 2025 20% of Chinese people will be over 60 years of age. In China the official retirement age is 60 for men and 55 for women, but most stay on the payroll. Shanghai's textile mills employ 450,000 people, but only half of these are workers – the rest are former workers, retired people who continue to draw 68% of a working employee's wages. By |

2000 there will be 150 million people who are over 60 – and not contributing in the least to the national economy.

Before 1949 life expectancy for the Chinese was 35: those old people who did live to a ripe old age were looked after in traditional large family units. Now couples, who these days are often the only child of their parents, face sole responsibility for all four parents. Widows and widowers are officially encouraged to marry – in fact, they are often unwilling to live with their married children because apartments are so cramped – but in some parts of China where people still believe that widows who remarry are immoral, there this policy is not popular.

Presenter: According to Angela Seligman, there are several problems facing Western countries in the future.

Angela Seligman: One of the problems as I see it is that a relatively small working population will have to support a large number of unproductive retired people. And of course 'younger' countries will be more competitive in the world market than 'elderly' countries. Another thing is that huge sums will have to be spent on health and welfare facilities for these old people.

Presenter: So, how can these problems be solved . . .?

(Time: 3 minutes 40 seconds)

**C** 🎭 Divide the class into an EVEN number of pairs, so that pairs of pairs can be formed later. You may need to have a couple of groups of three to start with.

Half the pairs look at Activity 23, which contains a bar chart showing the distribution of population under and over 25 in 1970 and 2000. The other half look at Activity 60, which contains a bar chart showing the distribution of the population in various countries today aged under 15, over 15 and over 65.

Make sure the pairs have enough time to discuss the facts and figures before they join another pair.

**D** Make sure each group has a chance to compare its decisions with the other groups.

---

# 9.4 Building paragraphs  Effective writing

**A** The answers to the questions are debatable: basically each new paragraph contains a new idea.

**B**  The original article was laid out like this, though other arrangements may be possible.

"We need cooperation and not polarisation," Professor Lehr said. Both the economy and society had to face the enormous challenge of adjusting to the demographic changes caused by a drastic fall in birth-rates, she said.

But she added that a minimum pension would not solve the problems linked to aging. "The Greys have opted for the wrong path."

At present, some 90 per cent of the two million West Germans who need care are looked after by their families, and 600,000 people live in homes. But staffing problems in hospitals and in the care sector have reached alarming proportions, and reports of "scandalous conditions" in old people's homes make headlines almost every week.

The anger of those involved in caring for the old has recently been fuelled by a decision of a Mannheim court which, in response to a complaint from residents in a small town in Baden-Wuerttemberg, ruled that old people's homes should not be situated in "high-quality residential areas."

The plaintiffs argued that they were "disturbed at night by the sound of ambulances and occasional screams from home inmates."

It was high time, Mrs Unruh said, that those in power in Bonn realised that West Germany was fast becoming a society hostile not only to children, but also to the aged.

She said her proposals for greater integration of the old and reduced dependence on the state welfare system had exposed the serious gap between private care provided by the family and the official welfare system in hospitals, homes and other institutions.

## 9.5  A discursive essay  Creative writing

**A + B + C**  Follow the procedure suggested in the Student's Book, perhaps recommending which alternative in **B** they should choose.

## 9.6  *Ages*  Idioms

**A**  *Answers*

1 Old World     New World
2 under age = too young (to drink, vote, etc.)
3 new blood = new, young members of group
4 old flame = someone you used to be in love with     for ages
5 newcomer     old hands = experienced members of staff

6 old boys / old girls = former pupil     old times
7 freshwater
8 fresh start = begin again
9 old masters = famous painters of the past
10 come of age
11 old wives' tale = belief handed down as traditional
    wisdom     fresh air = pure, cool air
12 Stone Age     space age     young at heart     as old as you feel

▶ A few more idioms, not included in the exercise:
for old times' sake = because of happy times in the past
brand new = completely new
fresh out of = just sold the last

# 10 It takes all sorts . . .

---

## 10.1 What do they look like?

**A** 📼 Pause the tape after each description for everyone (perhaps in pairs) to discuss which person they think was described.

*Transcript with* ANSWERS

Kate: This person looks quite naughty, like they've just gotten away with something. Um ... they're middle-aged, perhaps late forties early fifties ... um ... they look like they're the life and soul of the party and like they might tell some interesting and, ... well interesting jokes.      *2*

Andrew: This person is quite smart in appearance, aged probably about twenty- ... two, twenty-three. I should imagine ... um ... somebody who works in an office or a bank maybe, something like that. Um ... rather delicate way of ... of holding things. Um ... very nice attractive smile, very pleasant face and ... er ... obviously takes quite a pride in ... in their appearance.      *9*

Ann: This person has got a very kindly face ... um ... the sort of person that ... er ... you would trust to do anything for you. I would say late sixties, perhaps early seventies, wearing those ... um ... charming glasses ... er ... that are sort of half moon shape, so therefore is peering over the glasses at one. Um ... to sum it up: a favourite grandparent, I suppose.      *5*

Kate: This person looks like a business executive, very clean-cut, very efficient. They're probably in their mid to late fifties. Um ... they look like they take a great deal of trouble with their appearance, probably use hairspray and a lot of mouthwash, so they always have very pleasant breath.      *11*

Andrew: This person is very well turned out, hair very nicely cut and styled ... um ... wearing quite good clothes, probably from ... er ... a reasonably expensive shop, somebody aged around thirty ... er ... lively, bright personality, I should think. Enjoys socialising I'd say, probably a ... a great guest to have at a dinner party.      *10*

Kate: This person looks like they've just been caught by the camera and suddenly realise that they're having their picture taken and they aren't sure whether they're too happy about it or not. Um ... they're ... er ... about thirty to thirty-five years old and they look

118

like they're interested in people and things rather than posing, which makes me think they'd be very interesting to have a conversation with. They are self-conscious, which means they'd be interested in other people rather than talking about *themselves* all the time.    *4*

(Time: 3 minutes 25 seconds)

**B**   Ask for suggestions of other similar words that could be used – and encourage students to ask questions like this:
'What do you say when someone . . .?'
'What's the English word for . . .?'

**C**   If each person keeps the number of the picture he or she's describing a secret, this activity is more enjoyable.

**D**   Groups of four or five might be best here.

**E**   [image] In this Communication activity, student A looks at Activity 38 while B looks at 61. Each has a different photograph to describe.

## Extra activity

Get each member of the class to bring in photos of relatives, friends, film stars, pop stars, etc. Then, working in pairs, ask them to prepare descriptions of the people. Another pair has to identify the subject of each description from a collection of photos spread out on the table.

# 10.2   Modal verbs                                         Grammar

**A**   *Suggested answers and continuations*

1 They might tell me but ...
   – *it's possible that they'll tell me (perhaps slightly less possible than* may *in the last example)*
   ... I don't expect they will.
   They may have told me but ...
   – *it's possible that they told me*
   ... I can't remember whether they did.
   They might have told me but ...
   – *It's possible that they told me (perhaps slightly less possible than* may have *in the previous example)*
   ... my memory is a little hazy about it.

119

They may tell me but ...
*– it's possible that they'll tell me*
   ... they may not, it all depends.

2  We could have tea early because ...
   *– it's possible for us to have tea early today*
      ... we're both going out this evening.
   We were able to have tea early because ...
   *– it was possible for us to have tea early (that day)*
      ... we had finished our work.

3  You mustn't tell her that ...
   *– don't tell her*
      ... she's putting on weight.
   You don't have to tell her that ...
   *– it's not necessary to tell her*
      ... she has to cook the dinner.
   You needn't tell her that ...
   *– it's not necessary to tell her (same meaning as the previous example)*
      ... she has to do the washing-up.
   You oughtn't to tell her that ...
   *– it's not advisable to tell her*
      ... she's overweight.

4  I should have trusted him but ...
   *– it would have been a good idea to trust him*
      ... I'm ashamed to say I didn't.
   I had to trust him but ...
   *– I trusted him: I had no choice*
      ... I had serious misgivings about doing so.
   I shouldn't have trusted him but ...
   *– I trusted him, but I was wrong to do so*
      ... I did, I'm afraid.
   I didn't have to trust him but ...
   *– it wasn't necessary to trust him but I did*
      ... it seemed like a good idea at the time.
   I needn't have trusted him but ...
   *– it wasn't necessary to trust him but I did trust him (same meaning as the previous example)*
      ... it seemed the only solution.

5  She can't have lunch because ...
   *– it's not possible for her to have lunch (in the future)*
      ... she's got to catch a train at 12.30.

She can't be having lunch because ...
– *I'm sure she is not having lunch now*
    ... it's only 11.15.
She couldn't have lunch because ...
– *it wasn't possible for her to have lunch (in the past)*
    ... there wasn't time.
She can't have had lunch because ...
– *I'm sure she has not had lunch*
    ... she says she is starving.

6 He may not have seen her, so ...
– *it's possible he didn't notice her / meet her*
    ... you'd better ring up to find out if he did.
He can't have seen her, so ...
– *I'm sure he didn't see her / notice her*
    ... that's why he walked right past her.
He may not be seeing her, so ...
– *it's possible they are not going out together*
    ... don't assume he knows what she did last night.
He can't be seeing her, so ...
– *I'm sure they aren't going out together*
    ... he won't mind if he finds out what she was doing.
He may not see her, so ...
– *it's possible he won't notice her / meet her*
    ... you'd better phone her to tell her about the party.
He can't see her, so ...
– *it's impossible for him to meet her*
    ... she's going out with someone else tonight.

## B  *Answers*

 1 (in)ability
 2 possibility
 3 probability / certainty (assumption)
 4 probability / certainty (assumption)
 5 obligation / advisability / necessity
 6 probability
 7 permission / suggestion
 8 request
 9 ability / capability
10 probability
11 advisability
12 prohibition

## C  *Answers* (note the odd one out in 7)

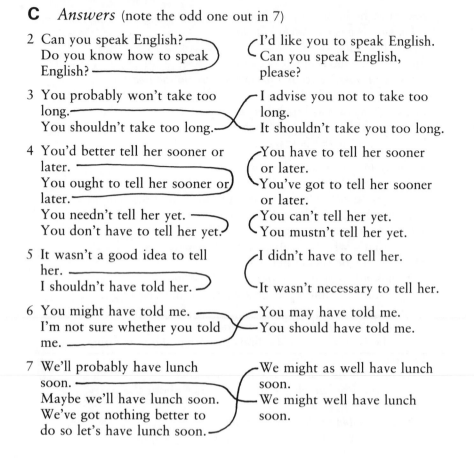

2 Can you speak English?
  Do you know how to speak English?

  I'd like you to speak English.
  Can you speak English, please?

3 You probably won't take too long.
  You shouldn't take too long.

  I advise you not to take too long.
  It shouldn't take you too long.

4 You'd better tell her sooner or later.
  You ought to tell her sooner or later.

  You have to tell her sooner or later.
  You've got to tell her sooner or later.

  You needn't tell her yet.
  You don't have to tell her yet.

  You can't tell her yet.
  You mustn't tell her yet.

5 It wasn't a good idea to tell her.
  I shouldn't have told her.

  I didn't have to tell her.
  It wasn't necessary to tell her.

6 You might have told me.
  I'm not sure whether you told me.

  You may have told me.
  You should have told me.

7 We'll probably have lunch soon.
  Maybe we'll have lunch soon.
  We've got nothing better to do so let's have lunch soon.

  We might as well have lunch soon.
  We might well have lunch soon.

## D  *Corrections*

Dear Jane,

As you **may** already know, we **had to** start looking for a new receptionist in our office last month. Mr Brown, our boss, **could** have chosen someone who already worked in another department but he **wasn't** able to find anyone suitable so he **had** to advertise in the local paper. There ought **to** have been a lot of applicants but surprisingly only a couple of replies came in and only one of those was suitable. I told Mr Brown that he **ought to / should / had better** get in touch with her at once. He decided we **didn't need to / needn't** phone her as there was no hurry, and we **might** as well send her a card. Unfortunately we heard no more from her, so we've had to start advertising again – in vain so far.

For the time being, the job's being done by Mr Brown's son who **shouldn't / oughtn't to** be working really because he's unhelpful and sometimes he **can** be quite rude to visitors. **I needn't / don't have to** tell you that we're all pretty fed up with the situation. Well, as I don't have **any more to say,** I'll stop there.

**E**   This activity looking at 'then' and 'now' gives everyone a chance to use some of the modal verbs in a free discussion. Point out that any archaic vocabulary items can be worked out from their context and that this will not hamper the discussion, e.g. *disport themselves* = show themselves; *raiment* = clothes; *inclement* = cold; *calls of nature* = toilet visits; *partaking* = eating.

---

# 10.3   Personalities                        Word study

**A**   Ask the pairs to report back to the class on their discussion.

**B**   *Answers*

clever ≠ stupid
generous ≠ mean/stingy
kind ≠ cruel
modest ≠ conceited
narrow-minded ≠ open-minded

prejudiced ≠ tolerant
relaxed ≠ nervous
shy ≠ self-confident
sensible ≠ silly/foolish
sophisticated ≠ naive

**C**   Note that these are words with similar meanings – there is rarely such a thing as an exact synonym.

*Answers*

clever = bright
cunning = crafty
excitable = highly-strung
fair = even-handed
forgetful = absent-minded
frank = direct
glum = miserable
good-natured = kind

jolly = cheerful
level-headed = sensible
reliable = trustworthy
self-confident = self-assured
snobbish = stuck-up
surly = grumpy
two-faced = insincere

**D**   *Answers*

| | | | |
|---|---|---|---|
| disagreeable | indiscreet | unkind | unpredictable |
| unapproachable | inefficient | unlikeable | unreasonable |
| inarticulate | unenthusiastic | illogical | unreliable |
| unbiased | inflexible | disloyal | disrespectful |
| incompetent | unfriendly | immature | insensitive |

| | | | |
|---|---|---|---|
| inconsiderate | unhelpful/helpless | disobedient | unsociable |
| discontented | inhospitable | disorganised | tactless |
| indecisive | unimaginative | impatient | thoughtless |
| undependable | unintelligent | impractical | intolerant |

**E + F**   As well as giving students a chance to use some of the vocabulary in free discussion, either of these activities could form the starting point for a paragraph-writing task.

## 10.4   Your lucky stars                    Reading

Follow the procedure outlined in the Student's Book. The initial reading and highlighting might be done as homework before the lesson.

▶ It may be interesting to find out how many members of the class start out as sceptics or believers and how many change their minds after doing this activity.

## 10.5   *Give* and *take*            Verbs and idioms

**A**   *Answers*

1 up   2 back   3 up   4 after   5 in   6 back
7 out   8 up

**B**   *Answers* (note the change in word order in some sentences)
1 take it all in     take down
2 takes up
3 take it on
4 Given / Taking account of     took her on
5 took it for granted / took it as read     take part in
6 take-off     taken in     take the day off
7 give or take
8 give-and-take     give way
9 take her for granted
10 take it out on
11 take to
12 take something apart / to pieces
13 taking account of
14 Giving away     gave rise to
15 take back

Remind everyone that they should highlight some of the expressions to help remember them.

Perhaps get everyone to work in pairs at the end and write a mini-exercise consisting of six sentences with gaps (.................) using the expressions from **B**. Then another pair can be asked to do the exercise.

# 11 Fame and fortune

## 11.1 Who do you admire?

Listening and vocabulary

**A** 📼 Pause the tape after each person has spoken, for students to make notes.

*Transcript*

Ishia:     I suppose somebody I've always admired is <u>Simone de Beauvoir</u>. I think that she probably had an enormous effect on women of my generation, apart from being a quite brilliant writer in my opinion, and a lot of other people's, er ... she also carried the philosophy of her work and her politics right through into her life and I suppose ... er ... I mean, although she was a feminist, she was a feminist in ... in what I consider to be the proper sense of the word. She adored men ... er ... and had lots of relationships with them, but it was the way that she conducted those relationships that was fascinating. Um ... I thought she was quite remarkable and ... and I ... her writing, which is so moving but also so honest and truthful ... er ... but contains all the ... the ideas that ... that we all aspire to, I ... I thought was ... was quite phenomenal.

Tim:     Gosh, who do I admire? You know <u>Benazir Bhutto</u>? She's an extraordinary woman. Her father ... er ... Zulfikar Ali Bhutto was the prime minister of Pakistan and he was ... um ... overthrown and executed when the army took over under General ... under President ... well, at that time General Zia who became President Zia. And ... er ... she fled the country and she continued in ... er ... spirited opposition to them ... to the regime from ... from exile. Finally when she returned to Pakistan, she was immediately jailed ... um ... but eventually, after a long per ... periods of ... of democratisation in ... in Pakistan and the ousting of President Zia and there was free elections, she eventually became prime minister ... um ... and she is one of the few, I think, great ... er ... women leaders in ... in what is otherwise a ... a ... particularly in Pakistan, a very male-dominated society.

Amanda: Yeah, one of the people that I really admire is <u>Cory Aquino</u>. And ... um ... she's ... she's remained powerful and ... er ... courageous despite everything that had been there to prevent her from doing that. Um ... her husband Benigno was shot down when he

returned from exile to the Philippines and she c ... you know
fought on through that, she became leader of the opposition to
the Marcos regime which is incredible ... er ... I don't know if you
know anything about Marcos, but that ... to remain alive against
supporters of the Marcos family, husband and wife, is incredible.
And anyway she was elected to become president when they were
overthrown in 1986, and despite everything she continued to hold
the country together.

Nigel: Someone I admire is <u>Jane Fonda</u>, not only is she a brilliant
actress, she's also stunningly beautiful. In fact, when she started
her acting career she wasn't really taken seriously as an actress,
she was thought upon more as a sex symbol really i... in films like
*Barbarella*. Um ... recently she's developed an interest in politics,
which I think's very important. And of course, recently she's
become very well-known for inspiring millions of people to keep
fit and stay healthy through the exercise routine she's developed.

(Time: 3 minutes)

**B** *Answers*

1 foremost / most eminent / leading    inspiration
  effort / hard work    serendipity / lucky chance
  outstanding / significant
2 notorious / infamous    publicity    reputation
  short-lived / ephemeral
3 evidently / clearly / plainly / undoubtedly
  respect / look up to / admire    fans / admirers    charisma
4 rags to riches    role model / idol / hero / inspiration

**C** Perhaps tell the class about some people YOU admire, to start
their discussions going.

# 11.2 Remarkable Charlie    Read and discuss

**A** As this is a particularly long text, it should be prepared for
homework, if possible.

**B** *Answers*

True statements: 2 3 6 8
False statements: 1 4 5 7 9 10

127

## C  🔲 *Answers*

*subversive* – undermining authority
*resilience* – ability to recover from setbacks     *self-*
*willed* – stubborn      *gags* – jokes      *inanimate* – not living
*bust* – broken      *adroitness* – skill      *charged* – filled
*corresponding* – matching      *reconcile* – harmonise and resolve
*effaced* – erased      *ominous* – threatening
*prudently* – wisely      *turbulent* – violent
*unfounded* – unsubstantiated      *charges* – allegations
*macabre* – horrifying

**D + E**   Follow the procedure outlined in the Student's Book.

---

# 11.3   **Walt Disney**                               Listening

## A  🔲 *Answers*

1 correspondence course
2 Oswald the Rabbit
3 talking cartoon film
4 Mortimer Mouse
5 Walt Disney himself
6 business manager      imaginative, creative part of the partnership
7 storyteller
8 Ub Iwerks
9 35      feature-length cartoon film      2,000,000      three
10 40      40      41
11 his artists and illustrators went on strike in 1941
12 commentary      editing
13 potential
14 55      $17,000,000
15 66      Disney World      71
   Experimental Prototype Community Of Tomorrow
16 taste      vulgarity      children of all ages

## *Transcript*

Presenter:    Walt Disney is well-known as the creator of Mickey Mouse
              and the inventor of Disneyland and Walt Disney World, but
              his creations are better known than his life. Peter Spencer is
              the author of a new book about Disney. What was Walt
              Disney's background?

Peter Spencer: Walter Elias Disney was born in 1901 in Chicago but
actually he was brought up in a small town in the Mid-West
near Kansas City, Missouri, which incidentally was later
used as the model for Main Street USA in Disneyland. Um ...
he first studied cartooning, you know, by doing a
correspondence course. During the First World War he
worked as a ... a driver for the American Red Cross but after
the war he returned to Kansas City where he met a guy
called Ub Iwerks. Now they ... er ... started to work together
on a series of experimental-type films ... um ... and after a
while they set off to California to join Walt's elder brother
Roy who was living there in Los Angeles.

Presenter: When did Mickey Mouse first appear?

Peter Spencer: Ah, well, Disney and Iwerks first invented a character called
Oswald the Rabbit but then in 1928 a new character was
born: cheerful, sometimes rather naughty, energetic mouse
with large funny ears. Yes, it was Mickey and he appeared
for the first time in the first talking cartoon film, called
*Steamboat Willie*. Er ... not many people know this but Walt
Disney actually provided the voice for Mickey. By the way,
he was almost called 'Mortimer Mouse', which doesn't have
the same kind of ring to it, or does it?

Well, Roy and Walt gathered a team of artists ... er ...
illustrators together ... um ... by this time Ub Iwerks had left
them and started his own company, this was in 1930, and
Disney Studios, as they called themselves, starting ... started
to produce the famous short cartoons with ... starring Mickey
and Minnie and Donald Duck and Pluto and Goofy. Er ...
Roy was the business manager and driving force behind the
company ... er ... making it very profitable and Walt was more
the ... er ... imaginative, creative part of the partnership.

Presenter: What kind of man was Walt Disney?

Peter Spencer: Well, according to the artists who worked for him Walt
actually couldn't draw very well ... er ... most of the
characters were actually drawn by Iwerks, but apparently he
was an amazing storyteller. He would act out the stories of
films doing all the voices and actions to show the illustrators
what he wanted them to do and then they had to go off and
try to recreate his visualisations.

Presenter: The most famous cartoon of all was *Snow White* – and the
best I still think.

Peter Spencer: Mm, yeah, it was the first feature-length cartoon and it was
released in ... er ... 1935. Now, *Snow White and the Seven
Dwarfs* required two million drawings and took three years'
work to make. Um ... obviously it was ... er ... very expensive,
particularly for those times. By the way, the British film
censor gave it an Adult certificate because he thought that it

would be too frightening for little children to see on their own.

Er ... that was followed by *Pinocchio* and *Fantasia* in 1940, *Dumbo* in 1941. In 1941 there was a bit of a setback because the artists and illustrators went on strike, because they felt that they were being very underpaid. This I'm afraid led to a great deal of bitter feelings and recriminations and ... er ... Walt's image of kindly 'Uncle Walt' took rather a knock and became slightly tarnished.

Presenter: By this time Walt Disney Studios was big business, wasn't it?

Peter Spencer: Oh, yes indeed, and once they settled the strike, they very cleverly diversified their output. In the forties and fifties they produced the famous True Life Adventures, you know those films where ... er ... they photographed animals in their natural habitat but they ... er ... dubbed on a jokey commentary and did tricky editing, it's ... er ... nowadays it's really rather ... um ... well rather awful to watch I think but they were very popular at the time.

And ... er ... the Disney Studios also started making ... um ... some rather low-budget live action feature films for children ... er ... something which the other studios didn't dare risk doing.

Er ... some of his films mixed live action with cartoons – er ... I'm thinking about *Mary Poppins*, which I think we've probably all seen, made in 1964, where cartoon characters and ... and the real life actors appeared together on screen and talked and danced and sang together.

Disney was one of the first to see the potential of television, all the other studios were afraid of this medium. Um ... so he started to produce films directly for television and ... and now of course there's a Disney Channel showing only Disney films.

Presenter: And then he dreamt up Disneyland, didn't he?

Peter Spencer: Ah, 'dreamt' is the right word. Disneyland was a creation of the land of his dreams: safe, happy, clean, fairy-tale world with its own Magic Kingdom. The original Disneyland was opened in Los Angeles in 1955 and it cost $17 million.

Walt died in 1966 but he was already working on plans for the Disney World in Orlando, Florida, which opened in 1971, and the EPCOT Center near Walt Disney World – that's the 'Experimental Prototype Community Of Tomorrow', by the way. And there's also a ... a Tokyo Disneyland, which was opened in ... um ... 1983.

Presenter: And ... and now there's even a EuroDisneyland near Paris, I think.

Peter Spencer: Yes, that's right. Um ... and the Disney Studios still continue to produce films in the ... the house style, the Walt Disney style and presumably it always will. Disney's films appealed

... um ... and still do appeal to children of all ages, but people often criticise them for their lack of taste and they say they're vulgar, but Disney said, 'I've never called this art. It's show business and I'm a showman.' Well, can you imagine a world without Mickey Mouse?

Presenter: Peter Spencer, thank you.

(Time: 6 minutes 30 seconds)

# 11.4 If they'd lived . . . Communication activity

**A** Allow enough time for a pre-task discussion before beginning the Communication activity.

**B** Student A has some facts about the short life of James Dean in Activity 25, student B has some facts about the life of Marilyn Monroe in Activity 47. They should spend some time studying the information before beginning their conversation.

**C** This is a follow-up discussion. The list may include some names that younger students are unfamiliar with – if so, tell them to concentrate on the names they do recognise.

# 11.5 Style, tone and content Effective writing

**A** All three paragraphs have features that you might consider more or less effective. Perhaps point out that clumsy or inelegant style is also ineffective – it may make people focus on the style instead of the content.

**B** Follow the guidelines in the Student's Book.

# 11.6 Household names Creative writing

**A + B + C** It sometimes requires a surprising effort of the imagination for students to realise that the rest of the world may not share their cultural background. These activities draw attention to the fact that one of the tasks that they may often have to do is to act as 'cultural interpreter' – explaining about their country to foreigners.

▶ Plenty of time should be allowed for the discussions in **A** and **B**.

# 11.7 *For, on* and *off* Idioms

## A Answers

2 on purpose
3 on behalf of
4 on condition that
5 for a walk
6 off work

7 on the way
8 on average
9 on strike
10 on television
11 on a diet

12 on foot
13 on hand
14 on the contrary
15 for a change

## B Answers

2 searching for
3 did she have on
4 comment on
5 on account of
6 rely on / count on
7 apologise for being
8 feel sorry for
9 depends on

10 it grows on you
11 walked on / went on walking / carried on walking
12 is an expert on
13 wind   on
14 fell for
15 insisted on waiting

► Some more expressions:

**on**   later on   on duty   on business   on display
   on fire   on no account   on toast   on the phone
   on time
**for**   for sale   wait for   ready for   vote for
**off**   off colour   off school   off the point   off your food
   well-off   walk off   jump off   When are you off?
**under**   under control   under pressure   under repair
   under suspicion
**with/without**   with/without exception   without delay
   with/without difficulty   share with

# 12 Rich and poor

## 12.1  Millionaires

**A**  Pre-listening discussion and task.

**B**  🔲  *Answers*

1 one fifth     250,000     oil     gas
2 $2,000,000,000     $25,000,000,000
3 shy, self-conscious     publicity and public appearances
   two     palace     an air hostess
4 capital     $400,000,000     1,788     257     564     18
5 jungle     swimming pools     Olympic
6 polo     ponies     air-conditioned stables
7 hotels     aeroplanes/planes/helicopters     mail order
8 health care     education     taxes

The information given in the recording is based on an article by
James Bartholomew in *Business* magazine.

## *Transcript*

Presenter:  A few years ago a man gave a birthday party in London for his
daughter and her friends – it cost £100,000. This generous father
was his Majesty the Sultan of Brunei – the world's richest man.
Lesley Andrews has been finding out about the man and his
amazing wealth. Lesley ...

Lesley  Thank you, Nigel. Well, actually, many people don't even know
where Brunei is: it is in fact in the north of the island of Borneo
in the South China Sea, bordered by the Malaysian state of
Sarawak. It's a small country, about one fifth of the size of
Belgium and it has fewer than 250,000 inhabitants. The Sultan is
Brunei's head of government, commander-in-chief of the armed
forces and he's also the religious leader.

  Brunei is a very rich country. It has a higher per capita income
than Japan, the USA or any European country. And its wealth,
Nigel, comes from reserves of oil and natural gas, which have
been developed and exploited by Shell.

  The Sultan himself earns more than $2 billion a year – that's
over £2,500 every minute. His total wealth is more than $25

billion, which makes him wealthier than the Queen of England, who by the way is worth a mere $7.4 billion.

However, when he was born, on the 15th of July 1946, Brunei was not then the affluent country it is today. The ... um ... huge oil and gas reserves were only discovered in the 1970s. During this time Brunei was a British protectorate and it didn't become fully independent until 1984.

Presenter: What sort of man is he?

Lesley: Well, he's a rather shy, self-conscious person. He avoids publicity and doesn't make many public appearances. He is married, he first got married when he was nineteen to his sixteen-year-old cousin, Raja Isteri. Then sometime, I believe in the 1970s, he met an air hostess on the Brunei international airline, called Mariam Bell – she's part Japanese and part Scottish – and she became his second wife. So he has two wives and they both have their own separate palace.

Presenter: Could you tell us about these palaces?

Lesley: Certainly. Well, one of them, which he built for the first wife, is the largest palace in the world – it's even bigger than the Vatican. And it cost $400 million. This palace stands on a hill overlooking the capital and has 1,788 rooms, including 257 toilets. And it has 564 chandeliers and eighteen lifts.

Now, as the Sultan wanted the palace built quickly, teams of architects and interior designers in the Philippines had to produce the designs within two weeks – and they ... er ... had to do this without even seeing the site where it was going to be built. The palace, I must say, really does look wonderful from the air, but closer up some people say that part of it resembles a multi-storey car park. And it's also said that the Sultan himself was disappointed because parts of it didn't come up to his expectations. Anyway, he built a smaller one for Princess Mariam, and this was built away from the capital in the jungle. This second palace isn't quite as big as the first but it still has five swimming pools, one of which is Olympic size, and it's full of all kinds of high-tech gadgets and equipment.

Presenter: So ... how does he spend his time and money?

Lesley: Well, his great passion is playing polo, he's got air-conditioned stables with over 200 ponies and he has his own polo club which has three polo fields, as well as a golf course and swimming pool. Oh, and he enjoys other sports too: he likes swimming, and he plays tennis and squash. He also likes driving fast cars, playing video games, piloting planes and shooting.

He also likes acquiring possessions such as hotels – he owns the famous Dorchester Hotel in London and the Holiday Inn in Singapore, for example. And ... er ... you know, Nigel, he buys aeroplanes too: he has his own fleet of planes and helicopters. One of his planes even has a jacuzzi in it!

Apparently, members of his family are keen mail-order

shoppers: they look through the latest Harrods catalogues, mark what they want to buy, then they fax the order through to London and the very same evening the goods are loaded onto the evening flight from Heathrow to Brunei.

So, as you see, Nigel, he does enjoy spending his money, but he also seems to be a very generous man who likes giving people expensive presents. And he believes in looking after his people: he provides free health care and free education for them all. Oh, and if you're a citizen of Brunei, you don't have to pay any taxes at all!

Presenter: Lesley, thank you.

(Time: 5 minutes)

**C** In this activity student A has information about seven billionaires in Activity 58 and student B has information about seven different billionaires in Activity 64.

Some of these people and families are well-known (e.g. the Benetton family), others are less well-known until you find out how they made their money (e.g. the Morita family who run the Sony empire). The fourteen people or families are just a multi-national selection of the world's better-known billionaires.

Incidentally, there are 145 individuals (only five of whom are women) and 80 families whose personal wealth exceeds $1 billion: 55 individuals and 27 families live in the USA; 40 individuals and eight families are Japanese; nine individuals and eleven families are German.

▶ Perhaps ask everyone to describe some of the richest people in their own country, and how they made their money.

# 12.2 Around the world                    Vocabulary

**A**   If possible, take a map of the world into class for this activity.

*Answers*

1 1,000       billion
2 inherit       unearned       investments       self-made man/woman
3 developing nations / the Third World       conspicuous consumption
4 interest rates       well-off
5 Third World       inflation rate
6 raw materials       shortage

**B**   Some other rich countries are Sweden, Australia and Saudi
Arabia. Some other poorer countries are Mali, Zambia and Pakistan.

By the way, the annual income of the USA (230 million people) is the
same as the total income of all Asia, Africa and South America (over
100 states and over 3,000 million people).

**C + D**   Allow quite a lot of time for these discussions, following
the procedure suggested in the Student's Book. Encourage vocabulary
questions.

# 12.3   Conditional sentences    Grammar

**A**   *Suggested answers*

1  When it rains our roof leaks.
   - *every time it rains water comes in*
   If it rains our roof leaks.
   - *on the occasions that it rains water comes in (perhaps less likelihood
   of rain than the previous example)*
   When it rained our roof would leak.
   - *every time it rained (in the past) water used to come in*
   If it rains our roof will leak.
   - *it may rain sometime in the future and in that case water will come in*
   If it rained our roof would leak.
   - *it's unlikely to rain, but if it did water would come in*

2  I'd go first class if I could afford to.
   - *I haven't got enough money*
   I'll go first class if I can afford to.
   - *I may have enough money*
   I'd have gone first class if I could have afforded it.
   - *I didn't have enough money, so I didn't travel first class*
   I go first class when I can afford it.
   - *sometimes I have enough money, sometimes I don't*
   I'll go first class when I can afford it.
   - *as soon as I have enough money I intend to travel first class*

3  She could get a rise if she asked her boss.
   - *She's unlikely to ask but if she did it's possible she'd be successful*
   She would get a rise if she asked her boss.
   - *she's unlikely to ask but if she did I'm sure she'd be successful*
   She might get a rise if she asked her boss.
   - *she's unlikely to ask but if she did it's possible she'd be successful*

*(perhaps slightly less likelihood of success than in the first example)*
She should get a rise if she asks her boss.
*– it's possible that she'll ask and if so it's probable she'll be successful*
She might get a rise if she asks her boss.
*– it's possible that she'll ask and if so it's possible she'll be successful*
She will get a rise if she asks her boss.
*– it's possible that she'll ask and if so it's certain she'll be successful*

4 I couldn't have gone there on holiday – unless I'd saved up all year.
*– it wasn't possible for me to go because I didn't save up*
I couldn't have gone there on holiday if I hadn't saved up all year.
*– it was possible for me to go because I did save up*

5 You should save your money in case you want to go on holiday.
*– save up because you might want to go on holiday*
You should save your money if you want to go on holiday.
*– save up because you want to go* OR *only by saving up could you afford to go*
You should save your money otherwise you'll want to go on holiday.
*– save up and this will prevent you wanting to go on holiday (strange idea!)*

6 If you should / If you happen to see him, give him my love.
*– there's a slim chance you'll see him*
If you see him, give him my love.
*– there's a good chance you'll see him*

7 If you won't lend me the money, I'll have to ask someone else.
*– if you refuse to let me have it*
If you don't lend me the money, I'll have to ask someone else.
*– if you can't let me have it*

8 If only I hadn't spent all my money and had saved some!
*– I wish I had been less profligate*
If I hadn't spent all my money and had saved some . . .
*– supposing I'd been less profligate*

## B 🔲 *Transcript with* ANSWERS underlined

Andrew: I'm wondering whether to buy a new hi-fi system to replace my old stereo. If I <u>buy</u> one, I <u>could get</u> one that plays compact discs. What do you think?

Bill: <u>Even</u> if I <u>could afford</u> to, I <u>wouldn't buy</u> a CD player. I think the quality of cassettes is perfectly adequate.

Claire:   <u>As long as</u> you're sure you <u>can afford</u> to, I think you
          <u>should go ahead</u> and buy a CD player.
Dave:     Well, <u>assuming that</u> you really <u>want</u> one, I <u>don't think</u>
          there<u>'s any reason</u> why you shouldn't buy one.
Emma:     I think <u>it'd be</u> a good idea, <u>provided that</u> you<u>'re sure</u> you
          really need one.
Frank:    <u>Providing that</u> you <u>buy</u> a system that <u>will play</u> both CDs
          and cassettes, you <u>can still go on buying</u> cassettes, which
          are much cheaper.

(Time: 35 seconds)

**C**   This group discussion helps to activate some of the language
items introduced in **B**.

**D**   *Corrected sentences*

1 If you **had** bought it last week, the price **wouldn't** have **gone** up.
2 *no errors*
3 She says that if it weren't for the tax system she'**d** be much better
off.
4 There wouldn't be so much poverty **if** less money **were/was** spent
on arms.
5 If you **don't** arrive in time they won't let you into the concert.
6 If **I had been** born rich I **wouldn't need** / **wouldn't have needed** to
work.
7 If you **let** me know **when** you **arrive I'll** meet you at the airport.
OR If you'd let me know **when** you arrived / **were arriving I'd have**
**met** you at the airport.
8 I'll be surprised **if** prices **don't** go up next year.

**E**   More free discussion – perhaps students should write down some
questions to ask before beginning their conversation.

**F**   *Suggested answers*

1 known      would be / was going to be      would have spent
2 you not have
3 Had      been      would/might/could have enjoyed
4 Should you wish
5 would/might      were it not

## 12.4   Sharing opinions                    Functions

**A** 🔲   Pause the tape after each speaker to allow time for
students to decide how they might reply – this can be done as a class
or in pairs. Encourage everyone to trust their feelings for what
sounds appropriate.

*Transcript*

Narrator:   What would you reply to these people?

Man:        Well, as I see it, millions of people in the world are worse off
            than us, but there's nothing *we* can do about it.

Woman:      I'd say that if you do have plenty of money, there's no point in
            spending it on private education for your children.

Man:        It seems to me that the only way to help the poor in the world is
            to find ways of helping them to help themselves . ... er ... not ... by
            ... er ... giving them free food.

Woman:      If you ask me, taxes for rich people should be really high – 95%
            or something – so that everyone is at the same economic level.

Woman:      It's quite obvious that in a capitalist society anyone who is
            intelligent can become rich – all they have to do is work hard
            and use the system.

Man:        Er ... in my view i ... it's worth making a lot of money ... er ... so
            that you can leave it to your children when you die.

Woman:      I can't help thinking that the reason why poor people are poor is
            that they don't work hard enough.

Man:        Don't you agree that if people are starving or have nowhere to
            live, it's the duty of better-off people to give them food and
            shelter?

Woman:      Look, let's face it, there's only one reason why people work and
            that's to make as much money as possible.

Man:        Surely, as long as you've got enough to live on, there's no point
            in making more and more money.

Woman:      If you're earning a good salary, surely you should save as much
            as you can for a rainy day.

Man:        I must say that one thing is certain: money doesn't buy
            happiness.

(Time: 1 minute 25 seconds)

**B** 🔲   In this case the tone of voice, as well as the actual words
used, expresses agreement or disagreement. Again, pause the tape
after each conversation for everyone to comment on what they have
heard.

Narrator: You'll hear some people reacting to various opinions – decide if they are agreeing or disagreeing with the opinions expressed. Pay attention to the tone of voice they use.

1 Woman: Aren't you glad you're not a millionaire?
  Man: Sure! *(sincere tone = agreement)*
2 Man: Don't you wish you could afford to spend your holidays in the Caribbean?
  Woman: Mm, ye-es. *(doubtful tone = disagreement)*
3 Woman: It's not worth saving your money, it's better to spend it.
  Man: Oh, sure! *(sarcastic tone = disagreement)*
4 Man: It's better to be happy than rich.
  Woman: Hmm. *(doubtful tone = disagreement)*
5 Woman: Well, basically, in a job the most important thing is how much you earn.
  Man: Oh, yes! *(sincere tone = agreement)*
6 Man: It's really important to save a little money every month – you never know when you might need it.
  Woman: I don't know about that. *(sceptical tone = disagreement)*
7 Man: The only way to survive on a tight budget is to keep a record of all your expenses.
  Man: I didn't know about that! *(surprised tone = agreement)*
8 Woman: Children these days get far too much pocket money.
  Woman: Mmm! *(sincere tone = agreement)*
9 Woman: In a family it should be the mother that controls the budget.
  Woman: Yes! *(emphatic tone = agreement)*
10 Man: If I inherited a lot of money it wouldn't change my life at all.
  Man: Oh, yes! *(sarcastic tone = disagreement)*

(Time: 1 minute 30 seconds)

**C** In this discussion exercise students take it in turns to be the chairperson, and introduce two or three topics asking the others to give their opinions. It might be interesting for the chairperson to 'score' the number of exponents from the speech balloons in **A** that each person uses.

Student A looks at Activity 2, student B at 39, student C at 73 and (in a group of four *only*) student D looks at 67.

---

# 12.5 Using synonyms and opposites – 1    Word study

**A** *Suggested answers* (some of these are debatable)

*comfortably off* = rich    *desperately poor* = very poor
*down on one's luck* = poor    *down to one's last penny* = poor
*feeling the pinch* = poor    *in dire straits* = poor
*in the red* = poor    *living from hand to mouth* = very poor
*loaded* = very rich    *low paid* = poor
*on the breadline* = very poor    *penniless* = very poor
*prosperous* = rich    *rolling in money* = very rich
*stinking rich* = very rich    *unable to make ends meet* = poor
*well-to-do* = rich

**B + C**   The tasks in sections B and C require students to use their judgement and feelings for appropriateness. Encourage the use of dictionaries during these exercises – if possible, have a number of English–English dictionaries available for consultation in class.

To save time, different groups could be assigned different groups of words in section C to deal with. Alternatively, or in addition, some of the work can be done as homework.

▶ No 'correct answers' are given here as this is largely a matter of feeling and opinion. If necessary, check any words you are yourself unsure of before the lesson.

---

# 12.6   *Look* and *see*                    Verbs and idioms

## A   *Answers*

1 for     2 off     3 out     4 through     5 up     6 up to
7 into     8 off

## B   *Answers*

1 look out for
2 look me up
3 look out for
4 have a look at     look alike
5 looks down on/looks down
  his nose at
6 gave me a funny look
7 I'll overlook
8 overlooks

9 Look here     onlookers
10 seen her current project
   through
11 see eye to eye
12 sightseers
13 see to
14 saw through
15 saw red
16 look back on

**C** *Suggested answers* (some of these are debatable)

1 She glanced at ...      ... the painting(?)      ... her lovingly(?)
  ... the person sitting opposite on the bus      ... the small print in
  the brochure      ... the view of the mountains(?)

2 She stared at ...      ... two men having a fight      ... a programme
  on television (?)      ... the painting      ... her lovingly
  ... the person sitting opposite on the bus      ... the small print in the
  brochure      ... the view of the mountains      ... someone arriving
  late(?)

3 He gazed at ...      ... a programme on television(?)
  ... the painting      ... her lovingly      ... the person sitting opposite
  on the bus      ... the small print in the brochure(?)
  ... the views of the mountains

4 She peered at ...      ... the person sitting opposite on the bus
  ... the small print in the brochure      ... the view of the
  mountains(?)      ... someone arriving late(?)

5 She noticed ...      ... two men having a fight      ... a programme
  on television(?)      ... the painting(?)      ... the person sitting
  opposite on the bus      ... the small print in the brochure
  ... the view of the mountains(?)      ... someone arriving late

6 He watched ...      ... two men having a fight      ... a programme
  on television      ... her lovingly(?)      ... the person sitting opposite
  on the bus(?)

# 13 Communication

---

## 13.1 Get the message? Vocabulary

**B** *Answers*

1 colloquial    informal    formal
2 expression
3 verbal
4 intonation    tone    gestures    body
5 saying    expression
6 proverbs
7 underline    italics    stress
8 regional
9 dialect
10 sarcastic
11 jargon
12 Received Pronunciation
13 bilingual
14 slang    appropriately

---

## 13.2 A 'typical' English conversation Listening

**A** 📼 *Suggested answers*

2 smile    raise an eyebrow encouragingly
3 50–60 centimetres for North Americans or Northern Europeans
   20–30 centimetres for Latin Americans
4 sitting next to each other    standing in a relaxed manner
   facing each other
5 handshakes    'Hello'    'Nice to see you'
6 'Lovely day'    'How are things with you?'

2 smile    friendly look
3 looking at your watch    'It's been nice talking to you'
4 move backwards    starting to go

## *Transcript*

Presenter:  OK, what is a conversation? Now, a conversation may seem to you and me just to be two people having a chat, exchanging words, exchanging ideas, but it seems that without the right kind of non-verbal behaviour it would probably be impossible to start. Sarah Newby explains why. Sarah.

Sarah:  Well, Terry, the stages of a typical conversation can be summarised in a most interesting way. There's nothing new about this analysis, like much of sociology we're just looking at human behaviour in a scientific way and drawing attention to its underlying structure.

Presenter:  OK.

Sarah:  So, let's begin with the so-called 'opening phase'. Now this begins by the two would-be participants making eye contact. In other words, one of them catches the other's eye ...

Presenter:  Right.

Sarah:  Right? And then both of them have to switch on 'conventional facial expressions'.

Presenter:  Oh, hang on, hang on.

Sarah:  W ... no no, all it means really is that th ... they smile or one raises an eyebrow encouragingly or something like that.

Presenter:  Oh, I see, yes.

Sarah:  Then they reach a ... a 'position of comfortable proximity'.

Presenter:  W ... what is ... what does that mean?

Sarah:  Well, er ... basically we're talking about distance. Er ... for North Americans or ... or ... or Northern Europeans 50 to 60 centimetres apart i ... is usual. But for Latin Americans 20 to 30 centimetres.

Presenter:  Wow! What happens when you get a North American talking to a Latin American?

Sarah:  Well, that actually is a very good point ...

Presenter:  Yeah?

Sarah:  ... because of course what usually happens is that ... that the ... the ... um ... North American will step backwards to try and make some kind of comfortable distance between them.

Presenter:  Because the Latin American is invading his personal space.

Sarah:  Absolutely right!

Presenter:  I know it.

Sarah:  Er ... then of course what they do is adopt an 'appropriate posture'.

Presenter:  Like ...?

Sarah:  Well, it could be ... er ... sitting next to each other, or ... or standing in a relaxed manner, or ... or facing each other.

Presenter:  OK.

Sarah:  Er ... at that point they exchange 'ritual gestures and phrases of greeting'.

Presenter:  W ... really? What, even here?

| | |
|---|---|
| Sarah: | Well, of course, things like handshakes, 'Hello', er ... 'Nice to see you' – all that sort of thing ... |
| Presenter: | I see. |
| Sarah: | Right? |
| Presenter: | Yeah. |
| Sarah: | Then they exchange 'stereotyped channel-opening remarks'. |
| Presenter: | Now you're going to have to explain that one. |
| Sarah: | Of course, of course: 'Lovely day!' er ... 'How are things with you?' |
| Presenter: | I see. |
| Sarah: | And then, of course, the ... the main business phase begins, so the actual discussion or conversation takes place. |
| Presenter: | The main bulk of the conversation. |
| Sarah: | Absolutely right. Then we come to the 'parting phase', the ... the actual ending of the conversation when one or both of them decide it's time to stop. So what they do is they exchange 'appropriate cordial facial expressions'. |
| Presenter: | Has to be cordial? |
| Sarah: | Usually. A smile or a friendly look is helpful. |
| Presenter: | OK. |
| Sarah: | And then of course we have the exchange of 'ritual gestures and phrases of parting'. |
| Presenter: | Wow. |
| Sarah: | This can take the form of ... of looking at your watch, er ... saying 'It's ... er ... it's been nice talking to you' ... |
| Presenter: | Oh, right. |
| Sarah: | ... and then what usually happens is a ... an 'increase of distance between them': y ... you start to move, move backwards, starting to go. Er ... then both partners break eye contact and the conversation is ended. |
| Presenter: | Well! Thank you very much indeed, Sarah. Now, ha, next time I meet someone I think I'll be watching myself to make sure I obey all the rules! |
| Sarah: | Haha! |

(Time: 3 minutes 10 seconds)

**B** 🔲 This extract is recorded SEPARATELY after the complete conversation on the tape. The missing words are underlined in the transcript.

## *Transcript*

| | |
|---|---|
| Sarah: | Then they reach a ... a 'position of comfortable proximity'. |
| Presenter: | W ... what is ... what <u>does that mean?</u> |
| Sarah: | Well, er ... basically we're <u>talking about distance.</u> Er ... for <u>North Americans</u> or ... or ... or <u>Northern Europeans</u> 50 to 60 centimetres apart i ... is usual. But for <u>Latin Americans</u> 20 to 30 centimetres. |

145

Presenter: Wow! What happens when you <u>get a North American talking to a Latin American</u>?

Sarah: Well, that actually <u>is a very good point</u> ...

Presenter: Yeah?

Sarah: ... Because of course what usually happens is that ... that the ... the ... um ... North American will <u>step backwards</u> to try and make __ <u>some kind of comfortable distance</u> between them.

Presenter: Because the Latin American <u>is invading his personal space.</u>

Sarah: <u>Absolutely right!</u>

Presenter: I know it.

Sarah: Er ...

(Time: 35 seconds)

**C** These questions are for discussion – there are no 'correct answers'.

**D** ⚅ In this role play everyone should stand up so that they can act out the situation more realistically. If possible, there should be space for people to come and go.

Student A's role is described in Activity 46, B's in 68 and C's in 74. In a group of four, two students can share C's role.

# 13.3 Gestures                              Reading

**A** *Suggested answers*

1 They both communicate information to an onlooker
2 An incidental gesture
3 A primary gesture
4 Sneeze, cough, sniff, sigh, etc.
5 Thumbs up, wink, point, applause, smacking lips, etc.
6 It's used ironically
7 Six or seven
8 ??
9 Eleven
10 ??
11 By approaching each culture with an open mind

**B** *Answers*

1 role
2 onlookers
3 distinguish between
4 distinction between

   5 manipulating
   6 censored
   7 illuminating
   8 animatedly
   9 incidental
10 primary

**C**   Many of these gestures can be 'acted' – people sometimes pretend to be puzzled, unhappy, etc.

**D**   Missing from the illustrations are: the rude British two fingers gesture and equivalent American one finger gesture. Also, the innocuous British 'Stop', which Greeks may confuse with the obscene *moutza* gesture. Note that some of the British ones shown here may be terribly rude to some nationalities – but this is something everyone should be aware of.

*Suggested interpretations*

   1 Everything's fine
   2 I'd like a lift (hitchhiking)
   3 Everything's OK
   4 Can I pay the bill? (in a restaurant)
   5 Two please
   6 He's stupid
   7 We understand each other
   8 I'm better than you (cocking a snook)
   9 Don't tell a soul, keep mum!
10 Come here
11 I'm warning you
12 to 15 *These are meaningless in Britain*

---

# 13.4   Joining sentences – 2    Effective writing

**A**   *Suggested answers* (possible changes are underlined)

1 A gesture is any action <u>which</u> sends ...
2 ... an abstract quality <u>which</u> has no simple equivalent ...
3 *no changes*
4 *no changes*
5 The office <u>that</u> she works <u>in</u> has fluorescent lighting, which gives ...
6 ... the new shopping centre, <u>that</u> we went to last weekend with David, <u>that</u> (?) used to go out ...

Paul has just got engaged to Tracy, who is the daughter of Claire and Frank. They are the owners of Acme Bookshops Ltd, which has just opened a branch in the new shopping centre. We went there last weekend with David, who used to go out with Tracy. Did you know that David's best friend is Paul? It's a small world, isn't it!

## B   *Suggested answers*

1 You might rotate your forefinger against your temple, indicating 'a screw loose'.
2 You might rotate your finger close to your temple, signalling that the brain is going round and round.
3 Realising what had happened, she called the police.
4 The first island discovered by Columbus was one of the Bahamas.
5 Albert Sukoff wrote a long article, doing so without the use of a single full stop.

## C   *Corrected sentences* (notice the presence or absence of commas)

1 The person **whose** phone number you gave me was not very helpful.
2 The most important point (**that**) he made was that we should approach each culture with an open mind.
3 The person **I spoke to / to whom I spoke** was rather rude, **which** upset me.
4 I'd like to thank Pat, without **whose** help the work would have been impossible.
5 **Considering** that you're so clever and you're the one that usually **knows** the answers (,) I'm surprised you got it wrong.

## D   *Suggested answers*

2 After hearing about their plans he was upset and angry.
3 Feeling absolutely furious, he pushed over the table, knocking our best glasses (on)to the floor.
4 While (he was) picking up the broken glass, he cut his finger, which started bleeding.
5 Taking his handkerchief from his pocket, he wrapped it round the cut.
6 After gathering up most of the broken pieces, which were on the floor, he apologised profusely.
7 Realising how stupid he had been, he offered to replace the broken glasses.
8 He intended to buy us a new set of glasses and, knowing they

were good quality ones, he went to a store in town which
had/has a good stock of glassware.

9  Looking round the store, he discovered the glasses were very
expensive, which gave him quite a shock.

10  Since breaking those glasses he has been careful to keep his
temper!

---

# 13.5  I ♥ sign language   Discussion activity

**A**  The sources of some of the slogans are:

Small is beautiful – E.M. Schumacher
Survival of the fittest – Darwin
The world's favourite airline – British Airways
Liberty, fraternity, equality – French Revolution
Man was born free and everywhere he is in chains – Rousseau
Feed the world – Band Aid
All you need is love – Lennon & McCartney
Workers of the world, unite – Karl Marx

**B**  *Answers*

1  CND peace symbol        4  hearts, clubs, diamonds, spades
2  Mercedes Benz logo      5  an environment-friendly product
3  Mickey Mouse            6  poison

**C**  *Answers*

1  Children / school                 10  Youth hostel
2  Railway crossing                  11  First aid
3  Elderly people                    12  Lost and found
4  Road leads to quayside / river    13  Elevator for handicapped
   bank                                  people
5  Cross wind                        14  Car ferry
6  Falling rocks                     15  Send-off deck (public
7  Uneven road                           terrace) at airport
8  Recreation or sporting            16  Left luggage
   facilities                        17  Customs and immigration
9  Walks                             18  Hotel information

**D**  The correct logos are in Activity 12.

# 13.6   What happened?          Creative writing

**A + B**   Allow plenty of time for **A**, before setting **B** for homework. There is no 'correct story', by the way. Point out to everyone that they should use the notes they made in **A** when writing the narrative in **B**.

# 13.7   Colours                    Idioms

**A**   *Answers*

1 with great success
2 slightly unwell
3 realistic details about a place
4 unable to distinguish between certain colours
5 different colours show different applications or categories: green for accounts, blue for imports, etc.
6 way in which different colours are used to decorate the room
7 understand his character for the first time (usually derogatory)
8 influence in a negative or biased way

**B**   *Answers*

1 blue-collar
2 out of the blue
3 reds
4 green
5 green with envy
6 saw red
7 red-handed
8 give (me) the green light
9 green
10 once in a blue moon
11 in the red
12 red tape

**C**   *Answers*

1 black look
2 in black and white
3 black market
4 black comedy
5 black eye
6 white wedding
7 white lie
8 white-collar
9 blackout
10 white elephant

# 14 The English-speaking world

---

## 14.1 English in the world  Reading

**B**  These are questions for discussion, but this information may be useful:

- English is spoken as a major first language in Australia, Belize, Canada (+French), Guyana, Ireland, Jamaica (and many other West Indian islands), UK, New Zealand, South Africa (+Afrikaans), USA, etc.
- English is used as a second language / lingua franca in Bangladesh, Botswana, Ghana, India, Kenya, Lesotho, Liberia, Malaysia, Malawi, Namibia, Nigeria, Pakistan, Papua New Guinea, the Philippines, Sri Lanka, Swaziland, Tanzania, Zimbabwe, etc.
- 10% of the world's population speak English as their mother tongue (Chinese 21%, Spanish 6%, Russian 6%, Malay 4%, Hindi 4%, Japanese 3%, Arabic 3%, Portuguese 3%, French 2%, German 2%)

---

## 14.2 Indirect speech  Grammar

**A**  *Suggested answers*

1  He told us that he had visited Australia in the summer.
   – *'I went there in the summer,' is what he said.*
   He told us that he visited Australia in the summer.
   – *'I (usually) go there in the summer,' is what he said.*
   He told us that he would be visiting Australia in the summer.
   – *'I'm going there / I'll be going there,' is what he said.*

2  She asked me if I had been to New Zealand.
   – *'Have you been there?' is what she said.*
   She asked me when I had been to New Zealand.
   – *'When did you go there?' is what she said.*
   She asked me whether I had been to New Zealand.
   – *same meaning as first example*

⟫→

3 David says he wants to visit his relations in Canada.
   – *he still wants to go there*
   David said he wanted to visit his relations in Canada.
   – *same meaning as previous example* OR *this is what he said some time ago so maybe he has gone there by now*
   David said he wants to visit his relations in Canada.
   – *same meaning as first example – perhaps emphasising that although he said it in the past he still wants to go*
   David said, 'He wanted to visit his relations in Canada.'
   – *another person wanted to go there, not David himself*

4 Ruth phoned to say that she would be flying to India the next day.
   – *she travelled the day after the phone call*
   Ruth phoned to say that she would be flying to India tomorrow.
   – *she is going to travel tomorrow*
   Ruth phoned to say that she was flying to India the next day.
   – *same meaning as first example*

5 I didn't find out when the show starts.
   – *the show is on soon and I need to know when it starts*
   I didn't find out when the show started.
   – *same meaning as previous example* OR *the show is over or has started already*
   I didn't find out when the show will start.
   – *same meaning as first example*
   I didn't find out when the show would start.
   – *the show has started or is over, I didn't know the starting time* OR *same meaning as first example*

**B** The class should be divided into groups of four or five – with a class of eleven students, one group should consist of five and the other of six students. Then, within each group, half the students should look at Activity 9, the other half at 44.

This is a straightforward transformation exercise, rewriting one short text into reported speech and then another into direct speech. However, Activity 9 contains a 'direct version' of text A and a 'reported version' of text B, while Activity 44 contains a 'direct version' of text B and a 'reported version' of text A. In the end there are several versions of each text to compare: the originals and the versions produced by the two pairs. Full instructions for this are given in both Activities in the Student's Book.

## C   *Answers*

1 admit    announce    call out    claim    cry out    deny
  explain    imply    insist    mention    mumble
  mutter    reiterate    repeat    reply    scream    shout
  suggest    whisper    yell
2 advise(?)    assure    convince    inform    notify    tell
  warn
3 advise    allow    ask    beg    encourage    instruct
  invite    order    permit    persuade    tell    urge

**D**  🎞  This exercise requires students to report the GIST of what is said in the recordings – just a couple of sentences, summarising the salient points. Pause the tape between each speaker.

There are no 'correct answers' to this – pay attention to the grammatical accuracy of what your students write.

## *Transcript*

Blain:   I was brought up in ... er ... Northern Canada ... um ... up in very tiny hamlets, I suppose you might call them, where there might be only two hundred people living. In one of the little towns I lived in – it wasn't a town, it was a camp – there were six families only and the nearest town was 180 miles away. The summers were very hot and the winters were *extremely* cold with masses of snow.

Rupert:  Well, I have very fond memories of my childhood: I was born in Holborn in the centre of London and I went to St George the Martyr Primary School but at the age of six we moved out to the country and we lived on a farm and that has very special memories for me. We were cut off from just about everything, we had a v ... phone eventually, an outside lavatory, all those sort of 'romantic' ideas about living in the country, which were reality then and ... er ... looking back on them, very happy memories.

Gay:     I was brought up in Greensboro, North Carolina, which is in the United States but it's down south and ... um ... it was great being a child there really because it was warm all the time and ... er ... we had a lot of kind of outdoor stuff that we did: we used to play a lot ... um ... outside, doing tennis and swimming and stuff like that. Um ... I think the weather really affected my childhood a lot because ... um ... there was a kind of sense of freedom and being spontaneous really.

Enzo:    I was brought up in Worcestershire in the Midlands and I'm of Italian parents, therefore I had quite a mixed, or mixed-up, childhood. My parents were from a Southern Italian village, therefore life at home was quite ... er ... Italian and the minute I walked through the door I suddenly had to become English and ... er ... Worcestershire being a very English part of the country, a very typical English part of the country, there ... er ... this was a ... a ... a big contrast. And I do have good memories about my childhood, although they're mixed up.

Nick:  I was brought up in ... er ... Huddersfield in Yorkshire, or near Huddersfield. Um ... and what I remember most is the fact that I was the doctor's son and so ... and we had the surgery in the house, so there were always people coming to ... er ... to be treated or to see my father and then when I was old enough to be out in the village people would see me as Dr Michael's boy and that was ... it was like a little identity without even having to work at it.

Ken:  Well, I was brought up in Dover, which is a small town on the south-east coast. Um ... I can remember happy sunshiney days ... er ... paddling in and out of the sea with my bucket and spade and ... er ... the weather always seemed to be hot and sunny then. Er ... there's also a big castle in Dover, which I used to think of as being exclusively mine because it ... it's a Norman castle and shaped like a fort, so a big treat was to be taken up there to see the flag flying on the top of the keep. I have very happy memories of my childhood, yes.

Karen:  I can't actually say where I was brought up because up until the age of fourteen I hadn't lived anywhere for longer than two years. I was brought up throughout Britain: in the areas around London, on the Isle of Man, through the Midlands, in the North of England and in Scotland. And consequently, as I was going to school, I had to learn each accent of the particular area very quickly because children can be very unkind if you don't fit in.

(Time: 3 minutes 40 seconds)

## E  Suggested answers

2  'No, you'll never guess . . . Give up? All right I'll tell you. I'm from Toronto, so I'm not American, I'm Canadian!' Kate said to me.

3  'What lovely handwriting you have!' Jane said to me.

4  'Why don't you enrol for a course in Japanese?' Jerry suggested.

5  'Look, I'm going to pay for everything. Yes, the drinks too,' Pippa said.

6  'Go on: you really ought to go in for it. You've got a good chance of passing, you know that,' Stephen said to me.

7  'Stephen, don't be too confident. It's a long time since I last took an exam, remember!' I said to him.

8  'Excuse me, I'm sorry to have to say this but would you mind not

talking so loudly. It is after midnight, you know,' I said to the people in the corridor.

**F** 🔲 Play the two passages to the class – the complete texts are printed in Activity 66 in the Student's Book and the recording lasts 2 minutes. Follow the procedure suggested in the Student's Book. Although both students in the pair will hear both passages, each one will be writing a report (i.e. a summary from notes) of a different one.

## Extra activity

Get each member of the class to recall or imagine what advice they were given by other people as a child, as a student, as an employee, as a parent, etc.

# 14.3  Spelling and pronunciation 1 – Consonants

**A** 🔲 Play the recording after everyone has done the exercise, either working alone or in pairs. This will give them a chance to make any corrections to the answers they have noted down. The recording lasts 40 seconds.

*Answers*

| | | | | |
|---|---|---|---|---|
| /tʃ/ | future | literature | march | picture | question |
| /ʃ/ | insurance | machine | moustache | opposite | partial |
| /ʒ/ | beige | decision | vision | prestige | |
| /dʒ/ | average | badge | cabbage | courage | damage |
| | injury | | | | |

**B** 🔲 Again, play the recording after everyone has done the exercise. The recording lasts 40 seconds.

*Answers*

| | | | | |
|---|---|---|---|---|
| /g/ | signature | guilty | gherkin | giggle |
| /dʒ/ | gesture | margarine | gypsy | gymnasium |
| | generation | ginger | George | genuine | engineer |
| | genius | | | | |
| /f/ | draught | laughter | | |
| [silent] | nought (Ø) | sign | thorough | sigh |
| | naughty | borough | drought | |

**C** 🔲 If any students are struggling with this exercise, perhaps give them a clue: only two words in each group except **h** should be underlined. The recording lasts 1 minute 50 seconds.

## Answers

| | | | |
|---|---|---|---|
| **b** | symbol | bribed | |
| **g** | hungry | ignorance | |
| **h** | rehearsal | behalf | inherit |
| **i** | yield | failure | |
| **p** | couple | hypnotise | |
| **t** | attitude | bright | |
| **d** | sadness | second-hand | |

**D** The only correct ones are: *advertisement    four o'clock reliable*

## Correct spellings

accommodation    argument    aggressive    committee developing    embarrassed    foreigner    independent medicine    pronunciation    receive    replacing responsibility    seize    skilful (US skillful)    therefore    until

**E** Follow the procedure in the Student's Book. Perhaps point out that the spellings given are the 'usual' ones in the respective dialects, and that in some cases either spelling can be used.

## Answers

**BrE** draught beer    favour    honour    humour jewellery    kidnapper    labour    pyjamas    quarrelling skilful    speciality    theatre    traveller's cheque    travelling TV programme    woollen

# 14.4 British and American English

Word study

As this is a tricky subject, your students may require some extra information: see below. It's also worth emphasising that misunderstandings between British and American people rarely happen because of linguistic differences.

Refer to a dictionary if you're unsure about the meaning or usage of any of the items in this section.

**A** 🖭 The answers are recorded on the cassette. Don't play the tape until everyone has finished the exercise (Time: 1 minute). Note that the words given in the two lists are simply the most common terms used in each dialect – words like *cinema* or *film* are sometimes used in AmE, for example, but *movie theater* and *movie* are used more often.

| AmE | BrE |
|---|---|
| apartment | flat |
| attorney | solicitor or barrister |
| to call someone | to ring someone up |
| checkmark | tick |
| closet | cupboard or wardrobe |
| downtown | city or town centre |
| drugstore or pharmacy | chemist's |
| the fall | autumn |
| faucet | tap |
| garbage/trash | rubbish |
| movie | film |
| movie theater | cinema |
| potato chips | potato crisps |
| schedule (/skedʒʊl/) | timetable |
| sidewalk | pavement |
| zipper | zip |
| zero | nought |

▶ Some more examples of vocabulary (the AmE form is first in each case):

sales clerk – shop assistant    sophomore – second year student
freshman – first year student    jelly – jam    jello – jelly
sedan – saloon    station wagon – estate car    hood – bonnet
fender – wing    windshield – windscreen    overpass – flyover

muffler – silencer    trunk – boot    spark plug – sparking plug
carburetor – carburettor    tire – tyre    traffic circle –
roundabout    gear shift – gear stick/gear lever

▶ Some examples of possible vocabulary confusions:

**BrE** biscuit = **AmE** cookie
**AmE** biscuit = **BrE** scone
**BrE** pants = **AmE** underpants or shorts
**BrE** subway = **AmE** pedestrian underpass
**AmE** pavement = **BrE** road surface

## B  *Answers*

| British English | | | American English | |
|---|---|---|---|---|
| 2 ground floor | lift | first floor | first floor | elevator |
| | | | second floor | |
| 3 trousers | waistcoat | | pants | vest |
| 4 underground | | | subway | |
| 5 queue | railway | | line | railroad |
| 6 motorway | petrol | | freeway/highway (*or* | |
| | | | turnpike/expressway/ | |
| | | | interstate) | gas |
| 7 torch | | | flashlight | |
| 8 toilet (*or* loo) | | | bathroom | |

▶ There are also a few differences in the GRAMMAR used in British
and American English, as shown in these examples of American
usage:

– Did you go there already?    Did you ever go there?
– They've already gotten off the plane.
  He's gotten much slimmer since I last saw him.
  *but* I've got plenty of time.
– If I would have known I could have helped you. (*in some US
  dialects only*)
– 'Do you have a dictionary? / Have you got a dictionary?'
  'Yes I do.'

# 14.5 *Say, call, speak, talk and think*    Verbs and idioms

## A  *Answers*

1  call   back = phone again another time
2  think   over = consider for a period of time
3  talk   into = persuade
4  talk down to = speak in condescendingly simple language
5  speak up = speak more loudly
6  talk   over = discuss
7  call   off = cancel
8  called up = drafted into the army
9  speak out = give one's opinions freely
10  call   up = phone

## B  *Answers*

1  say when
2  talk shop
3  not on speaking terms
4  It goes without saying
5  You can say that again!
6  easier said than done
7  No sooner said than done
8  speaks her mind
9  called his bluff
10  don't think much of
11  thinking aloud
12  thought better of it
13  talking point
14  think again

▶ Some more related idioms:
call someone names = insult
to say nothing of = without even mentioning
speak for yourself = give your personal opinion
so to speak = as it were, speaking metaphorically
talk of the devil = you are / here is the person we were just talking about
to say the least = without exaggerating

# 15 How strange!

---

## 15.1    Into the unknown . . .    Vocabulary and listening

Depending on the interests and beliefs of your class, this vocabulary session could include some work on religions, perhaps introducing some of these words. Perhaps ask the class to note down as many different world religions and sects as they can think of. This is not included in the Student's Book as it may be a sensitive area for some people.

faith    religion    priest    temple    mosque    cathedral
bishop    priest    archbishop    imam    altar
parts of a church/temple/mosque    bible    testament
atheist/agnostic    Hindu    Buddhist    Muslim    Jewish
Sikh    Christian: Catholic, Protestant, Orthodox, Anglican, etc.
born-again

### B    *Answers*

1 creepy / scary    supernatural
2 miracle    far-fetched    sceptical
3 déjà vu
4 illusion
5 scared stiff / terror-struck
6 fallacy
7 superstitious
8 coincidence

### D    💾    The recording is a starting point for further discussion and leads into the next section on urban legends. Possibly pause the tape at the place marked ★★★ for everyone to guess what happened in the end.

### *Transcript*

Woman: OK, well, this happened to one of my best girlfriend's best friends and her father, so I know it's true. They were driving along this country road on their way home from their cabin in the mountains and they saw this young girl standing there by the side of the road hitchhiking. So they stopped and they picked her up because it was really weird that she was out there alone at that time of night, it was really late, and she got in the back seat and then she told the girl and her father that she lived in this house about five miles up the road. And she didn't say anything after that but she just turned around and looked out of the window. OK, so they start driving to her house and she was still really quiet so they sha ... thought she was asleep. And then they got to the house, drove up to it, they turned around to tell her that they were there – and there was nobody in the back seat!

★ ★ ★

So they were very very confused and they didn't know what to do and they talked about it and they decided they'd knock on the door and they'd tell the people there what happened. OK, so the people in the house answered the door and guess what? They told them that they once had a daughter who looked like the girl that they had picked up, but she had disappeared a long time ago and was last seen hitchhiking on that very road and that that day would have been her birthday.

(Time: 1 minute 35 seconds)

# 15.2   Urban legends                              Reading

## A   *Answers*

1 Many of the hopes, fears and anxieties of our time
2 By the mass media: TV, the press, radio
3 A dragon in a cave, a mouse in a Coca Cola bottle

## B   *Answers*

1 Because we simply listen to the information we hear and pass it on, without paying attention to the form or content of our folklore
2 As they are passed from person to person
3 Killers and madmen on the loose, shocking or funny personal experiences, unsafe manufactured products
4 They are part of our modern folklore
5 Because they are not accounts of events that really happened
6 Because we enjoy them merely as stories – or we half-believe them
7 In groups of people of the same age, especially adolescents; among office workers and club members
8 Other people are inspired to tell similar stories

**D**   *Answers*

| | | |
|---|---|---|
| 1  acquire | 5  rumour | 8  merely |
| 2  widespread | 6  documentation | 9  anxiety |
| 3  alleged | 7  unselfconscious | 10  ancient |
| 4  aware | | |

**E**   The picture story in Activity 8 concerns 'the Baked Sunbather' (a man who used kitchen foil to create reflectors around him while sunbathing nude, fell asleep and was found later, baked alive). The one in 49 concerns 'the Poodle in the Restaurant'.

## 15.3   Sequencing ideas     Effective writing

**A + B + C**   Follow the procedure suggested in the Student's Book. Each of the paragraphs in **B** has its stronger and weaker points.

**D**   The class should be divided into an even number of pairs (or groups of three), so that pairs of pairs can be formed later. In this Communication activity each pair has an unusual picture to discuss and then write a description of. The one in Activity 34 is 'Shingle Street' by Glynn Thomas, the one in 45 is 'The Threatened Assassin' by René Magritte.

**E**   The pairs compare what they have written.

## 15.4   That's magic!     Communication activity

█▓█   Again this activity requires an even number of pairs, which will become larger groups later. Half the pairs look at Activity 17, the others at 70. Each pair has a magic trick to learn, which they will later perform to their 'audience'.

▶ Possible written follow-up:
Write a short report of what was done in this activity, following the guidelines suggested in 5.7.

162

## 15.5 Evangelists                  Read and discuss

**A**   This is an extract from a long article in *The Sunday Correspondent* about the phenomenon of evangelism in the USA. Besides interviewing the Rev Jim Whittington, the writer describes other evangelists: Oral Roberts, Jimmy Swaggart and Jim Bakker, whose trial is described in Communication activities 20 and 40 (see below).

The writer seems to be very sceptical of the Rev Whittington – and disapproves of his ostentatious wealth ('With a flash of diamond and gold from finger, wrist and chest ...'). He may be trying to be 'fair' but presumably the Rev Whittington's followers would say that he is distorting the truth.

**B**   Students should work in pairs for this activity. One should look at Activity 20, the other at 40. The idea is to exchange information about Jim Bakker and his trial and to discuss their reactions to it.

## 15.6 Transcendental meditation          Reading

**A + B**   Follow the procedure suggested in the Student's Book. Reading this text leads on to the Creative writing task in 15.8.

**C**   *Answers*
1 20 minutes twice a day = 40 minutes
2 No: it is compatible with any religious beliefs
3 Anyone
4 Your mind works better, tension and stress are dissolved and your body is better able to deal with illnesses
5 Maharishi Mahesh Yogi (who introduced the Beatles to it in 1967, by the way)
6 At one of 60 local teaching centres

## 15.7 My advice is . . .          Creative writing

**A + B + C**   Follow the procedure outlined in the Student's Book.

# 15.8   *Day* and *time*                                 Idioms

## A   *Answers*

| | |
|---|---|
| 2 decide to stop | 7 Eventually |
| 3 that's very unlikely | 8 a bad day |
| 4 special day | 9 terrified |
| 5 every single day | 10 I'm being unlucky |
| 6 make him happy | 11 That was a wonderful period. |

## B   *Answers*

1 Once upon a time
2 it's about time / it's high time
3 time limit
4 for the time being
5 time-consuming
6 time and time again     half the time / at times
   at times / half the time     wasting my time
7 good timing
8 take your time     in your own time
9 the time of your life
10 in time     on time

# 16 Travellers

## 16.1 Other places

Vocabulary

**A** **Extra questions** Ask the members of the class which nationality they would most like to be if they could choose a different one to be. Also, perhaps, if they could choose a person of another nationality to marry, which nationality would they choose and why?

**B** *Answers*

1 suspicious/wary
2 isolated/remote/inaccessible    hospitable
3 costume    folklore    customs
4 unspoilt    commercialised
5 coast    view
6 scenery/landscape
7 peaceful
8 crowded
9 border/frontier
10 journey    port    crossing

## 16.2 The travel writer

Reading

Jonathan Raban was born in 1942. Among his most interesting books are:
*Arabia* – about his journey in different countries in the Arabian peninsula
*Old Glory* – about his journey by boat down the Mississippi River
*Foreign Land* – a novel about a man who buys an old sailing boat
*Coasting* – about his journey around the coast of Britain in a sailing boat

**B** *Answers*

1 It has no point or pattern
2 Only partly – he is by turns engrossed, bored, alert, dull, happy, miserable, etc.

3 Because he needs time for his memory to make the story interesting
4 He is the person who wrote in the notebook and the person remembering the events later
5 Because it makes him feel he is working
6 Because irrelevant events are forgotten, important details are enlarged upon, links and patterns are discovered, plots are constructed, etc.
7 A few proper names, dates and facts
8 In a sailing boat

**C** *Answers*

2 collection
3 by nature
4 clear
5 unimportant things

6 excessive
7 grumbles
8 loses vitality

# 16.3   A rendezvous                                    Reading

One person looks at Activity 11, the other at 27.

Paul Theroux was born in 1941. He is a writer of both novels and travel books. His travel books include:
*The Kingdom by the Sea* – about his walk around the coast of Britain
*The Old Patagonia Express* – by train from North America to the very south of South America
*The Great Railway Bazaar* – by train through Asia
His best novels are considered to be: *The Mosquito Coast, Picture Palace, My Secret Life* and *The Family Arsenal*

# 16.4   Comparing and contrasting          Grammar

**A** *Suggested answers*

2 further/farther      than
4 the closest planet to
8 is much further/farther from the Sun than
12 about half the length of / half as long as a day on

13 is about two and a half times as long as
16 slightly shorter than a day on
18 20 days longer than

## D  *Suggested answers*

1 more      I enjoy coming home
2 more enjoyable
3 as comfortable and quick
4 about the same amount of time      as it does to
5 largest country
6 the largest population
7 of the smallest countries
8 I wish I had appreciated being younger
9 more eventful      a travel writer has to write about
10 see as much as I can of my own country
11 longer it takes to get to the top
12 to adjust to life at home again afterwards

## E  *Suggested answers* (these are debatable)

Perhaps more informal and more usual in conversation:
*is very like      is similar to      is identical to*
*is much the same as      reminds me of      seems like*
*has a lot in common with      In the same way ...*
*is quite different from      isn't the same as*
*stands out as*

Perhaps more formal and more usual in writing:
*is comparable to      is equivalent to      resembles*
*corresponds to      Similarly, ...      By the same token, ...*
*is very unlike      differs from      bears no resemblance to*
*has very little in common with      On the other hand, ...*
*In contrast, ...      Conversely, ...*

Possibly ask everyone to use the phrases above to write
some example sentences about the similarities and
differences between spending a holiday in:
  the country      the mountains      abroad
  a seaside resort      a large city      your own country

# 16.5 Using synonyms and opposites – 2

**A + B + C**  Follow the procedure suggested in the Student's Book. No correct answers are given here – use a dictionary if you are unsure of any words here.

# 16.6 Describing a place

**A**  Pause after each speaker for everyone to catch up with their notes and compare them with a partner.

**B + C**  Follow the procedure suggested in the Student's Book.

**D**  You may decide to stipulate which of the alternatives everyone should choose: the essay or the presentation.

## Transcript

Ishia: I always love going back to Rome. It's a city I've visited quite often and it's al … a great source of joy to me. I love flying in over the Mediterranean, seeing the sea, arriving in the plane, the doors open and that *wonderful* heat hits you. Driving through the city in order to get to wherever you're going to stay is not always the most fun part … um … the driving is … er … something to behold, but I love the area north of the Circus Maximus, which is … which is really the kind of … er … the Hampstead I suppose of Rome, which is very beautiful and very green, and full of palm trees and absolutely beautiful buildings. Um … there … it isn't sort of in the centre of Rome, which is awfully nice, and it's much cooler there, of course. Er … I … I suppose I like *all* aspects of Rome … er … particularly visiting the museums and the galleries which are really quite stunning, but to actually walk round the streets, see those beautiful buildings, sit in a restaurant, sit outside, have a cup of coffee, is a delight and I would recommend it to anybody.

Tim: As far as big cities go, I think New York's my favourite place. When I arrived there I felt as though I'd arrived in a movie, I came in a cab from the airport, and there were all the skyscrapers and the heat and the dirt and the yellow cabs and all the classic clichés that you think about America – they were all there. Um … I worked in a … a … in the PanAm building in the centre of New York. That meant travelling by subway every day, which was one of the hottest experience … experiences I've ever had! Because it was in the summer and it is very very hot in New York, so much so you arrive at your workplace and you have to change your clothes. The people of New York are terrific. I've got ... was very frightened I was going to be mugged, in fact, I thought that if you stepped out of your hotel at night you'd be shot, but it's proved not to be true. Um ... I find the people very friendly, very cosmopolitan, nobody was worried about the fact that I was English because they ... everybody talks with funny accents there. Um ... I find it a really wonderful place – a bit dangerous but really fast and really fun.

Juliet: I've been to Amsterdam many times now ... er ... it almost feels like my second home. Erm ... there's something about being in a city where there's a ... there's a lot of water which is ... seems to have a very ... erm ... gentle effect on people and also the fact that there's no ... um ... th ... the roads are very narrow, so car transport is quite limited and people tend to get around by bicycles. Um ... that again just seems to slow down the pace of the city. Um ... it's ... it's a very very lively place, there's a lot of ... a lot of outdoor activity, a lot of people sitting outside cafés and ... er ... drinking. Um ... there's ... there's ... people are very friendly as well. There's also a lot of cultural activity, there's the van Gogh Museum and there's ... um ... Rembrandt's House and ... erm ... the wonderful museum called the Rijksmuseum, so there's plenty to see as well. And ... er ... there's a lot of nightlife too: the infamous red light district, of course and ... er ... a lot of theatre and events like that. Um ... it's just a ... a beautiful city architecturally, lots of the ... very tall, slender houses. Um ... and ... er ... it's ... it's lovely to take a ... a w ... a ride along the canals as well, you can get on boats and things. It's just a ... a really pretty place to go, and, a really nice city.

Michael: I suppose one of the first things that would strike anybody going to Austin in Texas ... er ... specially coming from Europe would be how green it is – in Austin and around it because the image people have of Texas is of course a sort of dry, dust-blown prairie, but around Austin in that part of Central Texas there are hills and lakes and forests. And I think that's my first impression of Austin – going back there after a long time away was just how green it was. Um ... Austin is the capital of Texas and also ... er ... it's the home of the University of Texas, which means that there are lots of ... er ... young people in Austin and it's full of young people and full of nightlife for them and so, as a result, there's a lot of things that happen at night in Austin and, like a lot of Southern towns, what happens is that ... er ... specially on summer nights people just walk up and down the streets – families, er ... groups of boys or girls, and there are bars up and down the centre of town where they play live music all the time. And ... er ... it's really a lot of fun. Course there's lots of water sports and a

lot of outdoor things to do, as you might imagine, being Texas.
Um ... I guess one thing that also struck me ... er ... coming from ...
er ... Europe to America is that the way people drive in ... er ...
America, it's all so very disciplined, everybody sticks to the lines
that are painted on the roads and ... er ... you don't see so many
people ... um ... driving recklessly. Um ... I guess the ... the main
thing about Austin that I like is the ... er ... the culture that the kids
bring to the ... to the city ... er ... from the University. There's lots
of fringe theatre, there's not so much professional theatre, but a
lot of fringe theatre, and a lot of local music that's made, not just
country and western as you might expect but folk music and rock
music of all kinds – and classical music as well. There's a brilliant
auditorium in downtown Austin. All in all it's a ... I think it's an
atypical place ... er ... for Texas, which is one of the reasons I like
it.

(Time: 6 minutes 10 seconds)

## 16.7  *Come, go* and *run*                 Verbs and idioms

**A**  *Answers*

| | |
|---|---|
| 1 come off | 6 going in for |
| 2 going out with | 7 run out of |
| 3 gone off | 8 went / has gone off |
| 4 came up against | 9 run over |
| 5 go ahead | 10 go over/through |

**B**  *Answers*

1 run off
2 go for
3 go for
4 come up with
5 gone off
6 run out
7 come up to
8 went down with
9 go along with
10 go over      gone through/over

► Some other related idioms:

**come**   come by = obtain       come forward = present oneself
come off = succeed       come out = solve
come out with = utter

**go**   go back on = fail to keep promise
go down = be received       go off = proceed
go out = ebb       go without = not have
on the go = be active/busy

**run**   run away with = take and remove
run down = lose power       run over = summarise

# 17 Love stories

---

## 17.1 Talking about love – and stories

This exercise, in common with the rest of this unit, links the two themes of stories (i.e. books and literature) and love (i.e. relationships).

**B** *Answers*

The underlined words should be discussed after doing the exercise.

1 amusing     <u>best-selling</u>     entertaining     gripping
  <u>literary</u>     <u>poetic</u>     <u>popular</u>     <u>predictable</u>
  thought-provoking     well-written
2 empathise with     <u>feel sorry for</u>     <u>follow</u>
  identify with     laugh at
3 clear     <u>complex</u>     <u>hard to understand</u>     lucid
  readable     simple
4 <u>appendix</u>     <u>bibliography</u>     <u>blurb</u>     chapter     <u>character</u>
  <u>district</u>     <u>dustjacket</u>     extract     footnote     <u>foreword</u>
  <u>index</u>     page     paragraph     passage     <u>preface</u>
  quotation     section     unit
5 *These are a matter of opinion.*

**C** *Answers*

1 first person
2 relationship / love affair
3 partner / 'other half'
4 going out together / seeing each other / dating each other
5 bride and groom/bridegroom
6 dull / uninspiring / unrealistic – a relief / a breath of fresh air, etc.

**D** *Suggested answers*

love     is madly in love with     can't live without
        is crazy about     is devoted to     is infatuated with
        thinks the world of     adores     is keen on

| like | is attracted to    fancies    is fond of    admires |
| | gets on really well with |
| dislike | can't bear    doesn't think much of    is indifferent to |
| | doesn't get on with    is incompatible with |
| | has gone off    has fallen out with    puts up with |
| hate | detests    can't stand the sight of    loathes |

# 17.2   Small World              Reading

David Lodge, born in 1935, is the author of a number of entertaining novels, mostly dealing with university life, notably:

*Changing Places* – about an American professor and a British
     lecturer who exchange jobs for a year
*Nice Work* – what happens when a businessman and a feminist
     university lecturer are thrown together
*Small World* (this is an extract from it) – a 'romantic' novel
     satirising the world of academic conferences

**A + B + C**   Follow the procedure suggested in the Student's Book. The questions in **B** are for discussion, so there are no correct answers. The exercises can be done by students working in pairs or set for homework.

In Question 8, a *proposal* is a proposal of marriage – *propositions* are suggestions by men that Cheryl might like to spend the night with them.

**D**   This can be done in pairs, or by students working alone before comparing ideas with the rest of the class. Notice that it is not easy to find an example to fill every category, by the way.

## Suggested examples

1 *Just one of many things that made me smile:* 'Those who were rude or arrogant or otherwise unpleasant she put in uncomfortable or inconvenient seats, next to the toilets, or beside mothers with crying babies.'
2 *In a novel, information of this kind is usually lacking, though perhaps one might not previously be aware of the routine of the checker's job.*
3 *Again, a novel doesn't contain many 'opinions', but the passage opens with this one:* 'The job of check-in clerk . . . is not a glamorous or particularly satisfying one. The work is mechanical and repetitive . . .'

4 'Then the checker bears the full brunt of the customers' fury without being able to do anything to alleviate it.'
5 'With half her mind she despised these love stories, but she devoured them with greedy haste, like cheap sweets.'

**E** It might be amusing to discuss some 'typical' plots of romantic novels as a class. The blurb could be planned in class and then actually written as homework.

---

# 17.3   How romantic are you? Listening

**A** [cassette icon] Perhaps pause the tape at the point marked ★★★ for the discussion. Then play the second part so that everyone can find out if any of the later, less romantic, speakers express views that they have just expressed.

*Transcript*

Narrator: We asked a number of people this question: 'Do you believe in love?'

Andrew: Oh, yes, of course I believe in love, but then I'm just a silly old-fashioned romantic really at heart, I think.

Kate: I believe in love. I don't know exactly how to define it but I think it exists and I don't know how long it lasts.

Nigel: Yes, I believe in love. I don't believe in marriage, but I do believe in love and I think – that ... that sounds a bit cynical – but ... um ... I feel that often marriage can f ... can force love when y ... you have to keep it going because there's a marriage. So, yes, I believe in love for people and ... and specially I do for animals. Yes.

Ken: Yes, I think that love is the finest thing that money can buy.

Gay: Of course I believe in love. If I didn't really believe in love, I wouldn't want to be alive. For me there's everything from personal love to the love that is the healing force, which we need very much right now to help to work with things on the planet, like the rainforest and the things that we're working with.
★ ★ ★

Karen: Well, I have to frankly say that no, I don't, because after four disastrous marriages, it's all just an illusion, you know. It soon wears off.

Rupert: Yes, I believe in love ... er ... because there isn't anything else. Um ... there's not really a lot more I can say after that, but ... er ... yes, of course, I believe in love.

Blain: No, I don't believe in love. Love is a concept created by the marketing men to get men to buy things for women.

embarrassed but ... um ... enjoyed it a great deal, as did everybody else.

A wedding I went to a few years ago in Italy in a small Italian village in the south of Italy ... um ... was quite a typical ... er ... Italian wedding, where it was in the middle of summer and the bride and groom were married in the church: it was a typical white wedding and then what happened was that everybody got into their cars and all drove up into the country, up into ... up in ... out into the country, into the ... er ... um ... blaring their horns all the way for about thirty kilometres and every time they ... we passed anyone, we'd blare the horns in the cars. Anyway, when we arrived there we had this enormous spread of food, like ten, twelve courses that went on for hours and hours and hours. And at the end of it all what was interesting for me was that the best man auctioned off the groom's tie. And what he would do was he ... he ... he'd go round auctioning the tie, and what he would do is he'd cut a snippet of ... of the tie, depending on how much money each person gave and obviously the ... the ... er ... bride and groom's parents would give the most, therefore they got ... most part of the tie.

I've just been to an extraordinary wedding reception at the Café Royal ... um ... which was Turkish friend of mine and arriving in the middle of London in Piccadilly Circus and walking into the Café Royal was a bit like arriving at Istanbul Airport – full of people, full of children, full of bags and clothes, and I've never seen anything like it in my life, it was absolutely extraordinary. Wonderful food, everybody dancing around like crazy, and then of course the ... the wonderful moment where the groom and bride stand there and you have to pin money to them, which can be a bit embarrassing if you haven't brought much with you.

ael: I guess the biggest wedding I ever went to was my cousin's. She was married in Houston, this is about ... er ... six or seven years ago. And I'm afraid it was a typical ... um ... American wedding of total over-the-top excess. Um ... the bride and groom arrived in these huge stretched white limos, all the bridesmaids were all dressed in this horrible shade of pink, but it was all very expensive because all the bridesmaids were dressed in silk. And the ... the ... the groom and his best man were wearing ... er ... formal dress but one was red and the other was blue. And ... er ... we all had to wear formal clothes but we ... my family ... my part of the family turned up in black. Er ... haha ... and the guy was a dentist, you know, a big Houston dentist: dentists in Houston are *so* rich, you cannot believe how rich they are! The reception was in a big hotel in Houston and they had this really expensive rock band playing, I don't know how much ... they said they paid them something like two grand to play for the night, and they were

Kate: Um ... yes, I do. Of course I ... I believe in love. Um ... I don't believe it lasts for ever and I think it's something that you both have to work on ... er ... work at if ... if you're talking about a relationship between a man and a woman, or a man and a man, or a woman and a woman. Um ... but I think ... um ... having just had a baby recently I'm aware of the love between a mother and a child, which is overwhelming – something I'd never even thought of before.

Enzo: Love's a waste of time. You only get hurt – and you hurt other people.

(Time: 2 minutes 15 seconds)

**B**   Before doing this (which needs to be prepared for homework), spend some time with the class presenting a cassette of one of YOUR favourite songs to everyone.

I'd suggest one (or even two) of the following Beatles songs: *Yesterday, For No One, And I Love Her, When I'm Sixty-four, Girl*.

# 17.4   First meetings     Storytelling and listening

**A + B**   Follow the procedure suggested in the Student's Book before playing the recording.

**C**   Play the recording, perhaps pausing after each speaker for everyone to share their reactions.

*Transcript*

Kate: I was on my way home from junior high and in order to get to my house you have to walk by this baseball diamond. And there was a game of baseball going on and it looked kind of interesting so I stopped, there weren't very many people watching. And there was this guy and he wasn't really very good-looking but he had frizzly hair and glasses and he was really funny. He did this kind of monologue thing, which was great. And I went home and I told my mother I was going to marry him after talking to him for half an hour. And when I got to high school he was president of the student body and he asked me out and ... um ... we've got our picture in the yearbook together holding hands, and it's really nice.

Kerry: Well, I'd arranged to have a drink with a ... er ... friend of mine ... a ... a woman friend of mine who's a platonic friend of mine. And she ... er ... insisted on bringing this friend of hers which ... who she said I'd like to meet and ... er ... I thought she was trying to fix us up and I said, 'Please don't!' Um ... but she did bring this friend. Um ... and ... er ... we hit it off. And ... er ... after the wine bar we went to ... er ... to have a pizza and we all got ... um ... had a few more drinks and ... er ... the other woman who ... er ... ended up ordering a pizza that had a bunch of stuff on it that I really liked and she ... I ordered a pizza that had a bunch of stuff on it that she really liked, so we picked at each other's pizzas all night and we realised that we were ... sort of had an ideal relationship, so that we could order really any pizza on the menu and ... er ... we'd both be happy. And ... er ... anyway we ended up living together and still are.

Coralyn: Um ... we met at a party and it was a fancy-dress party. A friend of mine's twenty-first and it was quite big and I went dressed as Alice In Wonderland and ... um ... this person, this guy that ... um ... I married was dressed as the Cheshire Cat. And it just seemed so amazing that, you know, we were both from the same thing and we started chatting and ended up being together.

Jill: Well, I'd arranged to go to the cinema with a group of friends and ... um ... unfortunately I missed the train that would have got me to the cinema on time, so all my friends had gone in and I was left standing outside – the film had started, so I wasn't allowed in. And ... um ... there was a chap outside, he'd also missed the film and we started to talk and ... um ... we talked quite a bit and he said, 'Let's go down the road and see that film, because that one hasn't started at the Odeon.' So we went down there and ... um ... well, we've been going out ever since!

Carole: I ... I first met my partner ... er ... when he was on a boat and I was on the river bank, standing and looking generally into the distance and he was coming in to land with his boat and he threw me a rope and said, 'Would you mind catching this?' and I caught it and missed and tripped over it and fell in the river and he had to dive in and rescue me. And that was it!

(Time: 3 minutes)

# 17.5   Expressing feelings   Effective writing

**A**   *Suggested answers*

delighted  +  overjoyed    tickled pink    very happy
dismayed  +  disappointed    upset    sad    sorry    shocked
amazed  +  surprised    astonished    astounded
   taken aback
annoyed  +  irritated    angry    cross

---

puzzled  +  bewildered    confused    baffled
flustered

**B**   The letters could be 'delivered' to another pair respond in the roles of 'Pam and Max'.

   Possibly, to add piquancy to this task, everyone c either Pam or Max is an old flame of theirs, from w on bad terms!

▶ It might also be worthwhile spending a little tim discussing how one might begin and end a letter of someone who is ill, has been bereaved, has failed a perhaps a letter to Pam or Max years later when th (or after one of them has failed to turn up at the ch

---

# 17.6   A wedding . . .   Listening and

**A**   🔲   Pause the tape after each speaker for eve their notes.

**B + C**   Follow the procedure suggested in the Stu

## Transcript

Karen: I went to a fairly re ... typical wedding recently of my cousins, who was marrying the chap sh for four years. They'd actually bought the hou house full of all their stuff and they'd been pr white wedding. Er ... the whole family was the a competition to see which side of the family on either side of the church with more people. on to the reception, where ... um ... the bride's who are my cousin and her husband decided t wonderful fun for everybody to put no one ne they knew, which consequently made for a ver people shouting across the room.

Melinda: I went to a lovely wedding ... um ... a while ag were getting married were great friends of mi wedding in a registry office and contrary to m the wedding was very intimate ... um ... and ve they'd made up their own ... their own ceremo Afterwards we had a ... a vegetarian buffet and and a friend and myself had made up a ... um entertainment out of different little snippets of discovered about the bride and groom. And ...

terrible, they were awful. I remember my ... the main thing ... my main impression after a couple of hours of this ... um ... reception was of my brother wearing formal dress, because I normally ... I had never seen him in anything except jeans and a sweatshirt before, with a full beard and long flowing hair. I think the ... the main impression of this wedding was conspicuous consumption. It rained f ... drink and snowed food for three hours. It was horrible!

Tim: I don't think it really matters what kind of a ceremony you have to get married. I think the important part about it is that it's the day for the bride and groom and the extraordinary feeling is that everybody is there because of you and because they love you and that's the most wonderful feeling and it's a day which is unlike any other day in your life. I got married in a registry office with just my parents there and my wife's parents and nobody else, because we didn't want a ceremony, we just had a *huge* party afterwards, the biggest party that you've ... well, the biggest party I've ever thrown. Um ... and just the feeling of having all your friends there looking up with this kind of love coming up from them was ... was a really, really joyous experience and something that kind of cemented the marriage. I don't think you need a ceremony too much.

(Time: 5 minutes 40 seconds)

# 17.7 First paragraphs

Read and discuss

**A** The opening paragraphs are from:
*Emma* by Jane Austen (1816)
*A Tale of Two Cities* by Charles Dickens (1859)
*Three Men in a Boat* by Jerome K. Jerome (1889)
*Rebecca* by Daphne du Maurier (1931)
*Nineteen Eighty-Four* by George Orwell (1949)
*Conundrum* by Jan Morris (1974)

**C** In this Communication activity, each person has a summary of two of the books from which the extracts were taken. Student A looks at Activity 5, student B at 19 and C at 75.

**D + E** Both of these could be done or they could be alternatives. Students who don't need to concentrate on writing skills (e.g. those who aren't planning to take an exam) could leave out E.

# 17.8   Head over heels . . .                    Idioms

## A   *Answers*

1 needs his head examined = do something stupid
2 keep your head = don't panic
3 in two minds = be undecided
4 brainwave = brilliant idea
5 heads = the side of the coin with the Queen's head on
6 over my head = too difficult
7 make up my mind = decide
8 head over heels in love = madly in love
9 no head for heights = suffer from vertigo
10 a good head for figures = aptitude
11 take your mind off = help to forget
12 keep an open mind = remain unprejudiced
13 off his head = crazy
14 slipped my mind = forget
15 two heads are better than one = easier to solve problems with a
   partner

## B   *Answers*

1 play it by ear = improvise
2 catch someone's eye = attract attention
3 keep an eye on = watch carefully
4 see eye to eye = agree
5 took the words out of my mouth = just what I was going to say
6 keep a straight face = not laugh
7 with my eyes shut = without difficulty
8 couldn't believe my ears = be astounded
9 looks down her nose at = regard with disdain
10 follow my nose = find the way by instinct
11 two-faced = not hold consistent/honest opinions
12 lose face = lose respect
13 with his eyes open = fully aware of the risk
14 splitting hairs = make insignificant distinctions
15 in one ear and out the other = heard without making an impression

▶ Some other related idioms:
face up to = confront problem realistically
save face = avoid losing respect
with the naked eye = without binoculars
be nosy = inquisitive
be down in the mouth = be miserable

# 18 Body and mind

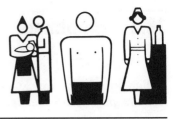

## 18.1 How are you?
Vocabulary

**B** *Suggested answers*

1 Doing exercises, swimming, jogging, working out, etc.
2 By dieting, by doing exercises, etc.
3 Flu, mumps, typhoid, malaria, whooping cough, polio, etc.
4 have drunk too much – they have a hangover     have overslept –
annoyed and perhaps have headache     have just run a marathon
– worn out     eat only junk food – guilty?     have had a bad
night – feel sleepy     have had a bad day – feel grumpy     have
had a busy day – feel exhausted
5 have sore feet – a chiropodist     need an injection – a nurse
are having a baby – a gynaecologist     need an operation – a
consultant / a surgeon     have a sore throat – no one or perhaps
the chemist     are having a nervous breakdown – a psychiatrist
6 hayfever – sneezing / runny nose     flu – headache / nausea /
temperature     migraine – splitting headache     food poisoning
– sickness and diarrhoea     sprained ankle – swollen ankle
schizophrenia – no sense of reality / split personality(?)     a cut
finger – bleeding     a broken arm – swelling, extreme pain, etc.
7 hayfever – tablets, perhaps     a cold – stay at home     bruise –
don't touch it     scratch – put a plaster on if it's serious     dog
bite – go to the doctor if it's serious     headache – take an
aspirin or paracetamol     toothache – go to the dentist     graze
– put a plaster on if it's serious     bee sting + mosquito bite – put
up with it or get something from the chemist     aching back –
exercises     sprained wrist – rest it and perhaps put a bandage on
it     a bad cough – take some cough medicine
8 consultant     matron     midwife     porter     sister
specialist     surgeon

181

## 18.2 **Emphasis**   Grammar and pronunciation

**A**  *Suggested answers*

1 Tim spends too much time eating and drinking.
 – *straightforward statement*
 Tim does spend too much time eating and drinking.
 – *emphasising that he does this, perhaps contradicting someone who maintains the contrary*
 Tim spends far too much time eating and drinking.
 – *emphasising that he spends a lot of time doing this*
 Tim really spends too much time eating and drinking.
 – *emphasising that he does this (as second example), but probably not contradicting anyone*

2 It was her arm that Jane hurt.
 – *not another part of her body*
 Jane hurt her <u>arm</u>.
 – *as the first example*
 It was Jane that/who hurt her arm.
 – *not another person who hurt their arm*
 Jane did hurt her arm.
 – *emphasising that this is what happened, perhaps contradicting someone who maintains the contrary*
 What Jane hurt was her arm.
 – *as the first example*

3 Ann's self-satisfied attitude makes me angry.
 – *straightforward unemphatic statement*
 What makes me really angry is Ann's self-satisfied attitude.
 – *emphasising how angry this makes me feel*
 It's Ann's self-satisfied attitude that makes me really angry.
 – *emphasising what it is that makes me feel like this*
 Ann's self-satisfied attitude does make me really angry.
 – *emphasising how angry this makes me feel (as the second example)*
 I'm angry because of Ann's self-satisfied attitude.
 – *straightforward unemphatic statement (as the first example)*
 I <u>am</u> angry because of Ann's self-satisfied attitude.
 – *emphasising that this is the case, perhaps contradicting someone who maintains the contrary*

4 <u>Chris</u> needs to take more exercise.
 – *not another person*
 Chris needs to take <u>more</u> exercise.
 – *she already takes some exercise but needs to do more of this*

Chris <u>needs</u> to take more exercise.
*– this is what she needs to do, but maybe she won't do this*
Chris needs to take more <u>exercise</u>.
*– not more care or more vitamins, etc.*

**B**  🔲  A short pause after each remark might be helpful.

## Answers

1 to 7: 'Terry had a stomachache because the plums he ate were
    unripe.'
not the <u>apples</u>  1  3        not a <u>headache</u>  4
not <u>overripe</u>  5              not <u>Sally</u>  2
it <u>is</u> really true  7        not the ones <u>you</u> ate  6

8 to 12: 'I need more time if I'm going to take up a new sport.'
not <u>money</u>  8  12            not <u>less</u> time  11
not a new <u>hobby</u>  10        not if <u>you</u> are going to  9

13 to 18: 'Most people like Helen because she has a friendly
    personality.'
not <u>everyone</u>  16                    they don't <u>dislike</u> her  *(none)*
not an <u>unfriendly</u> one  15  17      not a friendly <u>smile</u>  18
they don't like <u>another person</u>  13  14

19 to 24: 'Ted has a cough because he smokes 30 cigarettes a day.'
not <u>Helen</u>  21        not a <u>sore throat</u>  22  24
not <u>thirteen</u>  23     not <u>cigars</u>  19
not per <u>week</u>  20

## Transcript

1 No, Terry had a stomachache because the <u>plums</u> he ate were unripe.
2 No, <u>Terry</u> had a stomachache because the plums he ate were unripe.
3 No, it was the <u>plums</u> that were unripe.
4 No, Terry had a <u>stomachache</u> because the plums he ate were unripe.
5 No, Terry had a stomachache because the plums he ate were
    <u>un</u>ripe.
6 Terry had a stomachache because the plums <u>he</u> ate were unripe.
7 Terry <u>did</u> have a stomachache because the plums he ate were unripe.

8 No, it's more <u>time</u> I need if I'm going to take up a new sport.
9 No, I need more time if <u>I'm</u> going to take up a new sport.
10 No, I need more time if I'm going to take up a new <u>sport</u>.
11 No, I need <u>more</u> time if I'm going to take up a new sport.
12 No, I need more <u>time</u> if I'm going to take up a new sport.

13 No, most people like <u>Helen</u> because she has a friendly personality.

14 No, most people like Helen because <u>she</u> has a friendly personality.
15 No, the reason why most people like Helen is because she has a <u>friendly</u> personality.
16 No, <u>most</u> people like Helen because she has a friendly personality.
17 No, most people like Helen because she has a <u>friendly</u> personality.
18 No, most people like Helen because she has a friendly <u>personality</u>.

19 No, Ted has a cough because he smokes 30 <u>cigarettes</u> a day.
20 No, Ted has a cough because he smokes 30 cigarettes a <u>day</u>.
21 No, it's <u>Ted</u> who has a cough because he smokes 30 cigarettes a day.
22 No, Ted has a <u>cough</u> because he smokes 30 cigarettes a day.
23 No, Ted has a cough because he smokes <u>30</u> cigarettes a day.
24 No, what Ted has is a <u>cough</u> because he smokes too much.

(Time: 2 minutes)

**C** This should be studied by students alone or gone through with the class.

**D** *Suggested answers* (many variations possible)

1 It was eating unripe plums that gave Terry a stomachache.
It was the unripe plums that Terry ate which gave him a stomachache.
Terry was the one who had a stomachache after eating unripe plums.
2 What I need is more time if I'm going to take up a sport.
It's more time that I need if I'm going to take up a sport.
More time is what I need if I'm going to take up a sport.
3 What people like about Helen is her friendly personality.
What Helen has is a friendly personality and that's why people like her.
Helen does have a friendly personality and that's why people like her.
4 It's because Ted smokes too many cigarettes that he has a cough.
What Ted does is smoke too many cigarettes and that's why he has a cough.
It's Ted who has a cough because he smokes too many cigarettes.
The person who has a cough is Ted and it's caused by the number of cigarettes that he smokes.
5 What Katy did was worry about her health and this made her ill.
What happened was that Katy became ill because she worried about her health.
What Katy worried about was her health and this made her ill.
What made Katy ill was worrying about her health.

**E** 🔲 This is a partially controlled exercise, encouraging students to contradict each other. Each person has some information they think *may* be true and some information they know *is* true.

Student A looks at Activity 15 and student B at 76.

## 18.3 What is The Body Shop? Read and discuss

🔲 This is a 'jigsaw reading' activity. Student A has the beginning of the passage in Activity 7, student B the middle section in 22 and C has the last part in 33.

## 18.4 Using prefixes                                Word study

▶ Revise what was done in 10.3 on prefixes before starting **A**.

**A** *Answers*

| | | | | |
|---|---|---|---|---|
| **un** | acceptable | approachable | bearable | conscious |
| | desirable | faithful | foreseen | grateful | healthy |
| | natural | readable | sociable | willing |
| **dis** | contented | obedient | organised | respectful |
| **in** | appropriate | compatible | complete | convenient |
| | credible | decisive | discreet | excusable |
| | experienced | flexible | frequent | hospitable |
| | sane | sufficient | variable | visible |
| **im** | mortal | passive | personal | polite | probable |
| **il** | legible | literate | logical |

**B** *Answers*

| | | | | |
|---|---|---|---|---|
| **mis** | count | print | read | report | quote |
| **out** | bid | do | last | run | wit |
| **re** | consider | count | name | open | pack | play |
| | print | read | record | release | run |
| | sit an exam | tell | think | unite | use |
| **un** | dress | load | lock | pack | roll | screw |
| | wind | zip |

**C** *Answers*

| | | | | |
|---|---|---|---|---|
| **mid-** | air | fifties | life | point | twenties |

185

| | | | | |
|---|---|---|---|---|
| **over** | compensate | confident | crowded | dose |
| | enthusiastic | exposed | friendly | imaginative |
| | loaded | privileged | qualified | react |
| | simplify | staffed | value | weight |
| **under** | estimate | exposed | privileged | qualified |
| | value | weight | | |
| **self-** | assured | catering | confident | contained |
| | defence | discipline | explanatory | governing |
| | respect | satisfied | | |
| **ultra-** | cautious | fashionable | polite | |

▶ Some more prefixes, not included in the Student's Book.

| | | | | | |
|---|---|---|---|---|---|
| **Anglo-** | American | phone | Saxon | | |
| **anti-** | American | biotic | clockwise | nuclear | |
| | perspirant | septic | social | | |
| **co-** | educational | exist | founder | leader | pilot |
| | worker | | | | |
| **de** | brief | centralise | frost | value | |
| **Euro-** | cheque | dollar | election | parliament | |
| **Franco-** | British | phone | | | |
| **inter-** | class | departmental | firm | marry | |
| | personal | planetary | school | state | |
| **post** | date | | | | |
| **pre-** | cooked | date | recorded | school | |
| **pro-** | American | British | nuclear | | |
| **vice-** | captain | chairman | president | principal | |

## D  *Suggested answers*

1 ultra-modern    mid-way    outlived
2 impatient    misunderstand
3 overreacted    rewrite    unreadable/illegible/inaccurate
4 incompatible    self-satisfied/self-confident
   oversensitive/overimaginative
5 incredible    understaffed    reopened
6 self-discipline    disorganised

---

# 18.5  Bad feelings                                          Functions

**A**  🔲 Perhaps point out that sarcasm and sincerity can be seen in a speaker's face, as well as heard in the voice. Moreover, what is deemed sarcastic in some situations might be perfectly sincere in others – or even deliberately ambiguous, perhaps.

**B** Follow the procedure outlined in the Student's Book.

**C** In this Communication activity each person has to play the role of being in a different mood. Student A, looking at 29, pretends to be depressed; student B, looking at 54, pretends to be very angry; student C, looking at 71, pretends to be very bored. The emphasis here is not on 'acting' the mood successfully but on DEALING with the problem.

If this role play is not successful the first time, perhaps do it again with roles changed.

## Transcript

1 Man: What did you think of my work – was it good?
  Woman: Yes, it was really good. I liked it a lot.  *sincerely*

2 Woman: What did you think of my work – was it good?
  Man: Oh, yes, it was brilliant. I really enjoyed reading it.  *sarcastically*

3 Woman: Need any help?
  Man: Well, I was wondering whether it might be possible for you to help with the washing-up.  *sarcastically*

4 Woman: Feeling better?
  Man: Better?
  Woman: Yes, well, you weren't feeling too good yesterday – I was just wondering if you were feeling all right today.  *sincerely*

5 Man: Feeling better?
  Woman: Better?
  Man: Yes, I was very worried about you because you didn't come to the party I invited you to last night.  *sarcastically*

6 Woman: Any suggestions?
  Man: Well, I think it might be quite a good idea if you gave up smoking, for example.  *sarcastically*

7 Man: Any suggestions?
  Woman: I think it might be quite a good idea if we arranged to play tennis once a week.  *sincerely*

8 Man: How was your skiing holiday?
  Woman: Oh, it was wonderful – even though there wasn't much snow.  *sincerely*

9 Man: How was your summer holiday?
  Woman: Oh, we had a really good time – it was sunny almost every day.  *sarcastically*

10  Woman: Jane ... I wonder if you'd mind giving us your attention for a
moment? *sarcastically*

11  Man:    Chris?
Woman: Yes?
Man:    I was wondering whether it might be possible for you to take
notes during the lecture tomorrow. *sincerely*

12  Woman: Have we finished yet?
Man:    Yes, we have very nearly finished, don't worry. *sarcastically*

(Time: 1 minute 50 seconds)

## 18.6   First aid                      Communication activity

**A + B**   Follow the procedure in the Student's Book.

☒  Don't allow anyone to look at the 'right answers' in Activities
13, 48 and 57 until they have established what they THINK is the
correct treatment or procedure for each emergency.

## 18.7  *Hearts, hands, legs* and *feet*          Idioms

*Answers*

1  by heart = memorise
2  have someone's interests at heart = feel deeply
3  in good hands = well looked after
4  short-handed = not enough assistance
5  old hands = experienced staff
6  lose heart = lose courage
7  hold someone's hand = help as if a child
8  find one's feet = settle down
9  my heart isn't in it = not be enthusiastic
10  give someone a free hand = complete unrestricted freedom
11  in your hands = your responsibility
12  take it to heart = take too seriously
13  a change of heart = change decision
14  hasn't got a leg to stand on = no justification
15  have cold feet = feel afraid to commit yourself
16  underhand = cheating
17  keep one's hand in = retain a skill
18  give someone a hand = help
19  have the matter in hand = dealing with

20  break someone's heart = cause someone to suffer despair
21  put one's foot down = impose authority
22  put one's foot in it = cause embarrassment
23  light-hearted = not serious
24  put your feet up = relax
25  pull someone's leg = play a joke

▶ A few more idioms (these are connected with BACK and THUMB):
back out of = withdraw
back up = support
back down = yield
back-up = replacement
behind someone's back = without their knowledge
rule of thumb = a rough practical rule
thumb a lift = hitchhike

# 19 On business

---

## 19.1 On the job
Vocabulary

**B** *Answers*

1 application    CV/résumé
2 wages    white    salary    pension
3 competitors    redundant
4 budget    products    force    clients/customers
5 word processors
6 components    spare parts
7 chairman/chairperson    agenda    minutes
8 internal    memos
9 telex    fax    electronic
10 *Boxes clockwise from top left*: monitor    modem
   disk drive    floppy disks    mouse    keyboard    printer

---

## 19.2 Great business deals?
Reading and listening

**A** *Answers*

1 $24 worth of kettles, axes and cloth*
2 $80,000,000
3 $27,000,000
4 about 12 cents
5 about 800,000 square miles
6 about 1,600,000 square miles
7 $7,200,000
8 about 5 cents
9 $750,000,000 worth
10 an estimated 100,000,000,000 tons

* On a serious note: Perhaps you should remind everyone that the
European colonists and settlers in North (as well as Central and
South) America not only ruthlessly deprived the Indians of their land
and hunting grounds by theft, trickery and force of arms, but

actually killed most of them – millions of American Indians died in bloody massacres, in concentration camps and on death marches, from alcoholism, from starvation, and from imported diseases like smallpox, measles and cholera. Before 1492 over 10 million Indians lived north of the Rio Grande, by 1890 only half a million survived.

## B 🔲 Answers

**1933**   **Seller:** THE CANADIAN ....National....... Steamship.... COMPANY

| Place | Product | Price | Purchaser |
|---|---|---|---|
| Canada | Ten vessels | $ 20,000 per ship | Aristotle Onassis |

**Outcome:** Shipping began to boom when the world depression ended and he became a millionaire

**1923–5**   **Seller:** ARTHUR FURGUSON

| Place | Product | Price | Purchaser |
|---|---|---|---|
| London | Trafalgar Square | £ 6,000 | an American |
| London | Big Ben | £1,000 | a tourist |
| London | Buckingham Palace | £ 2,000 deposit | another tourist |
| Washington | The White House | $ 100,000 per annum | a Texan |
| New York | The Statue of Liberty | $100,000 | an Australian |

**Outcome:** Arthur Furguson was identified recognised, arrested and imprisoned for five years. After his release he retired to California and lived a life of luxury.

**1925–34**   **Seller:** 'COUNT' VICTOR LUSTIG

| Place | Product | Price | Purchaser |
|---|---|---|---|
| Paris | Eiffel Tower: as 7,000 tons of scrap metal | (not known) | André Poisson |
| USA | A machine to print bank notes | $ 50,000 | a millionaire |
| Chicago | A 'system' to double money on Wall Street | $5,000 | Al Capone |

**Outcome:** Victor Lustig was imprisoned in 1934 but escaped He was rearrested in 1945 and found guilty of printing $ 134,000,000 He died in prison in 1947.

## Transcript

1
In the ... er ... late 1920s, early 1930s, there was a ... a young Greek businessman who ... er ... made quite a lot of money ... er ... by importing tobacco into Argentina. Um ... he then moved up to North America ... er ... this was in about ... er ... 1933, when of course the world was in the middle

of a ... a trade slump. Er ... he ... er ... decided he wanted to get into shipping, and to get into shipping he needed ships so he ... he started looking around for some ships to buy with his tobacco fortune and he found ten vessels ... er ... which belonged to the Canadian National Steamship Company ... er ... the problem being that they were frozen into the ice in the St Lawrence River in Canada. They'd been rusting away there for two years and were now completely filled up with snow and ice. Er ... in fact the story goes that when he went aboard to ... er ... inspect one of the ships, he fell into a snowdrift and ... er ... ended up on the deck below. Well, the ships had cost $2 million to build ... er ... about ten years before, and the owners were prepared to let them go just for a ... a scrap price of ... er ... $30,000 each. He offered $20,000 and the owners accepted.

He left them there, stuck in the ice, there was nothing more he could do. Er ... but a few years later, the ... the world depression ... er ... came to an end and ... er ... world war seemed to be looming in Europe and, of course, that led in its turn to a ... bit of a shipping boom. So the young man, there he was with his ships and ... er ... he became one of the richest men in the world. His name was ... Aristotle Onassis.

2

Once upon a time there was an enterprising Scottish actor, called Arthur Furguson, who discovered that he could make a very good living selling things that didn't actually belong to him, in other words he was a con man. He first got the idea when he was sitting in the middle of Trafalgar Square (in London that is). Um ... this was in 1923, and he saw an American tourist admiring the stone lions and the fountains and Nelson's Column. He introduced himself as the 'official guide' to the Square and started to explain the history of the place. And while he was doing this he also slipped in a little mention that as Britain was heavily in debt, the British government was looking for the right kind of person to buy the Square. He said that he was the official government salesman and that the asking price was around £6,000. The American said that this was a good price and offered to pay by cheque right away, so Mr Furguson went off to okay this with his superiors – in other words he went off for an hour and a half and kept the American waiting. Well, he then came back and said, yes, they were willing to sell to the American at that price. The American wrote a cheque and Furguson gave him a receipt and the address of a company who would dismantle the Square and get it ready for shipping it to the States. Then he went off to cash the cheque.

Soon after that he sold Big Ben for £1,000 and took a down payment on Buckingham Palace of £2,000. Two years later he went to the United States and leased the White House to a Texas cattleman for 99 years for $100,000 per annum. Later he arranged to sell the Statue of Liberty to an Australian for $100,000, but unfortunately Furguson allowed the buyer to take a photograph of him and the Australian, feeling *slightly* suspicious, showed the photograph to the police. Furguson was identified and sent to prison for fraud for five years. When he came out he retired to California, where he lived in luxury until he died in 1938.

3

In 1925, in Paris, there was a man called Victor Lustig, he was actually a ... a Czechoslovakian but he was living in Paris. And one day, he noticed a news item in the paper that said that the Eiffel Tower was badly in need of repair. He used his connections and got hold of some official notepaper from the Ministry of Posts and wrote letters to five businessmen inviting them to a meeting with, as he signed it, 'Count Lustig', at a famous hotel. All of them attended this meeting and they were told in so-called complete confidence that the Eiffel Tower was in a terrible condition and would have to be demolished and rebuilt, and they were invited to submit tenders for 7,000 tons of scrap metal.

Well, after the meeting, Lustig got in touch with one of them, Monsieur André Poisson, and told him that the deal would go through more smoothly if he could manage to pay a little extra money, in other words a bribe. Well, Poisson being greedy, er ... agreed to this and paid the full price for the scrap metal *and* the bribe. Now, he paid it in a banker's draft, er ... so Lustig took the banker's draft and left the country. Now, Poisson was so ashamed of what he'd done that he didn't dare tell the police so Lustig came back again – and repeated the trick on another businessman. However, this time after this he left the country and emigrated to America, where he continued his trade on that side of the Atlantic.

Now, one of his deals here was to sell a machine, to a millionaire, that would duplicate bank notes and for this he got $50,000. In the 1920s he persuaded Al Capone, the famous gangster, that he had a system by which he, Capone, could double his money on Wall Street and Capone gave him $5,000 for this. However, Lustig, probably for obvious reasons, thought better of this deal and paid Capone back his money. He became an associate of Capone's and started a new line of business, printing bank notes. But in 1934 he was caught and imprisoned. However, he escaped. Eventually, after eleven years, in 1945, he was rearrested and found guilty of printing $134 million!! He died in prison in 1947.

(Time: 6 minutes 30 seconds)

# 19.3   Word order                    Effective writing

## A   *Suggested answers*

2 We should get in touch with them as soon as possible.
3 We should send them a fax immediately.
4 We also ought to send them a letter.
5 We shouldn't send them a telex every day.
6 We should never phone them in the morning.
7 We really shouldn't have taken so long to reply to their letter.
8 When will you have completely finished?

**B**   *Suggested answers*

1  They have a brand new office block in the heart of busy downtown Manhattan.
2  She's got a splendid well-paid job in an up-and-coming new computer software company.
3  The most reliable permanent member of our staff is taking early retirement.
4  I always stay in a lovely little traditional family hotel beside a beautiful mountain lake.
5  First I attended a long-winded monthly staff committee meeting and then I made an important business phone call.

**C**   *Suggested answers*

1  In 1968, Robert McCulloch, an American millionaire, found out that London Bridge was about to be demolished because a new one was to be built.
2  He decided to buy the stones, and have them shipped to America and rebuilt in the desert beside Lake Havasu in Arizona as a tourist attraction.
3  His offer of $2.4 million plus an extra $1,000 for every one of his sixty years of age was accepted.
4  It was only later that he realised he had made a slight mistake.
5  Apparently, he had assumed that it was Tower Bridge that he was buying and he hadn't realised that London Bridge was just an ordinary Victorian stone bridge!

**D + E**   Follow the procedure suggested in the Student's Book.

# 19.4   On the phone                              Functions

**A**   The questions in this section draw on everyone's previous experience of making phone calls. Students who lack this experience should listen carefully to those who have more experience during the discussion.

**B**   Follow the procedure suggested in the Student's Book. Encourage everyone to notice the mistakes made by the people on the recording.

## Transcript

| | |
|---|---|
| Woman: | Acme Trading, can I help you? |
| Jane: | Er ... hello, is Larry there, please? |
| Woman: | Jerry? |
| Jane: | No, Larry. Larry Allen. |
| Woman: | Oh, Larry. I ... I'm not sure, I'll find out for you. Hold the line, please ... Larry, someone on the phone for you. |
| Larry: | Find out who it is. |
| Woman: | Who's calling, please? |
| Jane: | Jane McCartney. |
| Woman: | Jean McSomething. |
| Larry: | Never heard of her. Tell her ... er ... tell her I'm in a meeting. |
| Woman: | Hello. |
| Jane: | Hello. Can I speak to him, please? I ... I just heard you speaking to him. |
| Woman: | I'm terribly sorry, madam, but he's not available at the moment. He's in a meeting. |
| Jane: | When will he be free, do you know? |
| Woman: | Oh, goodness – *I* don't know. Maybe after lunch. |
| Jane: | Oh dear ... um ... well, can you give him a message, please? |
| Woman: | Can't you call back later? |
| Jane: | Not really, I'd rather leave a message. |
| Woman: | Certainly, madam. What's the message? |
| Jane: | Can you tell him that Jane McCartney rang and I'd like him to call me when he's free. The number is 345 87 23. |
| Woman: | Oh ... er ... let me just find a pencil ... Right, I'm ready now. |
| Jane: | Could he call Jane McCartney on 345 87 23? |
| Woman: | Paul McCartney – 435 87 32. I've got that. Goodbye, thank you for calling. |
| Jane: | Good ... no, it's *Jane* and ... the number is 345 ... Ohh! |
| | |
| Narrator: | Second call. |
| | |
| Woman: | Good afternoon. Acme Trading. Can I help you? |
| Jane: | Hello, this is Jane McCartney. Can I speak to Mr Allen, please? ... Hello ... Hello! |
| Woman: | I'm just trying to connect you. |
| Jane: | Thanks. |
| Alan: | Hello. |
| Jane: | Hello, is that Mr Allen? |
| Alan: | Yes, Alan here. Who's speaking? |
| Jane: | This is Jane. |
| Alan: | Jan? |
| Jane: | No, Jane, Jane McCartney. |
| Alan: | I'm sorry I don't think I know you. Perhaps you've got the wrong person. This is Alan Hunter. |
| Jane: | I wanted Larry Allen. |
| Alan: | Well, I'm Alan Hunter. |

| | |
|---|---|
| Jane: | Oh dear, I'm sorry. I asked the telephonist to give me Larry Allen. |
| Alan: | Typical! |
| Jane: | Can you connect me back to the switchboard then, please? |
| Alan: | I'll have a go but it doesn't usually work. |
| Woman: | Hello, switchboard. Can I help you? |
| Jane: | Can you put me through to Mr Larry Allen, please? |
| Woman: | Certainly, madam, hold the line, please. |
| Colleague: | Larry Allen's phone. |
| Jane: | Hello. Is Larry there, please? |
| Colleague: | He was here a minute ago but he's just this moment left the office I'm afraid. He won't actually be back till after the weekend. Would you like to leave a message? |
| Jane: | Yes, could you tell him ... no, on second thoughts, no, there's no message. Goodbye. |

(Time: 3 minutes 15 seconds)

**C** 📷 This is a sequence of role plays in which students practise making their own phone calls. In each role play, two students are 'on the phone' (sitting back to back) while a third makes notes and gives feedback.

– The first role play is between student A in 21 and student B in 3, with C as 'observer' in 26.
– The second role play is between student C in 31 and student A in 42, with B as 'observer' in 14.
– The third role play is between student B in 30 and student C in 37, with A as 'observer' in 72.

(In a group of four two students should share one of the roles throughout the sequence of role plays.)

These instructions and the 'route' to be taken through the Communication activities are made clear in the Student's Book and in the Activities.

▶ This may sound complicated but it is actually quite straight-forward. If you're doubtful, follow the sequence through in the Student's Book before doing this with your class.

## 19.5 Could you take a message? Listening

**A** 📼 Play the three messages, perhaps pausing between them for everyone to complete their notes.

## Transcript

| | |
|---|---|
| Narrator: | You'll hear three phone messages – take notes as you listen to them. |
| Karen White: | Oh ... er ... hello. I've got a message for Jane Potter. Um ... this is Karen White, er ... KAREN WHITE – and ... er ... I'm calling from Chicago. Er ... Jane, as you know, you've agreed to do two presentations for us in July: one on the 14th at 11.30 and the other on the 15th at 12.30. Well, I'm afraid we've had to cancel the former and change the time of the latter to 14.15, just after lunch. Could you confirm that this is all right? Oh, yeah, and can you please send me a copy of your handout, so that I can run it off, you know, enough copies? See you on the 15th. |
| Stuart Hunter: | Hi ... er ... this is a message for Jane Potter. This is Stuart Hunter – STUART HUNTER – from Apollo International – APOLLO. It's about the order we've received for the HK 440 Vxi. We have one HK 440 Vxj in stock now that we can send off this afternoon. But we won't have the 440 Vxi till next month. The only difference between the Vxi and the Vxj is the power supply. The Vxi can be adjusted for 220 or 240 volts, but the Vxj only runs on 220 volts. This shouldn't matter for your requirements, but in any case can you phone me first thing to let me know whether you want to have the Vxj or wait till the Vxi is available. My number is 339 3987, extension 958. |
| Hilda Meyer: | Hello. This is Hilda Meyer – that's HILDA MEYER. Er ... I ... I'd like to leave a message for Jane Potter. I'm calling because my flight times have changed since I was last in touch with Jane and this may affect our arrangements. I haven't been able to get a flight on Monday 13th until the evening. Um ... the flight number is GJ 345 and it arrives at Gatwick not Heathrow Airport at 20.45. Now, I'll be staying at the Grosvenor Hotel – GROSVENOR – that's at Victoria Station, so if anyone meets me they should come to the airport by train not by car. If anyone *is* going to meet me, please let me know, so that we don't miss each other. Otherwise, I'll make my own way to the office on the Tuesday morning. So, I won't be able to meet Jane for dinner on the Monday – but if she's free I'd like to invite her to be my guest on the Tuesday evening. Thank you. |

(Time: 3 minutes)

**B** In this role play each person has some information to pass on to the other during a 'phone call'. The receiver of the information has to make notes. Student A looks at Activity 35, student B at 59.

## 19.6 Carrying out a survey

As explained in the Student's Book, the class is divided into two
groups. Group A will carry out a survey based on questionnaire A
and group B on questionnaire B. Follow the step-by-step procedure
outlined in the Student's Book.

## 19.7 Applying for a job     Creative writing

**A + B**   Follow the procedure suggested in the Student's Book. In
case members of the class are at a loss how to complete a CV, on
the next page is a sample that may be photocopied – it is adapted
from *International Business English* by Leo Jones and Richard
Alexander (CUP), which is recommended as a source for further
activities on the theme of this unit.

## CURRICULUM VITAE

Name:            MARY BRENDA SCOTT
Address:         44 London Road, Winchester SO16 7HJ
Telephone:       0962 8890 (home)    0703 77877 (work)
Date of Birth:   22 May 1972
Marital status:  single

### EDUCATION

| | |
|---|---|
| Churchill Comprehensive School, Basingstoke | 1983-1988 |
| Winchester Technical College | 1988-1990 |

### QUALIFICATIONS

| | |
|---|---|
| GCSEs Maths, English, French, Geography, History, Chemistry | 1988 |
| GCE 'A' Level Commerce, Economics, Spanish | 1990 |

### EXPERIENCE

| | |
|---|---|
| Office assistant, Totton Engineering, Totton | 1990 |
| Secretary to Sales Director, Totton Engineering, Totton | 1991-1992 |
| Personal Assistant to Export Manager, Millbank Foods, Southampton | 1992 to date |

My work with Millbank Foods has involved responsibility for giving instructions to junior staff and dealing with clients and suppliers in person and on the telephone. I have accompanied the Export Manager to Food Trade fairs in Germany, France and the USA.

### OTHER INFORMATION

I speak and write French and Spanish quite well (intermediate level). I am now taking an evening course in German conversation.

### OTHER ACTIVITIES AND INTERESTS

I play club basketball regularly and I sing and play guitar with a local country and western band.

### REFEREES

Mrs S.J. Grant, Personnel Manager, Millbank Foods, 34-42 South Dock Drive, Southampton SO8 9QT

Mr John Robinson, Sales Director, Totton Engineering, Cadnam Street, Totton SO23 4GT

© Cambridge University Press 1991

## 19.8    *Hard, soft, difficult* and *easy*        Idioms

*Answers*

1 hard up = short of money
2 hardware = computer equipment       software = computer
   programs
3 hard copy = printed material produced by computer
4 hard disk = not a floppy disk
5 hard-wearing = durable
6 hardware store = ironmonger's
7 uneasy = anxious, not relaxed       he's being
   difficult = obstinate       soft-hearted = compassionate
   easy-going = not getting worried or angry       have a soft spot
   for = feel affectionate
8 hard/difficult       soft-spoken = have a quiet, gentle voice
9 hard drugs = addictive, dangerous drugs
   soft drugs = marijuana, etc.
10 soft/easy       hard line = uncompromising attitude
11 hard-and-fast rule = fixed rule
12 hardback = not a paperback
13 hard-hearted = without compassion       give someone a hard
   time = make it difficult for them       make life difficult = create
   problems
14 soft drink = non-alcoholic cold drink
15 I'm easy = I don't mind
16 hard sell = aggressive selling techniques       soft sell = using gentle
   persuasion to sell
17 hard currency = dollars, etc.
18 take it easy = relax

▶ Some other related idioms:
**hard**       hard cash = notes and coins (not cheques or cards)
              hard drink = whisky and other spirits
              hard-headed = tough and shrewd
              hardwood = wood from deciduous trees
**soft**       a soft option = less difficult alternative
              softwood = wood from coniferous trees
**easy**       take it easy = don't get excited/worried
**difficult**  a difficult person = unpredictable, hard to deal with or
              please

# 20 The natural world

---

## 20.1 Fauna and flora Vocabulary

**B** Some of these drawings are supposed to be ambiguous, so that students are more likely to disagree about the fauna and flora represented and thereby 'cover' even more vocabulary!

*Suggested answers* (+ three extra species added to each group)

1 hare or rabbit   squirrel   bat   bear   gorilla
 hedgehog   leopard   deer   goat
 dolphin   +wolf   chimpanzee   baboon
2 owl   peacock   eagle or buzzard   penguin   sparrow
 parrot or macaw   pigeon or dove   stork   swan
 vulture   +seagull   starling   budgerigar
3 butterfly or moth   bee   wasp   beetle or cockroach
 ant   mosquito   snail   scorpion   spider
 caterpillar   +hornet   bluebottle   worm
4 frog   dinosaur (diplodocus)   lizard   snake   tortoise
 dragon   alligator   +tortoise   turtle   toad
5 rose   daffodil   poppy   tulip   daisy
 carnation   +dahlia   buttercup   chrysanthemum
6 palm tree   cactus   fir   oak   pine   mushroom
 bamboo   seaweed   +apple tree   beech   maple
7 crab   shark   octopus   squid   trout   sole
 lobster   oyster   mussel   eel   +cod   scallop
 mullet

**C** In this 'jigsaw reading' activity, student A reads the opening paragraph of *Metamorphosis* by Franz Kafka in Activity 55, while student B reads the blurb of *Woof!* by Allan Ahlberg in Activity 63. Besides discussing what they have read, you might like to ask your students to write a couple of paragraphs on this topic:
 'What would it be like if YOU woke up one morning to find yourself transformed into a cockroach, a dog – or another creature?'

## 20.2 The rise of the Greens

**A** This can be treated as another 'jigsaw reading' exercise, as suggested in the Student's Book. Or you may prefer to have everyone read both passages and then exchange their reactions.

**B** 🔲 **+ C** Follow the procedure suggested in the Student's Book.

### Answers

1 new and attractive alternative
2 Party       Movement
3 Friends of the Earth       Greenpeace
  the World Wide Fund for Nature
4 funds       the public's awareness
5 bikes       bike lanes
6 techniques       sites       routes       damaging       expensive
7 fashionable       environment-friendly
8 speak louder than words

### Transcript

Presenter: Who are the Greens? Well, not so long ago if you mentioned the Greens, people might have thought you were referring to little green men, stepping out of a flying saucer in a science-fiction film. But increasingly they're becoming an important political power. The Green Party's share of the vote went up from zero to 15% in the recent European elections. Helen Summerfield reports.

Helen: What kind of person is a Green? Sam Fuller stood as a Green Party candidate in the Euro-elections. Sam, would you describe yourself as a typical Green?

Sam Fuller: Well, there's no such animal. As you can see I haven't got long hair and I'm not a hippy. I'm dressed quite normally, and I usually wear a suit at work. But I suppose you could say that the more active Greens are I suppose predominantly middle-class, but their support comes from all sections of the community. What is happening more and more all over Europe is that people are becoming fed up with the existing political parties and the Greens represent a new and attractive alternative. We are a radical political force and unlike other parties we are against nuclear power and nuclear weapons.

Helen: The Green *Party* attempts to exert pressure on public policy and to influence industry from within national and local government, whereas the Green Movement is non-political. The three main non-political environmental pressure groups are the Friends of the Earth, Greenpeace and the World Wide Fund for Nature. These organisations have been working for many years, raising funds and raising the public's awareness of the need to protect the environment. They have many basic interests in common but individually they also run their own campaigns, for example to encourage people to use bikes and persuade local government to provide bike lanes where people can ride safely through towns and cities, and persuade the government to subsidise public transport so that fewer people will use cars. Sam Fuller again.

Sam Fuller: The most important part of all the Green Movement's activities is to propose specific solutions to specific problems. If a power station is planned or a new motorway is to be built we want to make sure it's done with the least possible damage to the environment. We try to propose alternative techniques, sites or routes which will be less damaging and in many cases less expensive too, as a matter of fact.

Helen: It may sound cynical to say this but as it becomes more fashionable for people to care about the environment, more and more members of the public will choose environment-friendly products. Companies that are not 'green' and who can't advertise their products as 'environment-friendly' or 'ozone-friendly' will lose business to firms who do have a green image. Even if they're doing it for the wrong reasons it doesn't matter if the results are good. In the same sort of way, political parties that don't have this fashionable green image will lose votes. Before too long governments may even fall if they aren't seen to be actually *carrying out* green policies, and not simply boasting about how 'concerned' they are. In protecting the environment, as in every other field, actions speak louder than words. And only actions will make any difference.

Presenter: That was Helen Summerfield reporting there.

(Time: 3 minutes 20 seconds)

**D** 📼 These short recorded extracts give students practice in using the 'clues' they hear to work out more information when they are listening to a conversation or a broadcast. Perhaps pause the tape after each clip.

*Transcript with* ANSWERS *after the* ■s

Narrator: Now you'll hear some recorded extracts from a conversation. In each case, the last word or phrase is not audible. Decide what the missing word or phrase might be. Listen to the example first.

1 Man:     . . . no, they live in Africa and they feed on leaves. I don't
           think they roar or make any noise. Oh, they've got these
           wonderful, long necks. You've been to the zoo, haven't you?
           Now, when you were there, did you see the ■ *giraffes*?

2 Woman:   . . . but actually they're not slimy at all, their skin is dry. And
           they aren't ... they aren't all dangerous because some types
           don't have a poisonous bite, in fact ... well ... to humans they're
           perfectly ■ *harmless (snakes)*.

3 Man:     . . . well, it's pollution, the overuse of chemical fertilisers and
           insecticides in agriculture all cause damage to ■ *the
           environment*.

4 Woman:   . . . carbon dioxide and other gases has led to an irreversible
           situation where the ozone layer is being damaged and the earth
           is likely to become warmer – this is known as the ■
           *greenhouse effect*.

5 Woman:   . . . felled and burned, all sorts of rare plants and animals are
           killed and we'll never see them again – these species'll all
           become ■ *extinct*.

6 Woman:   . . . all new cars take it, but if you're not sure about your car
           ask your garage if your car can be adjusted by them to run on
           ■ *unleaded petrol*.

7 Man:     . . . the reason why the trees are dying is basically the smoke
           and exhaust gases from industry, power stations and vehicles is
           full of sulphur dioxide and this poisonous substance falls to
           earth again as ■ *acid rain*.

8 Woman:   . . . yes, you see, paper, glass bottles and metal can all be used
           again more cheaply and without causing pollution or needing
           to cut down more trees. All these products can easily be ■
           *recycled*.

9 Man:     . . . may be true but the article I read said that we should cut
           down on the amount of energy we use if we want to conserve
           fossil fuels and reduce the pollution they cause. Apparently,
           the only way of producing electricity without pollution is by
           using ■ *nuclear energy*.

10 Man:    Hit it or something, go on, g ... kill it! I can't stand them!
   Woman:  Calm down, and don't be so silly. It won't hurt you – you're
           not a fly, are you? And I'm certainly not going to kill it
           because I like ■ *spiders*.

                                          (Time: 2 minutes 55 seconds)

**E**   This discussion is based on the ideas everyone heard in **D**.

# 20.3  The future and degrees of certainty

Grammar

▶ Ask everyone to look again at 10.2 on modal verbs before they begin these exercises.

## A  *Suggested answers*

1 I'll write to her tomorrow.
   – *offering or promising to do so*
   I'm going to write to her tomorrow.
   – *straightforward statement of intention*
   I was going to write to her tomorrow.
   – *I originally intended to do so, but now I won't OR I may not do so*
   I'll be writing to her tomorrow.
   – *sometime tomorrow this is what I'm going to do*
   I <u>will</u> write to her tomorrow.
   – *an emphatic offer or promise OR expressing determination to do so*
   I'm writing to her tomorrow.
   – *this is already planned (I've set aside time to do it tomorrow)*
   I'll have written to her tomorrow.
   – *I'm going to write today, so tomorrow the letter will have been written*
   I'll have to write to her tomorrow.
   – *it's necessary for me to do so tomorrow*

2 Are we going to make the first move?
   – *Do we intend to do this?*
   Shall we make the first move?
   – *Is it a good idea: do you agree with this suggestion?*
   Do we make the first move?
   – *Are we expected to do this (is this the accepted procedure)?*
   Will we make the first move?
   – *Is this what will happen in the future?*

3 I'm just going to phone them now.
   – *I'm going to make the call straight away*
   I'm about to phone them now.
   – *I'm going to make the call straight away (as first example)*
   I was just about to phone them now.
   – *my intention was to make the call but now I'm not going to OR I'm going to make the call straight away (as first example)*
   I'm phoning them now.
   – *I'm on the phone now OR I'm going to make the call straight away (as first example)*

I've phoned them now.
*– I have made the call and so you don't need to remind me again*
I'll phone them now.
*– I'm offering to make the call straight away* OR *I'm going to make the call straight away (as first example)*

4 Will you help us later?
*– I'm asking you to help us (a request)*
Are you going to help us later?
*– Is it your intention to help us?*
Will you be helping us later?
*– Is this what will be happening later?*
Won't you be helping us later?
*– I thought this is what would be happening later, but perhaps I was misled*
Are you helping us later?
*– Is it your plan to help us?*
Were you going to help us later?
*– Do you intend to help us* OR *Did you intend to help us (and now you've changed your mind)?*
Won't you help us later?
*– Please, I'm asking you to help us (a more persuasive, cajoling request than the first example)* OR *I though this is what you promised, but perhaps I was misled*
Aren't you going to help us later?
*– I thought this is what you intended, but perhaps I was misled*

## B Corrected sentences

1 I'm sure it **won't** rain tomorrow.
2 *no errors*
3 I'll have a drink while I'm **waiting** for her plane to land.
4 The meeting **won't/can't** begin until everyone **has** arrived.
5 *no errors*
6 **Shall** I help you to carry the shopping?
7 I'll be glad when it **is** time to go home.
8 *no errors*

## C Suggested answers

1 will be cut down / will have been cut down
2 will be devastated
3 will have been destroyed
4 will accumulate
5 will (have to) be imposed
6 will have become

7 will lead
8 will      be causing
9 will (have to) take
10 will have to come

**D**  *Suggested answers* (with second column rearranged)

| | |
|---|---|
| 2 She's very unlikely to be on time. | = I'm pretty sure she'll be late. |
| 3 I'm sure she'll be late. | = She can't possibly arrive on time. |
| 4 She'll probably get here on time. | = She's unlikely to be late. |
| 5 She may get here on time. | = I don't know if she's going to be late. |
| 6 I know she'll get here on time. | = She's not going to be late. |
| 7 I expect she'll be here on time. | = I doubt if she'll be late. |
| 8 I'm almost certain she'll be on time. | = There's a slim chance she'll be late. |

**E**  Notice that we tend to be suspicious of someone who says they are absolutely sure about something – just because they say they're sure it doesn't mean they're right!

*Suggested answers*

**100% (certain)**
   *It's going to get warmer.*
   *I'm absolutely sure it will get warmer.*
   *It's sure to get warmer.*
   *It's bound to get warmer.*
**very probable**
   *In all probability it's going to get a great deal warmer.*
   *There's a very good chance that it will get warmer.*
   *In all probability it will get warmer.*
**fairly probable**
   *I wouldn't be surprised if it got warmer.*
   *It's likely to get warmer.*
   *I bet it will get warmer.*
   *It looks as if it will get warmer.*
**50% (uncertain = it's possible)**
   *I guess it might get warmer.*
   *I suppose it might get warmer.*
**fairly improbable**
   *I'm fairly sure it won't get warmer.*

*I doubt if it will get warmer.*
*I don't think it will get warmer.*
**very improbable**
*I'd be surprised if it got warmer.*
*There's not much chance that it will get warmer.*
**0% (certain that it will NOT happen)**
*There's no likelihood that it will get warmer.*
*Of course it won't get warmer.*

**F**   Allow enough time for this freer discussion. There could be a written follow-up of this:

Write a paragraph reporting on the main points of your discussion OR, simply, write a one-page essay answering some of the questions for discussion in **F**.

---

## 20.4   Compound words                          Word study

### A   Compound nouns

You may like to point out to your students that in most compound nouns the main stress is on the first element but with a strong secondary stress on the second element:

| | | | |
|---|---|---|---|
| blackbird | /ˈblæk͵bɜːd/ | classroom | /ˈklɑːs͵ruːm/ |
| toy shop | /ˈtɔɪ ͵ʃɒp/ | lighthouse | /ˈlaɪt͵haʊs/ |
| greenhouse | /ˈgriːn͵haʊs/ | coursebook | /ˈkɔːs͵bʊk/ |
| rainforest | /ˈreɪn ͵fɒrɪst/ | | |

But in these NOUN PHRASES (i.e. adjective + noun) the main stress is often on the noun with a secondary stress on the adjective:

black bird   A crow is a large black bird /͵blæk ˈbɜːd/ with a yellow beak – it's much bigger than a blackbird /ˈblæk ͵bɜːd/.

green house   They have a green house with a red roof.

toy shop   Little Timmy was playing with his toy shop – we can also imagine him playing with toy soldiers (he probably bought his toy shop from a toy shop!!).

▶ However, in context, this pattern is often NOT followed, especially when we are making a special emphasis.

*Answers* (⬛ These are recorded on the cassette.)

charter flight    committee meeting    computer screen
drinking water    flight attendant    food chain
holiday brochure    language teacher    meeting point
ozone layer    palm tree    pet food    post office
pressure group    progress test    safety precautions
steering wheel    telephone call    traffic lights
typing paper    video recorder    waiting room
washing machine    wastepaper basket    water pressure
window cleaner    zoo keeper

## B  Compound adjectives

Again you might like to point out to your students that most
compound adjectives have the main stress on the second element but
with a secondary stress on the first element:

    self-employed  /ˌselfɪmˈplɔɪd/    duty-free  /ˌdjuːtiˈfriː/
    ozone-friendly  /ˌəʊzəʊnˈfrendli/    half-eaten  /ˌhɑːfˈiːtən/
    fourth-floor  /ˌfɔːθˈflɔː/

*Answers* ⬛ These are recorded on the cassette.

good-looking    green-fingered    hard-hearted    hard-working
heart-broken    home-made    ill-informed    loose-fitting
narrow-minded    quick-witted    record-breaking
self-employed    short-staffed    time-consuming    under-paid
user-friendly    well-behaved    well-meaning

# 20.5  The last frontier     Reading

Reading the two passages leads to the discussion in **C**, based on
what has been discovered.

## B  *Answers*

1 warm    southern circumpolar current
2 10%
3 4,000 metres/4 km
4 90%    75%
5 98%
6 Krill    it is the staple diet of most Antarctic wildlife

## 20.6   Spelling and pronunciation 2 – Vowels

**A**   *Some suggested rhymes*   (Some of these only work in R.P.!)

calm – farm      caught – bought      bird – third
sleep – creep      slip – hip      pot – got      look – cook
lunch – crunch      cool – fool      fall – hall      bite – fright
now – cow      toy – boy      there – hair      here – fear
make – fake      note – goat      fuel – dual      tired – hired
tower – power      royal – spoil      player – greyer
lower – grower

**B**   The two examples are recorded on the cassette as well as the three sentences that have to be highlighted in the Student's Book.

**C**   No correct answers are given for these homophones – consult a dictionary, if necessary, to settle any arguments.

**D**   *Answers*   These are recorded on the cassette.

i    mile – title      film – kitchen      fright – island      firm – sir
a    watch – yacht      father – castle      bald – yawn
     share – scarce      ache – vague      hand – factory
     says – any
ea   bear – pear      team – weak      break – steak
     threat – jealous      hearty – sweetheart      fear – dreary
     search – earnest
au   sausage – cauliflower      naughty – daughter
     laugh – draught
ei   receive – perceive      weight – neighbour
     leisure – Leicester      their – heir      foreign – ancient
     height – either
ie   chief – believe      fierce – pier
     friendship – unfriendly      die – pliers
u    bury – guess      bullet – butcher      butter – mustard
     business – busy      refuse – flute      murder – burst
o    monkey – frontier      lose – movement      folk – ghost
     crowd – shower      orange – soften      boy – joyful
     ordinary – glorious
ou   enough – rough      found – plough      bought – court
     cough – trough      soul – although
     through – throughout      should – could
     thorough – borough

oo food – loose    flood – blood    floor – door
foot – book

(Time: 3 minutes 5 seconds)

# E

## 📼 *Transcript and* ANSWERS

Narrator: Write down the words you hear. Listen to the example first.

| | | |
|---|---|---|
| 1 | handkerchief | I don't carry a handkerchief – I prefer to use tissues. |
| 2 | tissues | Have you got any tissues on you? |
| 3 | through | We walked through the park feeling excited. |
| 4 | excitement | Everyone shows their excitement before a long journey. |
| 5 | nuisance | It was a nuisance that we had to queue up. |
| 6 | queue | It was a very long queue. |
| 7 | gauge | I could see from the fuel gauge that I needed some petrol. |
| 8 | awkward | This can is quite awkward to open – can you give me some assistance? |
| 9 | assistance | I need your assistance. |
| 10 | whether | Can you tell me whether she's an acquaintance of yours? |
| 11 | acquaintance | She's not just an acquaintance, she's my fiancée. |
| 12 | fiancée | His fiancée's name is Rosemary, she's learning to play the flute. |
| 13 | practise | You have to practise a lot if you're learning to play a musical instrument. |
| 14 | allowed | Smoking isn't allowed in this building. |
| 15 | sighed | Everyone sighed when they realised it was the end of the exercise. |

(Time: 2 minutes)

## F *Correct spellings*

across    advertisement    aggressive    campaigning
diphthong    disrupted    enthusiastically    extinction
inconceivable    interrupted    replaceable    sanctuary
separate    seize    underdeveloped

## G Make sure everyone does this.

# 20.7 *Keep, hold, stand* and *turn*    Verbs and idioms

## *Answers*

1  held over = postpone
2  turn back = return
3  turned a blind eye = deliberately not notice
4  stand on ceremony = be very formal
5  keep in with = stay on friendly terms with
6  stand up for = support
7  keeps/kept a record = documents
8  holds the record = the fastest/biggest/etc.
9  keep a diary = write regularly in a diary
10  keep him company = stay with him
11  turning point = point where significant change takes place
12  turned down = reject
13  get hold of = reach
14  Hold it! = wait
15  stand up to = withstand
16  stands in for = deputise       hold the fort = take charge temporarily
17  keep your head = don't panic
18  stand on her head = do a headstand
19  stand in your way = prevent someone from doing something
20  kept it back = withhold

▶ Some other related idioms:

| | |
|---|---|
| **keep** | keep up with the Joneses = maintain same material standards as one's neighbours |
| | keep up appearances = continue to do what is expected in public, in order to hide something |
| | keep from = prevent oneself from doing |
| **hold** | hold off = not begin |
| | hold out = last |
| **stand** | stand out = be conspicuous |
| | standpoint = point of view |
| | stand-by = back-up |
| **turn** | turn in = go to bed |
| | turn against = become hostile to |
| | take (it in) turns = do one after the other |

# 21 Here is the news

## 21.1   In the news                          Vocabulary

**B**   *Answers*

1 constituency      proportional representation
2 majority      opposition
3 Senate      Representatives
4 Lords      Commons

▶ Make sure that each group talks about the political set-up in their country/countries.

**C**   *Answers*

The underlying **principle** of English justice is that the defendant is **innocent** until proved guilty.

   In England and Wales, if a person is **suspected** of a serious crime, they are **arrested** and then **questioned** by the police and **charged** with the crime. Then they may be held in **custody** or released on **bail** until their case is heard first at a Magistrates' Court, where they are represented by a **solicitor**. They may then have to wait some time before their case is heard in the local Crown Court or the Central **Criminal** Court (The Old Bailey) in London, where the **defendant** is represented by a **barrister** and the case is heard by a **judge** and a **jury** of twelve men and women. At the end of the **trial** they may be found not guilty and **acquitted** or found guilty and **sentenced**. They may be sent to jail, given a **suspended** sentence or put on **probation**, or perhaps made to pay a **fine**. If they feel they have been wrongly convicted they may **appeal** against their sentence.

▶ Make sure that each group talks about the legal system in their countries/country.

### Extra discussion ideas

Unless this is likely to be a sensitive area for your students, perhaps ask everyone to work in groups and ask their partners:
– which political party they support and why
– which world political leader they admire most and why

– in which political direction their country is likely to move in the future
– what their views are on the following political issues:

nationalisation    privatisation
devolution of power to the regions    the taxation system
spending on defence    public health care

## D   Suggested answers

The manager of the bus company said that some bus services will/may have to be withdrawn in order to save money.
A number of bus passengers are critical of the bus company manager's intention to withdraw some services.
The Minister (of Transport, presumably) said that he/she supports the bus company manager's proposal
The bus company manager has resigned because of all the controversy over the proposal to withdraw some services.
Members of the Cabinet disagreed about the proposal to withdraw bus services and the Minister of Transport has resigned as a result.

## E   Answers

AXE/SCRAP = reduce/dismiss    BACK = support
CALL = request    CLASH = disagree    CURB = restrict
GRAB = confiscate    LOOM = be imminent    OUST = replace
QUIT = resign    SLAM = criticise    SOAR = rise    SWOOP = raid
VOW/PLEDGE = promise

## F   Answers

BATTLE/CLASH/FEUD/ROW = disagreement    BID = attempt
BLAZE = fire    CHIEF = person in charge / leader
DRAMA = happening    FURY/OUTRAGE = anger
LINK = connection    RIDDLE = mystery    SPLIT = division
THREAT = possibility    WAR = rivalry

## G   Remind everyone to do this.

# 21.2   The wrong Wolff                Reading

*Answers*

1 Only one: *The Sun*
2 Two: *The Times* and *The Independent*

3 They were both German-born academics with the same name – an easy mistake to make, but one that should have been checked before publication. Moreover, the one that died was 73, while the famous one is only 61.
4 In case people would hear about the death at second hand.
5 They were both born in Berlin and came to live in London; when they both lived near to each other in Hampstead their phone numbers differed by one digit.
6 To make it ea-si-er for the read-ers of *The Sun* to fol-low. The *Guardian* report is written for more sophisticated readers.

# 21.3  Danger – Hippies!    Reading and listening

▶ IMPORTANT: Allow plenty of time for these integrated activities. The whole sequence is likely to require at least 90 minutes, together with time for preparation and follow-up at home.

Follow the procedure suggested in the Student's Book for each stage of the sequence.

All the activities should be done by students in pairs, though some of the reading can be prepared at home before the lesson. No 'correct answers' are given here, as most of the questions are a basis for discussion.

## 30 May 🔲 This is a listening activity.

*Transcript*

**Thursday 30 May**
Male newsreader: Here is the news. The group of 300 hippies who set up camp on a farm in Somerset earlier this week have promised to leave quietly. The convoy of 100 vehicles had been on the move for several days, after being prevented from setting up camp at Stonehenge, where they wanted to hold a free pop festival to celebrate the summer solstice. Wiltshire police banned this festival and escorted the slow-moving convoy out of the county into Somerset.

The hippies, who call themselves 'peace people', live off social security handouts and collect weekly unemployment benefit. There are also many school-age children amongst them. Their homes are primitive home-made tents, called 'benders', and ancient converted buses or vans. According to police many of these vehicles are unroadworthy and their drivers are breaking the law and causing a hazard to traffic. A number of hippies have been charged with drug offences since they first set up camp at the farm.

The owner of the farm at Lytes Cary near Somerton, Mr Les Attwood, who suffers from heart disease, claims that the uninvited campers have caused serious damage to his crops.

A High Court injunction ordering the hippies . . .

(Time: 1 minute 25 seconds)

**31 May**  This is a reading activity. Follow the procedure in the Student's Book.

**31 May to 9 June**  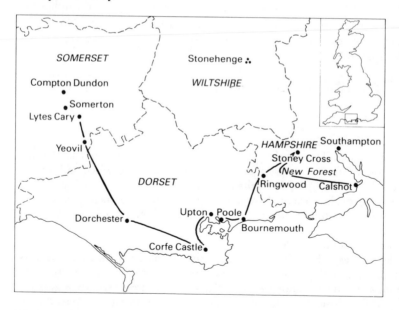 As they listen to the broadcasts, students have to mark the route on the map in the Student's Book AND note down the single most important event of each day. Perhaps pause between each news bulletin for everyone to complete their notes. Halfway through (at the point marked with ★★★ in the transcript) stop the tape for everyone to discuss what they have heard so far.

The news broadcasts, although they do report the events that actually happened, are slanted against the hippies in a decidedly non-BBC manner.

*Complete map*

*Transcript*

**Saturday 31 May**
Female newsreader: Here is the news. The so-called peace convoy finally left Somerset today but were met by 300 police in riot gear who blocked

the main road into Dorset. As Somerset police would not allow them to turn back into Somerset, for most of the day they were parked along the main Yeovil to Dorchester road. Finally, after the intervention of local MP, Mr Paddy Ashdown, the police agreed that the convoy could move on but only in five separate groups at half-hourly intervals. Local farmers, fearing that their own land might be invaded like Mr Attwood's, blocked all gates and access along the route. At the moment the five groups are reported to be heading in the direction of . . .

**Sunday 1 June**

Male newsreader: Here is the news. The so-called peace convoy reassembled last night near the village of Corfe Castle. This morning the convoy was forced to move on.

A police road block was set up at Upton and, after angry scenes, a police vehicle rammed the leading vehicle and forced it off the road. Following this incident, the twelve occupants of the vehicle were arrested. So far today there have been twenty arrests.

The convoy has just started moving again, but police are blocking all roads into the holiday resorts of Poole and Bournemouth. After leaving . . .

**Monday 2 June**

Male newsreader: Here is the news. Last night the 115 vehicles of the so-called peace convoy began a slow-moving journey through the outskirts of Poole and Bournemouth. At about midnight they crossed the Dorset border at Ringwood and drove into Hampshire finally stopping in the early hours at Stoney Cross, a picturesque beauty spot in the New Forest.

This morning, Hampshire police officers toured the area in loudspeaker vans informing them that they must leave by 3 p.m., but many vehicles are now out of fuel and the 300 hippies have apparently decided to defy the police by refusing to move on again.

Chief Constable of Hampshire, John Duke, described them as 'anarchists who were spoiling a beauty spot and harassing residents and holiday-makers alike'. He said that they were . . .

**Tuesday 3 June**

Female newsreader: Here is the news. In the House of Commons today the Home Secretary described the peace convoy as 'a band of medieval brigands, who have no respect for the law or for the rights of others'. In a statement to the House . . .

**Wednesday 4 June**

Male newsreader: Here is the news. In a court hearing today one member of the so-called peace convoy who was arrested at the weekend has been sent to prison after his hearse ran into a police vehicle and damaged it. Local residents near their camp in the New Forest have complained that . . .

**Thursday 5 June**

Male newsreader: Here is the news. This morning the Cabinet discussed the matter of the so-called peace convoy and some ministers are understood to have urged changes in the law to prevent a reoccurrence of the events of the past two weeks. According to the Home Office, the present situation remains a matter for the police to deal with and there is no likelihood of the army being called in . . .

**Friday 6 June**

Female newsreader: Here is the news. As expected this morning the high court issued an order for the so-called peace convoy to disperse and leave the area of Stoney Cross in Hampshire. They have been given one week to organise their departure so that they can leave in an orderly way. During the night a flock of sheep was attacked by stray dogs from the convoy and the owner of the flock, . . .

**Saturday 7 June**

Male newsreader: Here is the news. According to our reporter, the so-called peace convoy at Stoney Cross shows no sign of moving on, despite warnings from police. A large tent has been erected . . .

**Sunday 8 June**

Male newsreader: Here is the news. The 300 hippies in the New Forest today appealed for extra time to organise their departure. They say that their vehicles need repairs and that they will be unable to drive away for several days. The site at Stoney Cross has been described by local residents as 'noisy, unhealthy, dangerous and filthy'.

Meanwhile in London . . .

**Monday 9 June**

Female newsreader: Here is the news. The so-called peace convoy is no more. At 4.30 this morning, in a carefully planned operation, 440 police officers from four counties under the command of John Duke, Chief Constable of Hampshire, entered the camp, woke up the hippies and forced them to leave the site. 124 out of 129 vehicles were impounded because they were unroadworthy or unlicensed. 38 people were arrested for possession of drugs. The hippies, now on foot, started to walk through the rain in the direction of Ringwood but as the rain became heavier most of them accepted the offer of free buses to Calshot, where they were given food and free rail tickets to their homes. The police operation . . .

(Time: 5 minutes 30 seconds)

## Your reactions   Time now for a group discussion of the events so far.

**10 June and 12 June**   This can be set as homework, but should be discussed in class.

*Suggested answers*

1 Sympathetic
2 No need to go in at 4 a.m.; no need for so many police officers; no consideration given to the consequences of 'neutralising' the Convoy
3 Hmm: they seem more concerned with criticising the police and the Government. Perhaps the main point is that 'someone' is going to have to come up with a permanent solution, rather than a series of temporary ones.
4 To avoid further violence
5 He doesn't seem to like them very much
6 To point out that the police behaved kindly – 'the firm, caring operation by the police'

▶ Ask everyone to what extent reading the editorial and the letter has changed their view on the events of May to June.

---

# 21.4   **Semantic markers**   Effective writing

**A + B**   Follow the procedure suggested in the Student's Book. Perhaps highlight the relevant points in your own copy of the Student's Book.

**C**   *Suggested answers*

**Although it must be admitted that / Although** hard drugs can never be totally defeated, there are a number of steps that should be taken to reduce their use. **Furthermore / What is more** these steps must be taken at once – before it is too late.
   **Firstly / In the first place / First of all,** national governments throughout the world must control the use and supply of drugs within their borders. **This means that / It follows that** international organisations must coordinate individual states' policies. States which 'supply' drugs may be pursuing contradictory policies to states that 'consume' them and **as a result of this / consequently / this means that** time and effort is frequently wasted.
   Secondly, ...

## 21.5    **Reports and opinions**    Creative writing

**A + B**    Follow the procedure suggested in the Student's Book. Your students might prefer to use their own news photos instead of or as well as the ones in the Student's Book.

## 21.6    *Back, front* and *side*    Idioms

*Answers*

1  front-page news = important news
2  background = family, interests, etc.
3  on the side = unofficially
4  side-by-side = next to each other
5  behind my back = without my knowledge
6  front-runner = favourite
7  backhand = tennis stroke
8  back you up = support
9  backed out of = withdraw
10  National Liberation Front = political/military group
11  back-up copy = reserve
12  backwards = in reverse
13  back-bencher = non-office-holding
14  side-effect = secondary result
15  back to front = the wrong way round
16  a front = a way of hiding
17  front      back
18  from side to side = swaying
19  backed down = accept defeat
20  sidetracked = distract

# 22 Education

## 22.1 Schools and colleges

Vocabulary and listening

**B** *Answers*

1 nursery / nursery school / playgroup
2 primary     secondary     higher / tertiary
3 General Certificate of Secondary Education
   General Certificate of Education – Advanced level     Sixth
4 terms     semesters
5 public
6 degree     Bachelor of Arts     Bachelor of Science
   Bachelor of Education
   thesis (a dissertation is usually shorter than a thesis)
   Master of Arts (or MSc: Master of Science)
   Doctor of Philosophy (i.e. a doctorate)

**D** 📼 The descriptions of the three systems are greatly
simplified. Depending on the interest this arouses, you may like to
supply your students with more information.

**E + F** Follow the procedure suggested in the Student's Book. In E,
direct the class to the appropriate option.

*Transcript*

David:     Well, in Britain, from the ages of five to about eleven you start
            off at a primary school, and then from eleven to sixteen you go
            on to a secondary school or a comprehensive school and at
            sixteen you take GCSE examinations. After this, some children
            take ... er ... vocational courses or even start work. Others stay on
            at school for another two years to take A levels. And at the age
            of eighteen, after A levels, they might finish their education or go
            on to a course of higher education at a college or university, and
            that's usually for three years.

Michael:   Well, it depends on what state you're in but ... er ... most kids in
            the United States start school at about six ... er ... when they go to
            elementary school and that goes from the 1st grade up to the 6th

grade. Some kids go to a kindergarten the year before that. Then they go on to junior high school, that's about eleven, and that's the 7th, 8th and 9th grades. And then they go on to senior high school around age fourteen ... er ... starting in the 10th grade and finishing in the 12th grade usually. Some students ... er ... will leave school at sixteen and they'll start work, but ... er ... most of them stay on to graduate ... er ... from high school at age eighteen. In the first year at high school or college students are called 'freshmen', in the second they're called 'sophomores', in the third year ... er ... we call them 'juniors' and in the fourth year they're called 'seniors'. Now ... er ... er ... a lot of high school graduates ... er ... then go to college or university and they do a four-year first degree course. Some of them might go to junior college ... er ... which is a two-year course.

Nicolette: Well, in Australia, well in most states anyway, children start their primary education at five after perhaps a brief time in kindergarten. They will stay at primary school until they're about eleven, then they'll either stay there or go to an intermediate school for a couple of years. Then they start high school usually twelve or thirteen, which you start in the third form. Now, after three years at high school ... um ... you sit a general exam, some states call it School Certificate ... er ... and that is a sort of general qualification. After that you can leave school at sixteen or you can go on and sit your University Entrance examination, which then gives you entrée into a university or it's another useful qualification, and from then on you go to various sorts of higher education.

(Time: 2 minutes 40 seconds)

---

# 22.2   *-ing* and *to* __          Grammar

**A**   *Suggested answers and continuations*

1 We stopped to eat our sandwiches when ...
  *– we were walking along and then stopped in order to have a picnic*
   ... we saw a suitable place to sit down.
  We stopped eating our sandwiches when ...
  *– we were eating our sandwiches but stopped doing so, perhaps suddenly*
   ... it started to rain and we ran for cover.

2 I won't forget to meet her because ...
  *– this is something I'll remember to do (in the future)*
   ... I've made a note in my diary about it.
  I won't forget meeting her because ...

*– this is something I remember vividly (in the past)*
    ... it was a memorable occasion.

3 Sometimes she didn't remember to hand in her work because ...
    *– this is what she forgot (in the past)*
        ... she used to be so absent-minded
    Sometimes she doesn't remember to hand in her work because ...
    *– this is what she forgets to do (in the present)*
        ... she is so absent-minded.
    Sometimes she doesn't remember handing in her work because ...
    *– she does hand in the work but she forgets whether she has done so or not*
        ... she has such a short memory.

4 The lecturer went on to tell the audience about ...
    *– this is what she did next*
        ... the eventful voyage home.
    The lecturer went on telling the audience about ...
    *– she continued the same story, perhaps after an interruption*
        ... the theory of relativity.

5 We tried to get through to her on the phone but ...
    *– this is what we attempted to do*
        ... there was no answer.
    We tried getting through to her on the phone but ...
    *– this is the method we tried and perhaps another method succeeded*
    OR *this is what we attempted to do (as first example)*
        ... without success, so one of us went round to her flat.

6 I used to write a lot of 250-word essays but ...
    *– this was what I customarily did in the past*
        ... not any more: now I write much longer ones.
    I'm used to writing a lot of 250-word essays but ...
    *– this is what I am accustomed to doing (now)*
        ... this subject is really causing me difficulties.
    I usually write a lot of 250-word essays but ...
    *– this is what I normally do*
        ... recently I haven't written any.

7 I regret to tell you that your application was unsuccessful because ...
    *– I'm telling you this bad news now (rather formal style)*
        ... your qualifications are not suitable.
    I regret telling you that your application was unsuccessful because ...
    *– I'm sorry that I told you this, perhaps because you reacted so badly*
        ... I didn't think you'd burst into tears about it.

8 He'd like to study alone because ...
   – *this is what he wants to do now or soon*
       ... he has an important exam next week.
   He likes studying alone because ...
   – *this is what he always/generally prefers*
       ... he finds it easier to concentrate.
   Studying alone is what he likes because ...
   – *this is what he enjoys*
       ... he can spend all night at it if he wants to.

## B   Corrected sentences

1 Although I was looking forward to **meeting** her, I was afraid to make a bad impression.
2 **Smoking** is not allowed in the classroom but students are permitted **to smoke** in the cafeteria.
3 Everyone was beginning **to get** nervous before the exam, but once we began **to realise** that we were all in the same boat we began to feel better.
4 The man denied **having** committed the crime but he failed **to convince** the magistrate.
5 They made me **sit** down and wouldn't let me **leave** without **apologising** for being rude to them.
6 To get into university you have to **have** the right qualifications.
7 Don't forget **to make** notes before you start to write the essay, and remember **to check** your work through afterwards.
8 You can't expect **to achieve** success without **working** hard.

## C   Suggested answers

**Anne** ... agreed   arranged   attempted   began   chose
consented   continued   decided   failed   forgot
happened   hesitated   hoped   intended   managed
meant   preferred   pretended   promised   proposed
refused   tried   wanted   wished   **to read *War and Peace.***

**Bill** ... advised   allowed   asked   couldn't help   chose
encouraged   expected   forbade   forced   got
helped   intended   invited   meant   ordered
persuaded   preferred   recommended   taught   told
wanted   wished   **me to read *Crime and Punishment.***

**Cathy** ... appreciated   avoided   began   couldn't help
considered   contemplated   continued   delayed
denied   detested   disliked   enjoyed   felt like
finished   gave up   intended   missed   postponed

| | | | |
|---|---|---|---|
| practised | preferred | proposed | recommended |
| resented | spent | an hour | suggested | tried |

**reading *Don Quixote.***

**Dennis** ... delayed    detested    discovered    disliked
found    got    heard    imagined    missed    noticed
preferred    prevented    resented    saw    watched

**me reading *A Tale of Two Cities.***

**Elaine** ... admitted    assumed    decided    denied
discovered    dreamt/dreamed    expected    found
found out    forgot    guessed    heard    hoped
imagined    knew    noticed    pretended    realised    saw
suggested    thought    understood    **that I was reading *Emma.***

---

# 22.3   The Cat Sat on the test          Reading

▶ NOTE   There is more reading in this unit than in previous 'language units'. This reading passage and the one in 22.7 can be prepared at home.

## A   *Answers*

1  To educate the many rather than nurture the brightest few
2  Nearly half of them
3  So that they get term grades
4  Scholastic Aptitude Test      17      To assess students' suitability for college or university education
5  California Achievement Test      8, 10, 13 and 17      As a way of assessing students on a national, as opposed to local, basis

## B   *Answers*

1  So that the computer can mark the tests
2  The state (i.e. Maryland, Texas, etc.) and the local school board
3  There are none – the Cat (or the equivalent Iowa or Stanford test) is the only national assessment; the Sat is taken at the age of 17
4  Continuous assessment is carried out on students' class work, homework, occasional essays, and Scan-Tron exercises which produce term grades
5  In the UK pupils and teacher form a 'team against the examiner'; in the USA the teacher may be 'the enemy' because she assesses the students

6 Statements are more likely to be 'true'; choose the longest answer or answer (c)
7 Iowa and Stanford tests in some states
8 Reading vocabulary, spelling, language expression, maths (and other basic skills)
9 Ones who are not bright, white and middle class – especially poor black or Puerto Rican students
10 To boost their image in the market (i.e. to attract better applicants); some promising students don't apply, thinking they are not good enough

**C** *Answers*

*fuming* = very angry    *pernicious* = harmful
*nurture* = cultivate    *A-student* = bright pupil
*utilitarian* = practical    *quantification* = measurement
*continuous assessment* = evaluation throughout the course
*grades* = marks    *aspirants* = hoping to be admitted
*idiosyncrasy* = unconventional behaviour
*fast stream* = top class    *efficacy* = effectiveness
*much-vaunted* = over-praised

**D**  Besides discussing these questions, students will probably be keen to compare the American experience with their own.

---

# 22.4  First day at school                              Listening

Laurie Lee was born in 1914. His best-known book is *Cider with Rosie*, an account of his childhood in rural Gloucestershire. He is well-known as a poet and for two autobiographical works about his travels round Spain: *As I Walked Out One Midsummer Morning* and *A Rose For Winter*.

Evelyn Waugh (1903–66) is one of the foremost English novelists of the 20th century. His most enjoyable satirical novels are: *Scoop, Brideshead Revisited, A Handful of Dust* and *Black Mischief*.

**A + B + C + D**  ▭  Follow the procedure suggested in the Student's Book. These are straightforward readings from the two books, for everyone to listen to and then discuss.

*Scripts*

**A**  From *Cider with Rosie* by Laurie Lee.

The morning came, without any warning, when my sisters surrounded me, wrapped me in scarves, tied up my bootlaces, thrust a cap on my head, and stuffed a baked potato in my pocket.

'What's this?' I said.

'You're starting school today.'

'I ain't. I'm stopping 'ome.'

'Now, come on, Laurie. You're a big boy now.'

'I ain't.'

'You are.'

'Boo-hoo.'

They picked me up bodily, kicking and bawling, and carried me up to the road.

'Boys who don't go to school, get put in boxes, and turn into rabbits and get chopped up Sundays.'

I felt this was overdoing it rather, but I said no more after that.

I spent that first day picking holes in paper, then went home in a smouldering temper.

'What's the matter, Laurie? Didn't you like it at school then?'

'They never gave me the present!'

'Present? What present?'

'They said they'd give me a present.'

'Well, now, I'm sure they didn't.'

'They did! They said: "You're Laurie Lee, ain't you? Well, you just sit there for the present." I sat there all day but I never got it. I ain't going back there again!'

(Time: 1 minute 15 seconds)

**B**  From *Decline and Fall* by Evelyn Waugh.

The masters went upstairs.

'That's your little mob in there,' said Grimes; 'you let them out at eleven.'

'But what am I to teach them?' said Paul, in a sudden panic.

'Oh, I shouldn't try to teach them anything, not just yet, anyway. Just keep them quiet.'

'Now that's a thing I've never learned to do,' sighed Mr Prendergast.

Paul watched him amble into his classroom at the end of the passage, where a burst of applause greeted his arrival. Dumb with terror he went into his own classroom.

Ten boys sat before him, their hands folded, their eyes bright with expectation.

'Good morning, sir,' said the one nearest to him.

'Good morning,' said Paul.

'Good morning, sir,' said the next.

'Good morning,' said Paul.

'Good morning, sir,' said the next.

'Oh, shut up,' said Paul.

At this the boy took out a handkerchief and began to cry quietly.

'Oh, sir,' came a chorus of reproach, 'you've hurt his feelings. He's very sensitive; it's his Welsh blood, you know; it makes people very emotional. Say "Good morning" to him, sir, or he won't be happy all day. After all, it is a good morning, isn't it, sir?'

'Silence!' shouted Paul above the uproar, and for a few moments things were quieter.

(Time: 1 minute 20 seconds)

---

# 22.5  Making an emphasis                    Word study

**A**   Without the intensifiers, the paragraph seems rather limp:

Our class picnic nearly turned out to be a disappointment because of the rain and the number of people who dropped out at the last minute, but to everyone's amazement it was a success and we all had an enjoyable time. The people who had decided not to come must have been furious.

**B**   *Suggested answers*

**very/extremely**

| | | | | |
|---|---|---|---|---|
| clever | cross | different | disappointing | enjoyable |
| happy | helpful | powerful | proud | sleepy | surprised |

**absolutely**

| | | | |
|---|---|---|---|
| amazed | amazing | brilliant | catastrophic |
| disastrous | fantastic | idiotic | perfect | wonderful |

▶ Perhaps point out that *really* can be used to emphasise all the adjectives listed.

**C**   *Suggested answers*

**great**

| | | | | |
|---|---|---|---|---|
| amount | anger | detail | difference | disappointment |
| enjoyment | excitement | failure | friend | fun |
| happiness | help | improvement | power | pride |
| quantity | show | skill | strength | success |
| surprise | understanding | wealth | | |

**deep**

love    sigh    trouble

**big**

difference    help    improvement    surprise

**large**

amount    proportion    quantity

**heavy**
    sigh    drinker    smoker    snow    traffic
**high**
    pressure    price    quality    speed
**strong**
    opinion    smell    sense of humour
**absolute/complete/total**
    catastrophe    failure    fool    idiot    nonsense

## 22.6 Using stress     Pronunciation

**B** *Words with stresses marked* 🔲 These are recorded on the cassette.

acádemy   académic
árt   artístic
biólogy   biológical
bótany   botánical
chémist   chémistry   chémical
consúlt   consultátion
económics   económical
   ecónomy
éducate   educátional
exámine   examinátion
geógraphy   geográphical
grámmar   grammátical
hístory   histórical

lécture   lécturer
líterature   líterary
máths   mathemátics
   mathemátical
phýsics   phýsical
pólitics   polítical
sécond   sécondary
sécretary   secretárial
socíety   sociólogy
spécial   spécialise
   specialisátion   speciálity
statístics   statístical
zoólogy   zoológical

(Time: 1 minute 40 seconds)

**C** *Sentences with stresses marked* 🔲 These are recorded on the cassette.

2 Máths is an ínteresting súbject but I dón't wánt to be subjécted to a lóng lécture about it, thánk you very múch!
3 Whát a lóvely présent! I was présent when they presénted her with the awárd.
4 Wáit a mínute – I just neéd to make a minúte adjústment to this machíne.
5 Whén are you permítted to úse the emérgency éxit?
6 You neéd a spécial pérmit to úse this éntrance.
7 I've réad the cóntents of the bóok and nów I féel quite contént.

8 After our dessért, we wátched a fílm abóut some sóldiers who desérted and escáped into the désert and joíned a gróup of rébels.
9 Whén a métal óbject cóols dówn it contrácts.
10 This cóntract is inválid becáuse it hásn't been sígned.
11 The péople rebélled becáuse they objécted to the góvernment's pólicies.
12 I dón't nórmally mínd being insúlted – but I dó when such dréadful ínsults are úsed.

(Time: 1 minute 25 seconds)

## 22.7 That sixth sense  Reading and writing

**A**  These are questions for discussion, there are no 'correct answers'.

**B**  Perhaps get everyone to prepare the written task together with a partner. The completed letter could be 'delivered' to another student, who might reply in the role of Tom Smithies.

## 22.8 *Pick, pull, put* and *set*  Verbs and idioms

**A**  *Answers*

1 pick up a skill/language = learn, perhaps without being taught
2 put her up to it = give her the idea
3 pick me up = collect / give a lift    put yourself out = make special effort, cause inconvenience
4 putting me on    pulling my leg
5 pulled it off = succeed
6 set back = delay    put back = postpone
7 pick your pocket = steal from your pocket/handbag
8 put it together = assemble    set up = ready for use
9 set in = last a long time    put off = postpone
10 put them up = give them a bed    put them off = discourage
11 picking my teeth = using a toothpick    picking up the bill = paying
12 pulling out = leaving    pick-up = small truck    pulled in = drive off the road    pulling up = stop    picked up speed = go faster

# B  *Answers*

After she had **picked** our brains on the feasibility of the idea she **set** about **putting** forward her plans to the committee. Unfortunately, she didn't **put** the ideas across very well. As soon as she sat down, people began to **pick** holes in her arguments. They said she was trying to **pull** the wool over their eyes. She felt that everyone was **picking** on her unfairly and she knew that she was being **put** down. She **put** this down to her poor presentation and she felt terribly up**set**, but she had to **pull** herself together, **put** on a smile and **put** up with the humiliation.

pick someone's brains = use their knowledge
set about = begin
put forward = propose
put the idea across/over = communicate
pick holes = find fault
pull the wool over someone's eyes = deceive
pick on someone = victimise
put someone down = humiliate
put something down to = attribute
upset = unhappy or angry
pull yourself together = control yourself
put on a smile = pretend to smile
put up with = tolerate

▶ Some other related idioms:

| | |
|---|---|
| **set** | set out = begin (journey) |
| | set up = establish |
| | set to music |
| | set aside = not take into consideration |
| | set off = start sudden activity |
| | a setback = a cause of delay |
| **pull** | pull through = recover |
| **put** | put forward = move to earlier time |
| **pick** | pick someone up = make 'friends' |

# 23 Science and technology

---

## 23.1 Scientists and engineers
Vocabulary and listening

**B** *Answers*

1 screw/woodscrew    nut    bolt    washer    nail
   drawing pin    paper clip    hook    bracket    hinge
2 push-button    lever    handle    dial/gauge    knob
   switch    catch
3 hammer    mallet    chisel    screwdriver    pliers
   spanner    saw    electric drill

**C** These are questions for discussion – there are no 'correct answers'.

**D** *Transcript with* SUGGESTED ANSWERS

Narrator: What are they talking about? Listen carefully to these extracts and follow the instructions in your book.

1 Woman *(in a friendly, non-patronising tone of voice – talking to a group of adults):* . . . as you all know it's quite hard to use one at first because it feels very strange and unstable, quite frightening, especially for an adult, but they say that, once you've learned, you never forget. In fact, once you've got the knack it's easy, isn't it? Did you know that when they were first introduced in the 19th century, there was a law that you had to ring the bell all the time to warn people you were coming . . .
(BICYCLES)

2 Man *(in a superior, condescending tone of voice – talking to an adult):* . . . Yes, you see, it's the force of attraction between any two objects. The strength of the force depends on the mass of the objects and the distance between them. Er ... the most obvious effect is the way objects on the surface of the earth are attracted towards the centre of the earth . . .
(GRAVITY/GRAVITATION)

3 Woman *(in a patronising tone of voice – talking down to a child or an adult):* . . . as it comes down it goes relatively slowly – 100 to 1,000 miles per hour and you can't see it, but the return stroke

goes up from the earth to the cloud and it goes at over 87,000 miles per hour and that's the one you can see, you see, the one that goes back up. It's really just a very large, powerful spark. The distance in miles you are away from it is the time in seconds between it and the sound you hear . . .
(LIGHTNING)

4 Man (*in an enthusiastic tone of voice – talking to children but not talking down*): . . . Well, they were first discovered in 1895 and they can penetrate matter that is opaque to light. Some matter is more transparent to them than others, which means you can see inside somebody. They are actually quite dangerous and people who work with them wear special protective clothing . . .
(X-RAYS)

5 Man (*in a bored tone of voice, as if it's a lecture he's given too often – talking to a group of children or students*): . . . ordinary light consists of electromagnetic waves of different frequencies and phase. This is a bundle of waves of the same frequency and phase. You can create the beams from a ruby rod or a tube of carbon dioxide that's stimulated with flashes of ordinary light. The word is an acronym for Light Amplification by the Stimulated Emission of Radiation. Now, does anybody . . .
(LASERS)

6 Man (*in a friendly, intimate tone of voice, as if talking quietly to one person so that others can't hear*): . . . they're all types of fungus. There are many different kinds of them but the best known are the ones used in cooking and brewing. When they're mixed with sugar they cause the sugar to ferment and two things happen: first carbon dioxide is given off and second alcohol is formed, but when the proportion reaches 12% it's all killed off naturally . . .
(YEAST)

7 Woman (*in a good-humoured, slightly sarcastic tone of voice – talking to a small group or individual child or adult*): . . . Well, it might be useful to have them with you but usually they're too heavy to carry around so you have to go to a special place to consult it. They don't have an index or even a table of contents but they do have cross-references, but still it's relatively easy to use them . . .
(ENCYCLOPEDIAS)

8 Man (*loudly but neutral, addressing a large group of adults*): . . . in contact with each other, there's a resistance to movement between them. The main reason why we use ball bearings and lubricating oil is to counteract this: the main reason why rubber is used in tyres and shoes is to increase the effect of it . . .
(FRICTION)

9 Man (*patiently, as if explaining something for the third time but still not losing patience – talking to an adult or maybe a child*): . . . No, it's the process whereby materials are used again. Normally, it is

cheaper to do this because it's more energy-efficient. On the other hand, one material that's hard to deal with in this way is plastic – there are so many types that it's very difficult to separate . . . (RECYCLING)

10 Woman *(impatiently – talking to a class of children or students):* . . . and their molecules all contain hydrogen atoms some of which separate from the molecules when dissolved in water. The hydrogen atoms become electrically charged and they have a strong tendency to react with other substances. Vinegar? Yes, that's right, yes, that is one, yes. Another one that's used in all kinds of industrial processes is . . .      (ACIDS)

(Time: 4 minutes 30 seconds)

---

## 23.2   Astronaut wanted                    Reading

### A   *Answers*

1 Physical fitness and psychological tests
2 A former astronaut who is overseeing the tests and fielding questions from the press
3 More than 3,500 – the exact number is not given
4 150 are being tested this week
5 They are all 21–40, speak a foreign language, are British, and have a degree in science, engineering or medicine
6 Four

### B   *Answers*

1 She was not worried about the morning's medical fitness tests but was apprehensive about the afternoon's psychological ones
2 Because of the exercise they have been taking AND because of the camera lights
3 Because he has done research work on micro-gravity
4 They don't have to know Russian (but the training may well include Russian lessons)
5 Because they are a 'rarity': scientists who speak a foreign language
6 She is very scathing about it, criticising the poor train services and difficult timetables

(None of the people interviewed were shortlisted, by the way.)

### Extra discussion ideas
Work in pairs. Make a list of the pros and cons of YOURSELVES

taking part in an international space flight to:
– orbit the Earth        – land on Mars
– land on the Moon       – travel to another solar system

Then join another pair and compare your ideas. Decide which of the flights YOU would be most interested in taking part in and which you'd be least interested in.

## 23.3   How does it work?                    Listening

**B**  📼  *Answers*

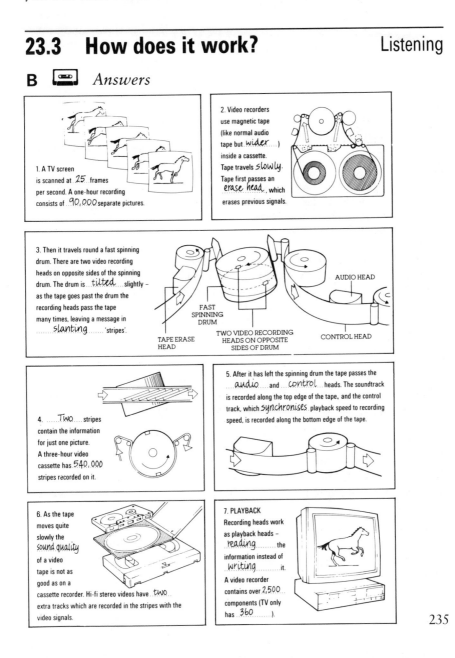

1. A TV screen is scanned at *25* frames per second. A one-hour recording consists of *90,000* separate pictures.

2. Video recorders use magnetic tape (like normal audio tape but *wider*) inside a cassette. Tape travels *slowly*. Tape first passes an *erase head*, which erases previous signals.

3. Then it travels round a fast spinning drum. There are two video recording heads on opposite sides of the spinning drum. The drum is *tilted* slightly – as the tape goes past the drum the recording heads pass the tape many times, leaving a message in *slanting* 'stripes'.

AUDIO HEAD

FAST SPINNING DRUM

TAPE ERASE HEAD

TWO VIDEO RECORDING HEADS ON OPPOSITE SIDES OF DRUM

CONTROL HEAD

4. *Two* stripes contain the information for just one picture. A three-hour video cassette has *540,000* stripes recorded on it.

5. After it has left the spinning drum the tape passes the *audio* and *control* heads. The soundtrack is recorded along the top edge of the tape, and the control track, which *synchronises* playback speed to recording speed, is recorded along the bottom edge of the tape.

6. As the tape moves quite slowly the *sound quality* of a video tape is not as good as on a cassette recorder. Hi-fi stereo videos have *two* extra tracks which are recorded in the stripes with the video signals.

7. PLAYBACK Recording heads work as playback heads – *reading* the information instead of *writing* it. A video recorder contains over *2,500* components (TV only has *360*).

235

## Transcript

Presenter: How does a video recorder work?

Woman: Right, well, to produce a colour TV picture an enormous amount of information is required: on a TV the screen is scanned at 25 frames per second, that means every second 25 separate pictures flash across the screen of your TV. A one-hour recording alone consists of 90,000 separate pictures. Video recorders use magnetically coated tape, it's the same as normal audio tape but wider, inside a cassette. This tape travels fairly slowly and as it travels, the tape first passes an erase head, which erases previous signals and then it travels around a fast spinning drum. There are two video recording heads on opposite sides of the spinning drum and the video track is recorded in diagonal stripes across the tape.

Well, the system works like this: this drum is tilted slightly at an angle from the tape so that as the tape goes past this rapidly spinning drum the recording heads pass the tape repeatedly many times, and thereby leaving a message in slanting 'stripes'. OK, so two stripes contain the information required for just one picture. A three-hour video cassette for instance would have 540,000 stripes recorded on it. Then after it's left the spinning drum the tape passes two more heads: the audio head and the control head. The soundtrack is recorded along the top edge of the tape and the control track, which synchronises playback speed to recording speed, is recorded along the bottom edge of the tape. Since the tape moves quite slowly the sound quality of a video tape is not as good as on a cassette recorder. Um ... and because of this hi-fi stereo videos have two extra tracks which are recorded in the stripes together with the video signals.

So to play back the tape the same process is used but with the recording heads working as playback heads, so ... er ... sort of reading the information instead of writing it.

A video recorder contains over 2,500 components, a television only has 360, but the greatest wear is on the recording/playback head, which may need replacing after only about three years.

(Time: 2 minutes 25 seconds)

**C** 📼 Students should make notes as they hear how compact discs work. It may help for them to see this diagram afterwards – it may be photocopied if required.

⟫→

# COMPACT DISCS

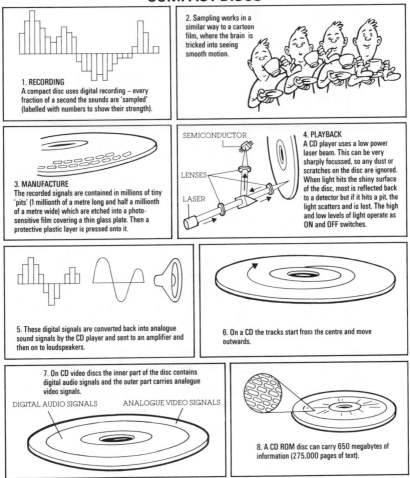

1. RECORDING
A compact disc uses digital recording – every fraction of a second the sounds are 'sampled' (labelled with numbers to show their strength).

2. Sampling works in a similar way to a cartoon film, where the brain is tricked into seeing smooth motion.

3. MANUFACTURE
The recorded signals are contained in millions of tiny 'pits' (1 millionth of a metre long and half a millionth of a metre wide) which are etched into a photosensitive film covering a thin glass plate. Then a protective plastic layer is pressed onto it.

SEMICONDUCTOR
LENSES
LASER

4. PLAYBACK
A CD player uses a low power laser beam. This can be very sharply focussed, so any dust or scratches on the disc are ignored. When light hits the shiny surface of the disc, most is reflected back to a detector but if it hits a pit, the light scatters and is lost. The high and low levels of light operate as ON and OFF switches.

5. These digital signals are converted back into analogue sound signals by the CD player and sent to an amplifier and then on to loudspeakers.

6. On a CD the tracks start from the centre and move outwards.

7. On CD video discs the inner part of the disc contains digital audio signals and the outer part carries analogue video signals.
DIGITAL AUDIO SIGNALS     ANALOGUE VIDEO SIGNALS

8. A CD ROM disc can carry 650 megabytes of information (275,000 pages of text).

© Cambridge University Press 1991

**D** For this Communication activity, the class should be divided into an even number of pairs, so that pairs of pairs can be formed later. Half the pairs look at Activity 62, where they see how a movie projector works; the other half look at Activity 56, where they see how a movie soundtrack works.

## Transcript

Presenter: How does a compact disc work?
Man: There are three headings I'd like to look at ... um ... to explain to you the workings of a compact disc. Let's look first at recording,

secondly at manufacture and thirdly at playback. OK: recording. A compact disc uses a digital technique. Now, digital recording means that it uses 'sampling'. Sampling means that every fraction of a second the sounds recorded are labelled with numbers to show their strength. This is similar to the way for instance ... um ... a cartoon character is animated. Now, in real life if you imagine somebody drinking a cup of tea, it happens in a very smooth motion; on a cartoon, say you're watching Mickey Mouse drinking a cup of tea, which would ... this would c ... consist of maybe 24 separate pictures per second which gives the illusion of somebody drinking and the eye can't detect the jerkiness of the action by the way the shutter works. Now sampling sound works in exactly the same way: the ear can't hear the gaps between the numbers.

OK, now let's look at the manufacture of a compact disc. What happens is that the recorded message, which is basically a series of ON and OFF signals is contained in millions of tiny 'pits' which are etched into a photo-sensitive film which covers a thin glass plate. These pits are tiny: they're about a millionth of a metre long and about half a millionth of a metre wide. OK, so this is then photographically developed, the plate I mean is photographically developed and then coated with silver. And then over the top of that a protective plastic layer is pressed onto it and this explains the longevity of a ... of a CD, unlike an LP. Um ... like LPs, but unlike cassettes, CDs are at the moment at any rate a playback medium only, you can't record onto them, yet.

OK, now let's look at playback. A CD player uses a low powered laser beam. Now, as a laser beam can be very very sharply focussed, what this means is that it can ignore any dust or scratches on the outer protective surface of the disc, unlike again an LP where the scratches show up in the sound, the analogue sound. So when the light hits the shiny surface of the disc, most of it is reflected back to a detector but if it hits a pit, the light scatters and is lost. Now, the high and low levels of light operate basically as a ... ON and OFF switch. So these digital signals are converted then back into analogue sound signals by the CD player and sent to an amplifier and then on to loudspeakers in the same way as a hi-fi, same way as a cassette or an LP. On a compact disc, the tracks go round and round, the same as again on a conventional LP, but the difference is that they start from the centre and move outwards.

Now, CD technology is also used for CD video discs ... er ... that's where the inner part of the disc contains the digital audio signals but the outer part carries analogue video signals. Er ... the other application of CD technology is that it is used in CD ROM discs which are for computers and these can carry an enormous amount of information: 650 megabytes which represents about

275,000 pages of text, that's on a single disc. Digital techniques are the present and the future and CDs and the development of high quality cassette tapes is leading to the total abandonment of the old LP format by many record companies.

(Time: 3 minutes 20 seconds)

## 23.4 A good introduction and conclusion

Effective writing

**A + B + C + D**   Follow the procedure suggested in the Student's Book.

## 23.5 Where next?

Reading

**A** *Answers*

1 Shortly after the earthquake in San Francisco (in October 1989, in which about 270 people were killed, most of whom were crushed in their cars on the lower deck of the Cypress Highway in Oakland)
2 About 3,000
3 Where it occurs and NOT its intensity
4 By detecting the foreshocks
5 They can't predict it with any degree of certainty
6 Because the most modern buildings withstood the earthquake – proving their calculations had been right

**B** *Answers*

1 When the tension between two tectonic plates moving in opposite directions is so great that the rock tears, releasing huge amounts of energy
2 In coastal areas – as these are heavily populated, loss of life is liable to be heavy
3 Because the Earth is 'creaking away' all the time and it is difficult to tell the difference between a creak and a quake
4 If the San Franciscans had been warned to leave the area in 1989, the highway in Oakland (where most of the victims died) might have been crowded with cars, and the loss of life would have been far worse

5 By isolating them from their foundations, using rubber or lead in shock-absorbing bearings
6 A computer in a building senses the earthquake and sends instructions for weights on the roof to be moved about – this minimises the amount of swaying

**C + D**  Follow the procedure suggested in the Student's Book.

---

## 23.6   Just say no . . .  Creative writing

**A + B + C**  Follow the procedure suggested in the Student's Book.
OR
As an alternative to the creative writing task suggested in the Student's Book, more technically-minded students may prefer this sequence of activities:

**A**  Work in pairs. You will both be writing an explanation of how an everyday process, or a household or office appliance works (e.g. a photocopier, fax machine, vacuum cleaner, toaster or microwave oven). One of you should write the FIRST half and the other the SECOND half.
When you have decided what you are going to write about, MAKE NOTES and agree on where your halfway point is to be.

**B**  Write your part of the explanation. Imagine that your reader is a non-expert lay person who can only follow a certain amount of technical detail.

**C**  Look at your partner's work and make any necessary amendments. Show your complete explanation to another pair and ask for comments.

---

## 23.7  *First, second, third and last*  Idioms

**A**  *Suggested answers*

1 I decided to catch a late train.  *– not an early one*
  I decided to catch the first train.  *– the first of the day*
  I decided to catch the early train. *– the only early one*
  I decided to catch the last train.  *– the last of the day*

I decided the train was late.   – *I worked out that it wasn't on time*

I decided to catch an early train. – *one of the early ones*

2 Her first husband   – *the first of her husbands*
  Her last husband   – *her most recent husband OR the final husband of several*

  Her latest husband   – *her current husband (of many)*
  Her ex-husband   – *her previous husband*
  Her second husband   – *the husband after the first*
  Her late husband   – *she is a widow*
  Her former husband   – *her previous husband*
  Her husband is late   – *he hasn't arrived yet*

3 A second-hand watch   – *not a new one*
  The second hand on a watch   – *the hand that shows the seconds*

## B   Answers

1 lasts     the last straw
2 first things first     first thing     on second thoughts
   at the latest
3 first come, first served
4 at first     lasted
5 second nature     on first name terms
6 last-minute     later on
7 at first hand     first-rate
8 second-rate     as a last resort
9 the last word
10 a second chance / a last chance
11 a second opinion
12 first cousins     second cousins
13 latest news     at long last
14 first aid     the week before last
15 in the third person     in the first person

▶ Some related idioms:

**last**   on its last legs = worn out
       last but not least = important
**late**   of late = recently
**first**   you can have first refusal = the right to decide first whether
       to buy
**second**   to second a proposal = support
**third**   Third World = less developed countries
       third party = person other than the two main people
       concerned

# 24 Utopia

---

## 24.1 The perfect society Reading and listening

**A**  As what constitutes 'good points' and 'bad points' is a matter of opinion, there are no 'correct answers' here. However, it might be a good idea to highlight what YOU consider to be good and bad about Pala in your copy of the Student's Book. Similarly, you could highlight the good and bad aspects of the other utopias described in **B** in the transcripts below.

**B**  📼  *Transcript*

Presenter:  I suppose everyone wishes the world could be a perfect place, where everyone lives in happy harmony. Well, we're going to hear about four visions of the perfect society. Going back to Ancient Greece first, Plato was born in 427 BC and he called his imaginary perfect society 'The Republic'. Er ... Philippa ...

Philippa:  Now, Plato's Republic has only got 5,040 citizens and that's the number that can be addressed by one orator. The political leaders of the Republic are called 'guardians'. Now, children in Plato's Republic go to school until they're twenty years old and then they do tests. The ones who fail these tests become businessmen, workers, farmers, and they're capitalists who are permitted to own property and to use money. The ones who pass the tests do another ten years of education and then they do more tests, and the ones who fail these tests become soldiers and *they* live in a communist society and they own no property and they don't have any money, they share everything. The ones who pass these further tests go on to study philosophy for another five years, and then they live practical lives in the world ... in the real world for another fifteen years and then when they're 50, they become 'guardians', the political leaders. And their only possession is in fact power. And in the Republic there are 360 guardians and each month 30 of these rule over the Republic.

Um ... marriage is interesting: in Plato's Republic marriage is completely controlled by the state and it's very selective and only the best marry the best. And ... er ... children: the ... the very ... the superior children are allowed to survive but in fact all the rest are killed at birth. And they're brought up not by their parents, but they're brought up collectively as a group.

Presenter:  Well, thank you, Philippa. Now, Thomas More lived from 1478

to 1535 and he actually invented the term Utopia, didn't he,
Terry?

Terry:    Yes. Yes, he took it from the ... from the Greek ... er ... and it
means 'No place'. Thomas More's Utopia ... um ... is on an island
800 kilometres round, somewhere in the Pacific ... er ... with
therefore, I suppose, a reasonably fair climate.

On the political side it's not ... er ... everything we'd ... er ...
consider right now, but ... er ... he had it ruled by a king, where
slaves did menial work, and where women were inferior to men.
On the plus side, however, all religions were tolerated. No
money changes hands, in fact there is no monetary system at all,
so ... er ... there's no ... no love of ... of property and acquisition,
therefore there's no greed, therefore no theft.

Um ... every adult male works six hours a day at a job that he
likes to do and a job which serves the needs of the community.
Er ... he doesn't receive payment, as I said, in money: he receives
what he needs from a ... a common store – food, drink, that sort
of thing for his family. E ... each group of 30 families ... er ... elect
a leader, and every ten leaders elect a chief ... er ... the chief
becomes a member of the national council. The national council
elects one king, who rules for life, so ... i ... it's a sort of
democratically elected king.

Er ... education ... well, that emphasises vocational subjects,
obviously subjects which will be useful to the people who work,
for the benefit of the community, so it all ties in. And ... er ... war
is only acceptable when it's absolutely necessary, there are to be
no common squabbles or ... um ... little petty rows.

Presenter: Fine! H.G. Wells, who was born in 1866 and died in 1946, also
had a vision of Utopia. Polly ...

Polly:    Um ... well, Wells's Utopia is a world state, so that means one
government for the whole world. And in this world government
the state owns all the land and all the sources of power and
food. But individuals can still own and inherit property, so you
can have some personal things. He's really into high-tech, he has
these visions of these amazing electric trains that go at 300
kilometres per hour and they've got libraries and sofas and
reading rooms – it's really just extraordinary. And he thinks that
most work should be done by machines, which is a nice idea, so
people have a lot of free time.

Now, his world is governed by this special ruling class and you
have to take a test to qualify, and if you qualify you're not
allowed to smoke or drink or gamble, but you can tell the rest of
the world what to do!

Um ... personal details of every person on the planet are kept in
what I guess is a huge computer in Paris, and this information is
used to control population and labour and tell the underlings
how to live their lives. Um ... and if you want to have children,

243

you have to produce this record that shows you're healthy, and you have enough money and you're the right age. And after you have your children, the state takes them away from you and they take them to this place where they teach you good habits and make you want to ... er ... learn, except I don't know how they make you do that.

Presenter: Hm, fine! And finally, Shangri-La. James Hilton wrote about this magic land in his novel *Lost Horizon*, which was made into a film in 1937 and I believe remade in 1973, wasn't it, Tony?

Tony: Yes, that's right. Shangri-La is high in Tibet, and it's surrounded by mountains and it's inaccessible to the whole of the world, so it's idyllic. Now, in Shangri-La people live to be at least 200 years old or more. They all eat magic berries that keeps them young, and they practise yoga and they all follow the teachings of Buddha. The inhabitants of Shangri-La devote their entire lives to contemplation, research and the pursuit of wisdom. They're all good-mannered, honest and sober – and very happy.

(Time: 6 minutes 50 seconds)

---

## 24.2   Special uses of the Past      Grammar

**A**  *Suggested answers*

1 I was hoping we could have a talk today.
   *– slightly pessimistic about the chances of talking, perhaps trying to persuade someone*
   I had hoped we could have a talk today.
   *– pessimistic about the chances* OR *regretting the impossibility of it*
   I hope we can have a talk today.
   *– straightforward expression of hope* OR *more forceful request for time to talk*
   I'm hoping we can have a talk today.
   *– straightforward expression of hope, perhaps emphasising that I've got this constantly in my mind*

2 I wonder if you could help me.
   *– straightforward request.*
   I was wondering if you could help me.
   *– rather tentative request*
   I wondered if you could help me.
   *– very tentative request*

3 Were you wanting to see the manager?
   *– very indirect enquiry, possibly deferential or maybe slightly sarcastic*

Do you want to see the manager?
– *straightforward enquiry*
Don't you want to see the manager?
– *surprised tone, perhaps suggesting that you seem to have changed your mind*
Did you want to see the manager?
– *slightly indirect enquiry, possibly deferential*
Didn't you want to see the manager?
– *surprised tone, perhaps suggesting that you should be in there talking to him/her now*
Would you like to see the manager?
– *inviting someone to meet the manager*

4 I wish there was more time.
– *regretting the shortage of time now or always*
I wish there had been more time.
– *regretting the shortage of time in the past*
I wish there were more time.
– *regretting the shortage of time now or always (as first example)*
If only there were more time.
– *regretting the shortage of time now or always (as first example)*

## B Answers

2 didn't
3 went
4 were / was / had been

5 knew / had known / could work out / could have worked out, etc.

## C Correct continuations with √ incorrect ones with X

1 It's past midnight and I think it's time …
… I went to bed. √      … for me to turn in. √
… I call it a day. X
2 It's terrible, she behaves as if …
… she owned the place. √      … she weren't a guest. X
… it was her own home. √
3 He spoke to me as if …
… I were a half-wit. √      … I was simple-minded. √
… I have no brains. X
4 I wish …
… she were less outspoken. √
… she wouldn't speak her mind so frankly. √
… I was less sensitive to disapproval. √
… I can tolerate criticism better. X

5 I'd rather ...
  ... you didn't tell me off. ✓    ... you don't scold me. ✗
  ... not to blame me. ✗
6 I wouldn't mind if ...
  ... he isn't such a daydreamer. ✗
  ... he weren't so forgetful. ✓    ... he was less absent-minded. ✓
7 If only ...
  ... the world is a better place. ✗
  ... the world were a better place. ✓
  ... the world be a better place. ✗
  ... the world should be a better place. ✗

## D  *Some suggested continuations*

1 It's high time you had your hair cut.
2 I'd much rather you smoked out in the garden.
3 She looked at me as if I was crazy.
4 I'd like to suggest that we all go out together after the lesson.
5 It'd be much better if you wrote to her.
6 I do wish this wasn't the last unit.

## E  *Correct continuations with* ✓ *incorrect ones with* ✗

2 If any unforeseen problems ...
  ... should arise, let me know. ✓
  ... were to arise, keep me in the picture. ✗
  ... arise, don't keep me in the dark. ✓
  ... are to rise, tell me at once. ✗
3 I insist ...
  ... that she should be informed. ✓
  ... that she is given the information. ✓
  ... she be informed. ✓    ... to inform her. ✗
4 It's important ...
  ... that we were on our guard. ✗
  ... that we are as careful as can be. ✓
  ... to be extremely careful. ✓
  ... that we should show the utmost care. ✓
5 I propose that ...
  ... we take a vote on it. ✓    ... we should ask for a show of hands. ✓
  ... the matter be put to a vote. ✓    ... we held a ballot ✗
6 We demand ...
  ... that payment is made at once. ✓
  ... that payment be made at once. ✓
  ... to be paid at once. ✓    ... that payment was made at once. ✗

# 24.3   *Lay, lead, leave, let and lie*   Verbs and idioms

## A   *Answers and suggested continuations*

| | | |
|---|---|---|
| 1 lied | lying | ... didn't take any notice of him. |
| 2 lay | laying | ... the food in the oven caught fire. |
| 3 lay | lying | ... the others cooked the supper. |
| 4 left | leaving | ... they thanked us for having them. |
| 5 let | | ... the hall was already full of people. |
| 6 led | leading | ... reacted differently. |

## B   *Answers*

1 took the lead = be in front
2 take it lying down = not tolerate without resisting
   led me on = mislead
3 leaves me cold = doesn't excite me
4 let alone = far from
5 leading article = editorial
   laid off = lose their jobs (temporarily)
   a pack of lies = completely untrue
6 let off steam = give vent to your feelings
7 letting go = stop holding
8 lies = is situated
9 let it be = not interfere
   leave well alone = not interfere unnecessarily      lead to = cause
10 lay my cards on the table = be frank about my intentions
11 let = allow      leave of absence = unpaid holiday
   left over = remaining      let her down = disappoint
   let her go = allow to leave
12 layout = arrangement      a lay person = non-expert
13 leave = entrust      lay on = arrange      left out = omitted
14 let up = stop
15 leading up to = precede      leave me alone = not disturb or molest

▶ Some other related idioms:
**lay**   lay it on thick = exaggerate
   hens lay eggs
**lead**   lead time = time before product can be delivered
   a leading question = a question that encourages someone to
      answer in a particular way
   lead someone up the garden path = mislead
   lead someone astray = encourage them to do something wrong

**leave** leave it at that = do no more
**let** let sleeping dogs lie = don't cause unnecessary problems
**lie** lie in wait for someone = hide in order to catch them
your whole life lies before you = you're still young

---

## 24.4  Reading aloud                    Pronunciation

**A + B** 〔▭〕 The complete article is printed in Activities 52 and 65 of the Student's Book. Follow the procedure suggested in the Student's Book.

*Complete article with catenation marked in the first paragraph*

BRASILIA – UTOPIA IN THE HEART OF BRAZIL

Brasília, the capital city of Brazil, was designed as a futuristic Utopian city in the 1950s by Lúcio Costa and Oscar Niemeyer, both followers of the great French architect Le Corbusier. Brasília is a purpose-built city twelve hundred kilometres from the coast on a red dirt plateau where no one lived – or wanted to live. It's the most photogenic city in the world with sweeping avenues, beautiful ceremonial buildings and fantastic sunsets.

   The parliament building, shops, hotels, flats, leafy suburbs for the middle classes, schools, the university and the ministries are all located in separate zones. But looking more closely at the spectacular buildings you can see that they are falling to bits because they were built on the cheap. In a city where temperatures are normally over 30 degrees, the main indoor shopping centre is not even air-conditioned. And the poorer workers and their families are accommodated in large, squalid shanty towns on the edge of the city.

   It's a city designed for the automobile with magnificent multi-lane highways but no pavements or pedestrian crossings because, in the future everyone would have a car. Unfortunately, even today only one in eight of the citizens of Brasília has access to a car and the public transport system is chaotic. Most of the time the highways are empty but twice a day they are jammed with cars and pedestrians have to dodge the traffic to get across.

   The one consolation for the very rich is that there are regular flights to Rio. It's scarcely surprising that on Friday afternoons all the flights out are fully booked.

(Time: 2 minutes)

**C** 〔▨〕 Perhaps play the whole tape through again at the end.

# 24.5   The best of all possible worlds   Reading

**A** 🔲 This is an authentic letter from James Rodengen in Costa Rica.

## *Script of letter*

Dear Friend,

Most of us have dreamed at one time or another of finding a place where we can be truly happy . . . a Shangri-La with an ideal climate, remote from turmoil and confusion; where the air is fresh and free from pollution and the only noise we hear is that of the wind in the trees, the roar of the sea and the song of the birds – but still close enough to civilization to enjoy the benefits of a thriving, metropolitan city.

There is such a Paradise, and you can reserve your own special corner for only $150 down payment and interest-free monthly payments of $150 at absolutely no risk. If you examine your property any time within one year and are not completely satisfied, **every cent you paid will be refunded** with no questions asked.

We are talking about the Beaches of Nosara on the West Coast of Costa Rica, a country known throughout the world for its peace, tranquility and solid, democratic government.

First, let me emphasize that Costa Rica is not threatened by the conflict in Central America and most definitely **IS NOT** what is generally known as a "Banana Republic".

But to assure your dream for tomorrow, it's up to you to take action today. I hope to hear from you soon.

Sincerely,      James M. Rodengen

Apartado 1084
Centro Colón
San José
Costa Rica 1007

(Time: 1 minute 30 seconds)

**C**   Announce a deadline for this group activity, so that everyone knows how long they have and so that there is enough time for the presentations in **D** later. Let them know how long their presentation should be, too.

**D**   Make sure there is enough time for each group to do their presentation.

249

# Acknowledgements

The author and publishers are grateful to the following for permission to use copyright material identified in the text:

Dover Publications, Inc. for the pictograms from *Handbook of Pictorial Symbols* by Rudolf Modley used in the chapter titles; University of Cambridge Local Examinations Syndicate for the Certificate in Advanced English syllabus description on pp. 17–18; Cambridge University Press for the extract from *The Cambridge Encyclopedia of Language* by David Crystal on p. 86; Longman Group UK for the extract from *Call for the Dead* by John Le Carré (Longman Simplified English) on p. 86; Anna Tomforde and *The Guardian* for the extract on p. 116; The Hogarth Press for the extract from *Cider with Rosie* by Laurie Lee on p. 227; Chapman & Hall Ltd and Little, Brown and Company for the extract from *Decline and Fall* by Evelyn Waugh, copyright 1928 by Evelyn Waugh, © renewed 1956 by Evelyn Waugh, on pp. 227–8; James M. Rodengen for the letter on p. 249.

Artwork by Pavely Arts